FUNDAMENTALS OF GOVERNMENTAL ACCOUNTING AND REPORTING

BY BRUCE W. CHASE, PH.D., CPA

Notice to readers

Fundamentals of Governmental Accounting and Reporting is intended solely for use in continuing professional education and not as a reference. It does not represent an official position of the American Institute of Certified Public Accountants, and it is distributed with the understanding that the author and publisher are not rendering legal, accounting, or other professional services in the publication. This course is intended to be an overview of the topics discussed within, and the author has made every attempt to verify the completeness and accuracy of the information herein. However, neither the author nor publisher can guarantee the applicability of the information found herein. If legal advice or other expert assistance is required, the services of a competent professional should be sought.

You can qualify to earn free CPE through our pilot testing program.
If interested, please visit https://aicpacompliance.polldaddy.com/s/pilot-testing-survey.

ISBN 978-1-119-73666-0 (paper)
ISBN 978-1-119-73675-2 (ePDF)
ISBN 978-1-119-73673-8 (ePub)
ISBN 978-1-119-73676-9 (obk)

Course Code: **733983**
FGAC GS-0420-0A
Revised: **February 2020**

V10018914_060820

Table of Contents

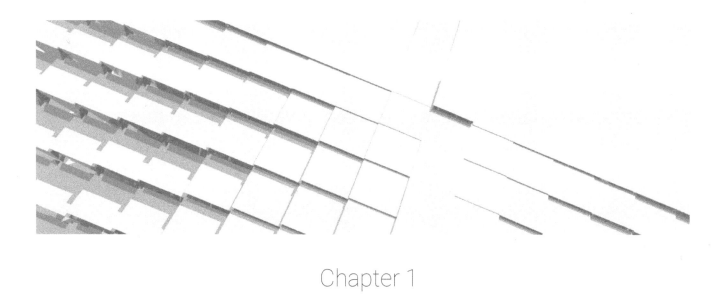

Chapter 1

The Governmental Environment and GAAP

Learning objectives

- Recognize the unique aspects of the governmental accounting environment.

- Identify which organizations must follow GASB standards.

- Recognize authoritative guidance on generally accepted accounting principles (GAAP).

Governmental accounting versus for-profit accounting

The practice of state and local government accounting can be succinctly distinguished from that of for-profit accounting, which is already familiar to many of us. Several elements of governmental accounting are very distinct from for-profit accounting. One core difference is that the purpose of government is not to make a profit but to provide services to the citizenry. There are different users of the financial statements than in the for-profit sector. The accounting is different — there is even a different standards-setting board, the GASB, which typically issues new rules each year. Like the FASB, however, the GASB is subject to the auspices of the Financial Accounting Foundation (FAF).

This course focuses on the fundamentals of governmental accounting. *Governmental accounting* is the composite activity of analyzing, recording, summarizing, reporting, and interpreting the financial transactions of governments.

Governmental environment

Key environmental differences between government and business

The state and local governmental environment is different in several ways from the business environment. These differences influence financial reporting objectives. The GASB's white paper, *Why Governmental Accounting and Financial Reporting Is — and Should Be — Different,* identifies the following five environmental differences between governments and for-profit businesses[1]:

- *Organizational purposes.* Businesses are in the business of making money. The purpose of governments is to enhance or maintain the well-being of citizens by providing public services. Many of these services are provided with no direct relationship to how much recipients pay. For example, a local library is supported by tax revenue, not by fees charged to the people who actually use the library.
- *Sources of revenue.* One difference between government and business is their revenue streams. Governments receive substantial revenue from nonexchange transactions, such as taxes and grants. Taxes are provided by involuntary resource providers. The primary source of revenue for businesses is voluntary exchange transactions.
- *Potential for longevity.* The legal structure of the government is also different from that of a business. Each state has its own requirements pertaining to the roles and responsibilities among the different levels and branches of government. Because governments have the ability to tax, they rarely go out of business. This longevity is reflected in a long-term view in financial reporting.
- *Relationship with stakeholders.* Citizens delegate government operations to elected officials. The public has the right to hold the government to a higher standard of accountability for raising and spending of public funds. Accountability says that these elected officials must provide information about both stewardship and interperiod equity, which addresses a question: Are current-year revenues sufficient to pay for services provided that year or will future taxpayers be required to assume the burden of paying for services long since provided?
- *Role of the budget.* Control over the level of taxes and the spending of those resources is achieved by budgets legally adopted by elected officials. *Demonstrating accountability with budget authority* is a key objective of governmental financial reporting.

Knowledge check

1. Which statement is accurate regarding the governmental environment?

    a. The state and local governmental environment is different from business in a number of ways, and these differences influence financial reporting objectives.
    b. Few governments' resources come from taxes.
    c. The organizational purpose of a government is identical to a business.
    d. Governments are often concerned with going out of business.

---

[1] To download a copy of the white paper, revised in April 2013, go to http://gasb.org/jsp/GASB/Page/GASBSectionPage&cid=1176156741271.

2. Which statement accurately describes the relationship between the government and its stakeholders?

   a. The primary source of revenue for a government is voluntary exchange transactions.
   b. A similarity between government and business is how resources are provided.
   c. Governments are accountable to citizens and taxpayers and must provide them information on how financial resources are used.
   d. Budgets are rarely legally adopted by elected officials.

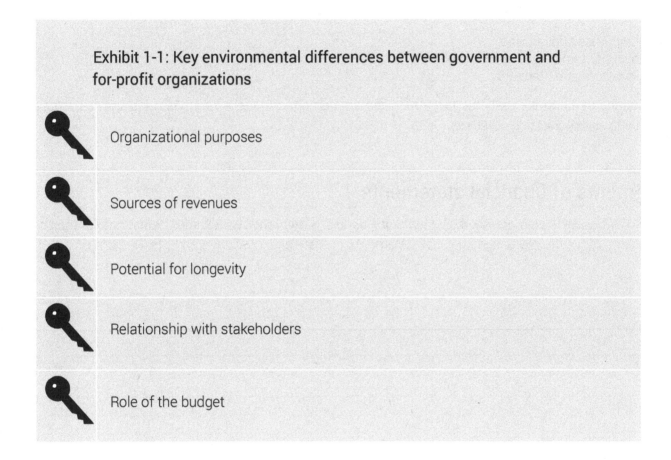

Exhibit 1-1: Key environmental differences between government and for-profit organizations

Organizational purposes

Sources of revenues

Potential for longevity

Relationship with stakeholders

Role of the budget

Objectives of financial reporting

These and other differences in the respective environments result in governments having unique financial reporting objectives. *Accountability* becomes the *paramount objective* of financial reporting. The GASB states that financial reports should include information that can be used for the following:

- Comparing actual financial results with the legally adopted budget *(budgetary information)*
- Assessing financial condition and results of operations *(financial information)*
- Assisting in determining compliance with finance-related laws, rules, and regulations *(compliance information)*
- Assisting in evaluating efficiency and effectiveness *(performance information)*

These financial reporting objectives for governments are much broader than those for businesses. To meet these objectives, governments are required to produce several different types of financial statements that include an expansive amount of information.

Users of financial statements

The primary users of governmental financial statements are

- taxpayers and citizens,
- oversight and legislative bodies, and
- investors and creditors.

Although not a primary user, the government's management often relies on the financial statements for planning and monitoring purposes.

Elements of financial statements

GASB Concepts Statement No. 4, *Elements of Financial Statements*, establishes definitions for the seven elements of historically based financial statements of state and local governments. See exhibit 1-2.

Exhibit 1-2: The seven elements of state and local government financial statements

	Elements of a statement of financial position
1	**Assets** are resources with present service capacity that the government presently controls. A *resource* is an item that can be drawn on to provide services to the citizenry.
2	**Liabilities** are present obligations to sacrifice resources that the government has little or no discretion to avoid.
3	A **deferred outflow of resources** is a consumption of net assets by the government that is applicable to a future reporting period.
4	A **deferred inflow of resources** is an acquisition of net assets by the government that is applicable to a future reporting period.
5	**Net position** is the residual of all other elements presented in a statement of financial position.
	Elements of the resource flows statements
6	An **outflow of resources** is a consumption of net assets by the government that is applicable to the reporting period.
7	An **inflow of resources** is an acquisition of net assets by the government that is applicable to the reporting period.

GASB Concepts Statement No. 4 elements differ from the 10 interrelated elements described in FASB Concepts Statement No. 6, *Measurement of Elements of Financial Statements*. FASB Concepts Statement No. 6 applies to business and not-for-profit organizations. The 10 interrelated elements are assets, liabilities, equity or net assets, investments by owners, distributions to owners, comprehensive income, revenues, expenses, gains, and losses.

GASB Statement No. 63

GASB Statement No. 63, *Financial Reporting of Deferred Outflows of Resources, Deferred Inflows of Resources, and Net Position,* provides financial reporting guidance for deferred outflows of resources and deferred inflows of resources. GASB Concepts Statement No. 4 introduced and defined those elements as a consumption of net assets by the government that is applicable to a future reporting period and an acquisition of net assets by the government that is applicable to a future reporting period, respectively. Previous financial reporting standards, however, do not include guidance for reporting those financial statement elements, which are distinct from assets and liabilities.

GASB Concepts Statement No. 4 also identifies net position as the residual of all other elements presented in a statement of financial position. GASB Statement No. 63 amends the net asset reporting requirements in GASB Statement No. 34, *Basic Financial Statements — and Management's Discussion and Analysis — for State and Local Governments,* and other pronouncements by incorporating deferred outflows of resources and deferred inflows of resources into the definitions of the required components of the residual measure and by renaming that measure "net position" rather than "net assets." GASB Concepts Statement No. 4 also resulted in the amendment of paragraph 31 of GASB Concepts Statement No. 3, *Communication Methods in General Purpose External Financial Reports That Contain Basic Financial Statements,* to reflect all elements of GASB Concepts Statement No. 4 and to conform the language of GASB Concepts Statement No. 3 to GASB Concepts Statement No. 4.

GASB Statement No. 65

GASB Statement No. 65, *Items Previously Reported as Assets and Liabilities,* establishes accounting and financial reporting standards that reclassify — as deferred outflows of resources or deferred inflows of resources — certain items previously reported as assets and liabilities. This statement also recognizes — as outflows of resources or inflows of resources — certain items previously reported as assets and liabilities.

In addition, GASB Statement No. 65 provides that reporting a deferred outflow of resources or a deferred inflow of resources should be limited to those instances identified by the GASB in authoritative pronouncements that are established after applicable due process. Prior to the issuance of this statement, only two such pronouncements have been issued. GASB Statement No. 53, *Accounting and Financial Reporting for Derivative Instruments,* requires the reporting of a deferred outflow of resources or a deferred inflow of resources for the changes in fair value of hedging derivative instruments; GASB Statement No. 60, *Accounting and Financial Reporting for Service Concession Arrangements,* requires a deferred inflow of resources to be reported by a transferor government in a qualifying service concession arrangement. This statement amends the financial statement element classification of certain items previously reported as assets and liabilities to be consistent with the definitions in GASB Concepts Statement No. 4.

GASB Statement No. 65 also provides other financial reporting guidance related to the impact of the financial statement elements, deferred outflows of resources and deferred inflows of resources, such as changes in the determination of the major fund calculations and limiting the use of the term "deferred" in financial statement presentations.

Unique concepts in government accounting

Several unique accounting practices have evolved for state and local governments because of their unique environment, the need to meet financial reporting objectives, and the financial statement elements detailed earlier. Several aspects of the system of accounting used by governments are similar to those used by businesses, such as the use of debits and credits, journals, and ledgers. Additionally, many transactions continue to be recorded under government accounting in the same way that they are recorded in for-profit accounting. Still, there are several key differences, as follows:

- **Measurement focus and basis of accounting (MFBOA).** The activities of government can be broadly grouped into two categories, each of which uses a different MFBOA. The two categories are as follows:
  - *Business-type activities.* These are the activities a government carries out primarily to provide specific services in exchange for a specific user charge. These user fees are often intended to cover the cost of providing such services. Common examples of business-type services are water and sewer services. Accounting for this type of activity is very similar to a for-profit organization.
  - *Governmental activities.* These are the activities that occur in a government organization related to the acquisition, use, and balances of spendable financial resources and related current liabilities, **except for** those activities accounted for as business-type or fiduciary activities. Police services and education are common examples of government services that qualify as governmental activities. Accounting for these types of activities requires a different MFBOA.
- **Fund accounting.** To assist in demonstrating accountability, governments have long reported activities in separate funds. A fund is a fiscal accounting entity with a self-balancing set of accounts in which cash and other financial resources, all related liabilities and residual equities (or balances), and changes therein, are recorded and segregated to carry on specific activities or attain certain objectives in accordance with special regulations, restrictions, or limitations. Funds are used to separately account for financial activities based on legal requirements or management needs.
- **Budgetary reporting.** To meet one of the financial reporting objectives, governments must be able to compare actual financial results with the legally adopted budget. Budgets represent much more than a plan for a government: they represent a legally binding document and are often recorded in the accounting system.

Knowledge check

3. Which statement is accurate regarding budgetary reporting?

   a. To meet one of the financial reporting objectives, governments must be able to compare actual financial results with the legally adopted budget.
   b. Budgets are never recorded in the accounting system.
   c. Budgets are generally reviewed by a government every five years.
   d. Budgets are nonauthoritative plans for governmental operations.

Which organizations are required to follow GASB standards?

The GASB is responsible for accounting standards for state and local governments. Before covering accounting standard process, let's cover which organizations must follow these standards:

- **General-purpose governments.** State, city, county, and town governments follow these rules and are referred to as *general-purpose governments*. Such governments are government organizations that provide a wide range of services to their citizens (such as police, firefighters, road construction and maintenance, and public works).
- **Special-purpose governments.** Other independent governmental entities are considered *special-purpose governments*. Such governments provide only a single function or a limited number of functions. The most common examples are independent school districts, water and sewer authorities, and other special districts set up to provide a variety of other types of services.

A summary of the types of governments found in the United States, based on the 2017 *Census of Governments*, follows:

Counties	3,031
Municipalities	19,495
Towns and townships	16,253
Independent school districts	12,754
Special districts	38,542
Total	90,075

Other entities also may have to follow the accounting standards for state and local governments. For example, some not-for-profit museums, colleges, libraries, commissions, and boards may meet the definition of a government and, therefore, must follow GASB standards.

Entities that meet at least one of the following criteria must follow GASB standards:

- Officers of the entity are popularly elected.
- A controlling majority of members of the entity's governing board is appointed (or approved) by officials of at least one state or local government.
- A government is able to unilaterally dissolve the entity, with the entity's net assets reverting to a government.
- The entity has the power to enact and enforce a tax levy.
- The entity has the ability to directly issue federally tax-exempt debt.

If the only criterion met is the ability to directly issue federally tax-exempt debt, the presumption that an entity is governmental may be rebutted based on compelling, relevant evidence.

GAAP and standards-setting organizations

For external financial statements to be useful, they must be prepared consistently over time and be comparable with those of other similar entities. To this end, external financial statements must be prepared in accordance with generally accepted accounting principles (GAAP). The following is a list of organizations that have responsibility for setting accounting standards for different types of organizations:

- The GASB has the primary responsibility for setting accounting standards for state and local governments (see earlier criteria for organizations that must follow GASB standards).
- The FASB has the primary responsibility for setting accounting standards for nongovernmental entities.
- The Federal Accounting Standards Advisory Board (FASAB) has the primary responsibility for setting standards for all agencies of the federal government.
- The International Accounting Standards Board (IASB) has been recognized by the Council of the AICPA as the body to establish international financial reporting standards for both private and public entities.

Additionally, a consultative body, the Governmental Accounting Standards Advisory Council, assists the GASB. The council consists of representatives who have an interest in governmental accounting and reporting.

In November 2013, the FAF adopted a new policy that clarifies the characteristics of the information that the GASB may address in setting standards for financial accounting and reporting for governments. A brief summary of the *GASB Scope of Authority: Consultation Process Policy* follows:

a. Governmental stakeholder's debate: (*a*) the types of reporting that should (and should not be) subject to GASB standards and guidelines and (*b*) the GASB's appropriate role.
b. The FAF established the GASB to carry out the FAF's mission with respect to the governmental accounting and financial reporting information.
    i. Governmental standard-setting responsibility was given to the GASB; however, FAF trustees retained oversight of that responsibility.
c. The FAF and GASB will institute processes and procedures to clarify the GASB's authority to issue concepts, statements, and guidance (scope).
d. The GASB's and FAF's Standard-Setting Process Oversight Committee will consult (consultation) on the pre-agenda phase about meeting certain characteristics that the GASB determines may be included in potential standard-setting activity.
e. The consultation will focus on whether information the GASB is considering for standard-setting activity is financial accounting and reporting information within the context of its standard-setting mission.
f. The consultation will not focus on a specific standard-setting project.

The GAAP hierarchy

Historically, the GAAP hierarchy for state and local governments resided in the AICPA auditing literature rather than GASB accounting literature. Following a move by FASB in 2008, the GASB issued in 2009

GASB Statement No. 55, *The Hierarchy of Generally Accepted Accounting Principles for State and Local Governments,* to place the GAAP hierarchy in GASB literature. In June 2015, the board issued GASB Statement No. 76, *The Hierarchy of Generally Accepted Accounting Principles for State and Local Governments,* to replace GASB Statement No. 55. An important feature of GASB Statement No. 76 is the elevation of GASB implementation guides in the GAAP hierarchy. The following illustration summarizes the GAAP hierarchy for state and local governments.

GAAP Hierarchy

Category A

Officially Established Accounting Principles — Governmental Accounting

Standards Board (GASB Statements)[2]

Category B

GASB Technical Bulletins, GASB Implementation Guides, and literature of

the AICPA cleared by GASB

In searching for the proper treatment of an item under GAAP, one would start by looking at category A of GAAP and then category B. For example, if the accounting treatment for a transaction or other event is not specified by a pronouncement in category A, a governmental entity should consider whether the accounting treatment is specified by a source in category B.

If the accounting treatment for a transaction or other event is not specified within a source of authoritative GAAP as described in categories A or B, a governmental entity should consider accounting principles for similar transactions or other events within categories A or B, and then may consider nonauthoritative accounting literature from other sources that does not conflict with or contradict authoritative GAAP. A governmental entity should not follow the accounting treatment specified in accounting principles for similar transactions or other events in cases in which those accounting principles either prohibit the application of the accounting treatment to the particular transaction or other event or indicate that the accounting treatment should not be applied by analogy.

Nonauthoritative accounting literature includes the following:

- GASB concepts statements
- The pronouncements and other literature of the FASB
- The pronouncements and other literature of the FASAB
- The pronouncements and other literature of the International Public Sector Accounting Standards Board
- The pronouncements and other literature of the IASB
- AICPA literature not cleared by the GASB

---

[2] All GASB Interpretations heretofore issued and currently in effect also are considered as being included within Category A and are continued in force until altered, amended, supplemented, revoked, or superseded by subsequent GASB pronouncements.

- Practices that are widely recognized and prevalent in state and local government
- Literature of other professional associations or regulatory agencies
- Accounting textbooks, handbooks, and articles

The appropriateness of nonauthoritative accounting literature depends on its relevance to particular circumstances, the specificity of the guidance, and the general recognition of the issuer or author as an authority. For example, GASB concepts statements would normally be more influential than other sources in this grouping.

GASB statements, updates, and current projects

This course reflects GASB statements issued through GASB Statement No. 91, *Conduit Debt Obligations.*

Current major GASB projects include the following:

- Conceptual Framework — Disclosure Framework
- Conceptual Framework — Recognition
- Financial Reporting Model
- Public-Private Parnerships and Availability Payment Arrangements
- Revenue and Expense Recognition

The governmental environment and GAAP

As we have established, state and local governments operate in a different environment than do businesses. Because of these differences, state and local governments have different reporting objectives, follow different accounting methods, and have an expanded list of financial statement users. Accounting standards are set by the GASB for entities that meet the definition of a government.

	Key foundational points
1	Governmental accounting is the composite activity of analyzing, recording, summarizing, reporting, and interpreting the financial transactions of governments.
2	The governmental environment has a strong influence on the financial reporting for this sector of the economy.
3	The GASB sets the accounting standards for state and local governments.
4	The state and local governmental environment is different in a number of ways from the business environment and these differences influence financial reporting objectives. Governmental environment components include organizational purpose, sources of revenue, potential for longevity, relationship with stakeholders, and role of budget.
5	Unique concepts in governmental accounting include MFBOA, fund accounting, and budgetary reporting.

Practice questions

Please note that the following practice questions are not required reading material.

1. Which is a characteristic that distinguishes government from business enterprises?

    a. Organizational purposes.
    b. Sources of revenues.
    c. Role of the budget.
    d. All the above.

2. Which is **not** a financial reporting objective of state and local government?

    a. Comparing actual results to budget.
    b. Assessing cash flows.
    c. Assessing results of operations.
    d. Assisting in the evaluation of efficiency and effectiveness.

3. Who is a primary user of government financial reports?

    a. The citizenry.
    b. Legislative and oversight bodies.
    c. Investors and creditors.
    d. All the above.

4. What is a key accounting difference for state and local governments?

    a. Budget reporting.
    b. MFBOA.
    c. Fund accounting.
    d. All the above.

5. Which characteristic used to determine whether an organization is a government can be rebutted with compelling, relevant evidence?

    a. The majority of governing board members are appointed by governmental entities.
    b. An entity that has the power to enact and enforce a property tax levy.
    c. An entity has the ability to directly issue federally tax-exempt debt.
    d. The potential for unilateral dissolution with the net assets reverting to a government upon dissolution.

6. Which organization currently sets the primary accounting standards for state and local governments?

    a. FASB.
    b. GASB.
    c. AICPA.
    d. NCGA.

7. In the left column are four sources of GAAP for state and local governments. Draw a line from the respective source of GAAP to the appropriate category of GAAP to which it belongs in the right column.

AICPA Audit Guide content cleared by GASB
GASB Statement No. 54, *Fund Balance Reporting and Governmental Fund Type Definitions*
GASB Interpretation No. 6, *Recognition and Measurement of Certain Liabilities and Expenditures in Governmental Fund Financial Statements*
The GASB *Guide to Implementation of GASB Statement 53 on Accounting and Financial Reporting for Derivative Instruments*

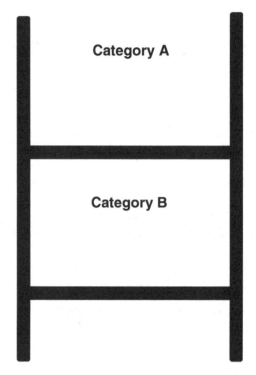

Category A

Category B

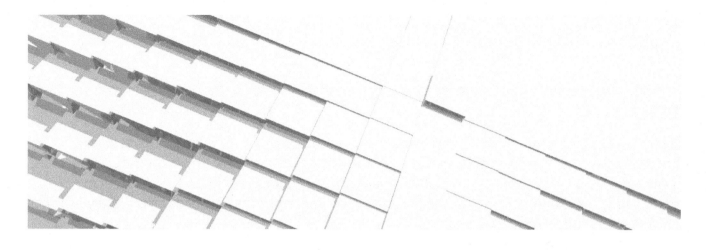

Chapter 2

Fund Accounting and the Financial Reporting Model

Learning objectives

- Recognize funds and identify why they are used.

- Determine how many funds are needed.

- Recognize the fund structure used by governments.

- Recognize the financial reporting model used by governments.

Reporting two ways: Fund and government-wide statements

Governments report financial activities in two ways: by fund and for the government as a whole.

Fund fundamentals

Funds

Before we explicitly define fund, we must understand why governments use funds. One reason is because governments receive resources from a variety of sources for a variety of purposes. For example, a city may receive resources from the state to maintain roads or from the federal government to run a reading program. Governments may also hold restricted resources for such things as employee pensions or a reserve for future debt payments. Governments must be able to demonstrate that they are using resources for the purposes for which they were given.

In addition, governments are engaged in a diverse range of activities with different operating objectives. For example, many activities are provided without direct charge (for example, police service), whereas some services are set up to recover full costs (for example, water and sewer services). Governments will want to separately measure these types of activities to see if they are meeting their different financial objectives.

To meet the overall objective of accountability, governments must be able to demonstrate compliance with legal and other restrictions placed on resources and be able to properly measure the costs of different activities. To do this, governments use several smaller accounting entities — funds — to provide financial information. Fund accounting provides the means to report financial activities based on different legal requirements and operating objectives.

The GASB defines a *fund* as follows: "A fund is defined as a fiscal and accounting entity with a self-balancing set of accounts recording cash and other financial resources, together with all related liabilities and residual equities or balances, and changes therein, which are segregated for the purpose of carrying on specific activities or attaining certain objectives in accordance with special regulations, restrictions, or limitations."

This definition contains several important concepts. First, funds are not separate legal entities but are created by accounting. The "self-balancing set of accounts" concept relates to the fact that each fund will record activity under its own accounting equation; therefore, separate financial statements can be prepared for each fund. Financial reporting by governments emphasizes the activities of funds and fund types. The final part of the definition gives several reasons for having separate funds.

Number of funds

How many funds does a government need? Will 5, 10, 20, or even 50 be enough? It depends. Often, an accounting system is able to track several different activities within one fund. For example, a government may use one fund to account for all federal restricted operating grants. Another government may set up a separate fund for each major grant. What is important is that both governments must be able to demonstrate that they used the resources in compliance with any restrictions placed on them. In addition, separate funds must sometimes be used because of accounting or legal requirements. The following rule should be used to determine the number of funds: In general, a government should use the minimum number of funds necessary for sound financial management and to meet legal and accounting requirements.

As the number of funds increases, so do the complexities in budgeting, accounting, and other administrative matters; at the same time, flexibility decreases. An organization must maintain a balance between too many and too few funds. Therefore, the number of funds that a government should use becomes a matter of professional judgment.

All governments need at least one fund, its "general fund." Whether to use additional funds is a matter of legal requirements and professional judgment.

Creating a new fund

A government can establish a new fund at any time. For example, a new fund may be mandated by new accounting standards or a change in a state's constitution. A grant or other restricted revenue source may also require the creation of a separate fund. Also, a government may start a new activity that it wants to track separately.

A new fund should be established when legally required or when new accounting standards are promulgated. In other cases, management needs to determine whether the desired level of financial control and management can be achieved by accounting for an activity within an existing fund or whether a separate fund is required.

Fund structure

Government activities are diverse and can be grouped into three broad categories: general activities of the government financed primarily by taxes and grants, business-type activities financed primarily by user fees, and activities where the government performs the role of an agent or under a trust agreement. Accordingly, funds used by a governmental organization fall into the following three categories:

1. *Governmental funds.* These are used to account for the general operations of a government. The emphasis of financial reporting is on the flow of expendable financial resources. The accounting is designed to measure the change in available financial resources, as opposed to "net income." Governmental funds are supported primarily with taxes.
2. *Proprietary funds.* These are used to account for the business-type operations of a government. The emphasis of financial reporting is like that of a business. The accounting is designed to measure operating income, financial position, and cash flows. Proprietary funds are supported primarily with fees for services.
3. *Fiduciary funds.* These are used to account for resources established under a trust agreement or a custodial relationship. These resources cannot be used to support a government's own programs. The accounting is designed to measure resources held for others and changes in those resources.

Within these three major categories of funds, 11 different types of funds can be used. All funds used by governments are defined as 1 of the 11 fund types. Often a government can have more than one fund of a particular type or, in some cases, have no funds of a particular type.

The following illustration shows the 11 fund types grouped by fund categories.

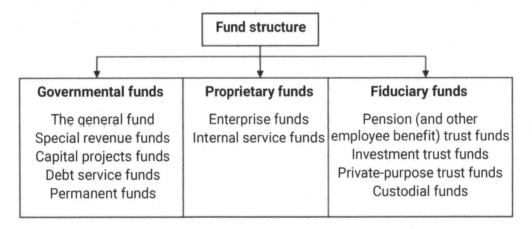

Governmental funds

1. *General fund.* This is used to account for and report all financial resources not accounted for and reported in another fund.
2. *Special revenue funds.* These are used to account for and report the proceeds of specific revenue sources that are restricted or committed to expenditure for specified purposes other than debt service or capital projects. The term *proceeds of specific revenue sources* establishes that one or more specific restricted or committed revenues should be the foundation for a special revenue fund.

Those specific restricted or committed revenues may be initially received in another fund and subsequently distributed to a special revenue fund. Those amounts should not be recognized as revenue in the fund initially receiving them; however, those inflows should be recognized as revenue in the special revenue fund in which they will be expended in accordance with specified purposes. Special revenue funds should not be used to account for resources held in trust for individuals, private organizations, or other governments.

The restricted or committed proceeds of specific revenue sources should be expected to continue to make up a substantial portion of the inflows reported in the fund. Other resources (investment earnings and transfers from other funds, for example) may also be reported in the fund if those resources are restricted, committed, or assigned to the specified purpose of the fund. Governments should discontinue reporting a special revenue fund and instead report the fund's remaining resources in the general fund if the government no longer expects that a substantial portion of the inflows will derive from restricted or committed revenue sources. Governments should disclose in the notes to the financial statements the purpose for each major special revenue fund, identifying which revenues and other resources are reported in each of those funds.

3. *Capital projects funds.* These are used to account for and report financial resources that are restricted, committed, or assigned to expenditure for capital outlays, including the acquisition or construction of capital facilities and other capital assets. Capital projects funds exclude those types of capital-related outflows financed by proprietary funds or for assets that will be held in trust for individuals, private organizations, or other governments.
4. *Debt service funds.* These are used to account for and report financial resources that are restricted, committed, or assigned to expenditure for principal and interest. Debt service funds should be used to report resources if legally mandated. Financial resources that are being accumulated for principal and interest maturing in future years should also be reported in debt service funds.
5. *Permanent funds.* These are used to account for and report resources that are restricted to the extent that only earnings, and not principal, may be used for purposes that support the reporting government's programs; that is, for the benefit of the government or its citizenry. Permanent funds do not include private-purpose trust funds, which should be used to report situations in which the government is required to use the principal or earnings for the benefit of individuals, private organizations, or other governments.

Proprietary funds

1. *Enterprise funds.* These are used to account for operations that are financed and operated in a manner similar to a business enterprise, in which fees are charged to external users for goods and services.
2. *Internal service funds.* These are used to account for activities that provide goods or services to other funds, departments, or agencies of the primary government and its component units, or to other governments, on a cost-reimbursement basis.

Fiduciary funds

GASB Statement No. 84, *Fiduciary Activities*, which is effective for fiscal years beginning after December 15, 2018, establishes criteria for identifying and reporting fiduciary activities. The criteria for identifying fiduciary activities primarily focus on (*a*) whether a government controls the assets of the fiduciary activity and (*b*) the beneficiaries with whom a fiduciary relationship exists.

Governments with activities meeting the criteria will present a statement of fiduciary net position and a statement of changes in fiduciary net position, with certain exceptions.

It is important to note that *agency funds* will no longer be reported under GASB Statement No. 84.

1. *Pension (and other employee benefit) trust funds.* These are used to account for resources for pension plans and postemployment benefit plans other than pension plans that are administered through qualifying trusts and other employee benefits plans for which resources are held in a trust meeting specified criteria and contributions to the trust and earnings on those contributions are irrevocable.
2. *Investment trust funds.* These are used to account for the external portion of investment pools and individual investment accounts that a government holds in a trust or equivalent arrangement that meets specific criteria.
3. *Private-purpose trust funds.* These are used to account for all other trust agreements meeting specific criteria for which the government itself is not a beneficiary that are not required to be reported in pension (and other employee benefit) or investment trust funds.
4. *Custodial funds.* These are used to account for fiduciary activities that are not required to be reported in pension (and other employee benefit) trust funds, investment trust funds, or private-purpose trust funds. Custodial funds should report fiduciary activities that are not held in a trust or equivalent arrangement that meet specific criteria. The external portion of investment pools that are not held in a qualifying trust should be reported in a separate external investment pool fund column, under the custodial fund classification.

A government is not required to report all 11 fund types. As stated earlier, the number of funds that a government should use becomes a matter of professional judgment. Many activities of a government can be accounted for in the general fund; separate funds can be used if needed to increase accountability. However, a government should use the minimum number of funds necessary for sound financial management and to meet legal and accounting requirements. There are only a few instances where generally accepted accounting principles requires the use of specific funds to report certain activities. It is important to note that all governments should have a general fund and there can be only one general fund.

Knowledge check

1. Which statement is correct regarding the creation of new funds?

    a. A grant or other restricted revenue source may require the use of a separate fund.
    b. Governments never start a new activity that they want to track separately.
    c. The governing board cannot create a new fund at any time during the year.
    d. A new fund can be created only at the start of the year.

2. Which statement is accurate regarding fiduciary funds?

    a. Investment trust funds are used to account for the external portion of investment pools reported by sponsoring governments.
    b. Private-purpose trust funds are governmental funds.
    c. Private-purpose trust funds are used to account for resources held by the government in a purely custodial capacity.
    d. There are five types of fiduciary funds.

Overview of the financial reporting model

Before we move on, a basic understanding of the reporting model used by state and local governments would be useful. Remember that accountability is the key financial reporting objective and that fund accounting is one method used to fulfill this objective. One aspect of financial reporting by governments is an emphasis on the activities of funds and fund types. However, governments must also provide financial information about the results of operations and financial condition of the overall government. To meet both needs, governments produce two types of financial statements: fund financial statements and government-wide financial statements.

Fund-based statements provide financial information about each major fund of a government. As will be discussed more in future chapters, governmental funds use a different measurement focus and basis of accounting (MFBOA) than do proprietary funds and fiduciary funds. Because of this difference, it would not be appropriate to report financial information measured differently in the same financial statements. To do so would be like comparing apples and oranges. As a result, separate fund-based statements are reported for each fund category.

The separate fund financial statements for each fund category are as follows[1]:

- Governmental funds
  - Balance sheet
  - Statement of revenues, expenditures, and changes in fund balances (also called "resource flows statements" in GASB Concepts Statement No. 4, *Elements of Financial Statements*)
- Proprietary funds
  - Statement of net position or balance sheet
  - Statement of revenues, expenses, and changes in fund net position (also called "resource flows statements" in GASB Concepts Statement No. 4)
  - Statement of cash flows (also called *resource flows statements* in GASB Concepts Statement No. 4)
- Fiduciary funds
  - Statement of fiduciary net position
  - Statement of changes in fiduciary net position

Government-wide statements are intended to provide information about the financial resources and activities of the overall government. The statements report information about governmental activities and business-type activities and a total for the primary government. Producing these government-wide statements from the fund-based statements is not as simple as it may seem. Several adjustments must be made to the information in the fund-based statements to produce meaningful government-wide statements. The major adjustments are as follows:

- Information in the government-wide statements must be reported using the same MFBOA. To accomplish this, governmental funds information must be converted to the same MFBOA used by proprietary funds.

---

[1] Appendix A provides examples of both fund financial statements and government-wide financial statements.

- The resources and activities of internal service funds are reported with governmental activities if they mainly serve governmental funds. If they mainly serve enterprise funds, they are reported with business-type activities.
- Certain intragovernmental activities are eliminated.
- Fiduciary funds are not reported in the government-wide statements.

Fund financial statements must provide a reconciliation to the government-wide statements. The reconciliation provides a summary of the preceding adjustments.

The two government-wide statements[2] are

- statement of net position and
- statement of activities (also called "resource flows statements" in GASB Concepts Statement No. 4).

Governments are required to report both fund financial statements and government-wide statements in their general-purpose external financial statements. GASB requires that general-purpose financial statements contain the following, at a minimum:

- Management's discussion and analysis (MD&A)
- Basic financial statements
  - Government-wide financial statements
  - Fund financial statements
  - Notes to the financial statements
- Required supplementary information (other than MD&A)

The relationship of the different elements required for general-purpose financial statements can be seen in the chart that follows. As discussed previously, the fund financial statements and government-wide statements provide different information about the government's financial resources. The arrow between the two types of statements emphasizes the fact that the two statements must be reconciled. The reconciliation is presented as part of the fund financial statements or in an accompanying schedule.

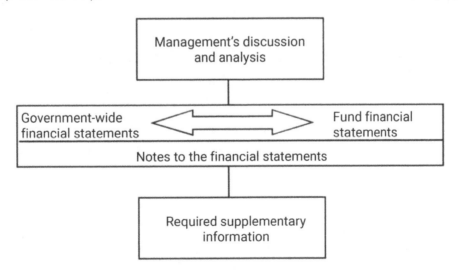

---

[2] See footnote 1.

Summary

To meet the financial objective of accountability, governments use funds to report financial resources and activity. Funds are separate accounting entities for which financial statements can be prepared. There are 11 different fund types that fall into three categories: governmental funds, proprietary funds, and fiduciary funds. Governmental funds use a different MFBOA than do proprietary and fiduciary funds.

Financial reporting by governments must include information about individual major funds and fund categories as well as information about the overall government. Therefore, governments report both fund financial statements and government-wide financial statements. Separate fund financial statements are reported for each of the three fund categories. Two government-wide statements are reported for the overall government: the statement of net position and the statement of activities. The fund financial statements must be reconciled to the government-wide financial statements.

Knowledge check

3. Which statement is accurate regarding the fund financial statements?

    a. There are separate fund financial statements for each fund category.
    b. All funds report a statement of cash flows.
    c. Only fiduciary funds report fund financial statements.
    d. All fund financial statements use the same MFBOA.

	Key foundational points
1	Fund accounting provides the means to report activities based on different legal requirements and operating objectives.
2	Funds used by governmental organizations are categorized as governmental, proprietary, or fiduciary.
3	Governments prepare fund financial statements and government-wide financial statements.

Practice questions

Please note that the following practice questions are not required reading material.

1. What is a characteristic of a fund?

    a. Fiscal entity.
    b. Accounting entity.
    c. Contains self-balancing set of accounts.
    d. All the above.

2. What is a fund category used by governments?

    a. Expendable funds.
    b. Current funds.
    c. Plant funds.
    d. Proprietary funds.

3. Which is a governmental fund?

    a. Private-purpose trust fund.
    b. Enterprise fund.
    c. Permanent fund.
    d. Internal service fund.

4. Which is a proprietary fund?

    a. Debt service fund.
    b. Special revenue fund.
    c. Permanent fund.
    d. Enterprise fund.

5. A statement of revenues, expenditures, and changes in fund balance is required for which?

    a. A proprietary fund.
    b. An internal service fund.
    c. The general fund.
    d. All the above.

6. A government-wide financial statement includes which?

    a. Statement of revenues and expenses.
    b. Statement of activities.
    c. Statement of cash flows.
    d. Statement of changes in net position.

7. Which is **not** a fund financial statement?

    a. Statement of revenues, expenditures, and changes in fund balance.
    b. Statement of cash flows.
    c. Statement of activities.
    d. Statement of changes in fiduciary net position.

8. Which fund would report a statement of cash flows?

    a. Enterprise fund.
    b. Private-purpose trust fund.
    c. Special revenue fund.
    d. All the above.

9. A government decides to open a new park and to charge a fee to cover a portion of the cost. Discuss the possible fund types in which this activity may be reported.

10. For each of the following individual funds, indicate in the blank space the fund type (for example, a capital projects fund) in which it typically belongs:

    _____ Water and sewer utility fund.
    _____ Endowment fund for purchase of library books.
    _____ City Hall construction fund.
    _____ General long-term bond redemption fund.
    _____ Central print-shop fund.
    _____ Parking deck fund.
    _____ Federal grant fund.
    _____ State grant for new bridge fund.
    _____ High school graduate scholarship fund.
    _____ Fleet center fund.
    _____ Employee retirement fund.

11. For each of the following individual funds, to which fund category does it belong: governmental (G), proprietary (P), or fiduciary (F)?

    _____ Enterprise fund.
    _____ Permanent fund.
    _____ Debt service fund.
    _____ Investment trust fund.
    _____ General fund.
    _____ Special revenue fund.
    _____ Capital project fund.
    _____ Private-purpose trust fund.
    _____ Internal service fund.
    _____ Pension (and other employee benefit) trust fund.

Chapter 3

Budgeting

Learning objectives

- Determine the unique role of budgets in the governmental environment.

- Distinguish how budgets are recorded in the accounting system.

- Determine what encumbrances are and how they are used.

- Identify how budget information is reported in the financial statements.

No taxation without representation

What does that historic phrase have to do with budgets? A great deal, as it turns out. Many services of government are paid for with taxes, something most people have to pay. However, only people who we elect can impose those taxes on us. They also are the ones who decide how those resources are to be spent by legally adopting a budget. Governments must show that they spent resources only for purposes approved by our elected officials.

The role of budgets

Why are budgets so important in government? The answer is that budgets are based on the historic notion of "no taxation without representation." Governments can raise taxes only for purposes approved (appropriated) by the elected representatives of the people.

Matters related to the budget are some of the most important decisions that elected officials make. Generally, it is a legally adopted budget that confers authority to levy taxes and spend money. The budget process typically lasts for months and involves public hearings. Elected officials have to balance the need for services against how much taxpayers are willing to provide.

Once approved, budgets become legal contracts between the government and its citizens. Elected officials formally pass an appropriation act, resolution, or ordinance (approved revenues and expenditures), giving government legal authority to spend money. Government officials must demonstrate compliance with legal budgets as part of their financial reporting. Budgets consist of both estimated revenues and appropriations. Although the budget for estimated revenues is often used to set tax rates, it does not have the same legal impact as appropriations. Most governments cannot legally exceed appropriations.

Although all funds may have budgets, they play a special role for *governmental* funds. Typically, services provided by governmental funds are paid for by taxes; there is often little relationship between the revenues generated and the services provided. Elected officials decide how tax revenues are going to be spent when they approve budgets for governmental funds.

Budgets for the businesslike activity of proprietary funds are usually flexible and often not legally adopted. For these activities, there is a relationship between revenues and expenses. Elected officials are usually more concerned with rates charged by business-type activities than the amount of projected expenses. For example, if an activity generates more revenues than projected, it is likely to also generate more expenses.

Governments adopt an annual budget, which in most cases is for the general fund. Special revenue funds also normally have legal budgets. Legal budgets for debt service funds are less common because debt covenants often specify payment requirements. Capital project funds are usually budgeted on a project basis and often have no annual appropriated budget. Generally, permanent funds also do not usually have legally adopted budgets.

Budgets for governmental funds may be approved on some basis other than generally accepted accounting principles (GAAP). For example, a budget can be developed on a cash basis or a budget may include commitments to acquire goods or services before the end of the year (encumbrances). For reporting purposes, a presentation that compares budgeted amounts to actual amounts should report the actual amount of revenues and expenditures on the same basis as the budget.

Budgets can be approved at any level of management control. For example, the budget can be approved at the fund, function, department, activity, or object level. The more detailed the level of management control at which the budget is approved, the less flexibility the government has in reallocating resources internally. A balance should be achieved between legal budgetary control and efficient management control.

Knowledge check

1. Which statement is correct regarding the role of budgets?

    a. Budgets consist solely of estimated appropriations.
    b. The budget process does not typically involve public hearings.
    c. Elected officials have to balance the need for services against how much taxpayers are willing to provide.
    d. Budgets have no authoritative role in a government's spending.

2. Which statement is correct regarding a proprietary fund budget?

    a. A proprietary fund budget must be legally adopted.
    b. There is often little relationship between the revenues generated and the services provided by the business-type activities of proprietary funds.
    c. Proprietary fund budgets are usually flexible.
    d. Elected officials are more concerned with projected expenses than the rates charged for business-type activities.

Recording the budget

Because of their legal significance, budgets are often integrated in the accounting system of governments. In many automated systems, budgets can be loaded into the system in different ways. Accounting systems can produce a variety of reports comparing amounts budgeted to actual amounts for revenues and expenditures. In a manual system, the budget can be recorded by a journal entry. To facilitate comparison with actual amounts, budget amounts are recorded as opposite of the actual amounts. For example, estimated revenues would be debited, whereas actual revenues are normally credited; appropriations are credited, whereas expenditures are debited. A sample budget journal entry follows:

	DR	CR
Estimated revenue	75,000	
Appropriation		65,000
Budgetary fund balance		10,000

The preceding entry includes a credit to budgetary fund balance. This account is used to facilitate the use of double-entry accounting. The credit to budgetary fund balance can also be interpreted as the projected impact the budget will have on fund balance.

At the end of the year, the budget is closed by simply reversing the preceding entry as follows:

	DR	CR
Appropriation	65,000	
Budgetary fund balance	10,000	
Estimated revenue		75,000

Once the budget has been recorded, no additional entries are required to the budget accounts during the year unless the budget is revised. For example, if appropriations were increased, then the entry would include a debit to budgetary fund balance and a credit to appropriations. A governing body can revise a budget at any time by taking legal action through its budget process.

Encumbrances

Government managers use budget information to monitor spending. The *available appropriation*, which represents the amount of the current appropriation remaining to be committed or spent, can be arrived at by subtracting actual expenditures and outstanding commitments from the appropriated amount. Subtracting both actual expenditures and outstanding commitments provides a better indication of what amount is available to spend.

Governments often use encumbrances to record outstanding commitments in the accounting system. An *encumbrance* does not represent a liability or expenditure; it is a budgetary tool used to control spending. Amounts are usually encumbered when goods or services are ordered. When the goods or services are received, the encumbrance is removed and the actual expenditure and liability is recorded.

Encumbrances usually represent purchase commitments and, often, are only estimates of the costs of goods or services to be received. The actual cost for the goods or services received may differ from the encumbered amount. When this happens, the encumbrance should be removed for the same amount at which it was established and the expenditure recorded for the actual amount.

For example, assume a government orders goods estimated to cost $15,000. In a manual system, an encumbrance is recorded as follows:

	DR	CR
Encumbrances	15,000	
Budgetary fund balance		
Reserve for encumbrances		15,000

When the item is received, the encumbrance is removed and the expenditure recorded. Assuming that the actual invoice for the preceding encumbrance is for $14,990, the entry to record this transaction is as follows:

	DR	CR
Budgetary fund balance		
Reserve for encumbrances	15,000	
Encumbrances		15,000
Expenditure	14,990	
Accounts payable		14,990

Note that the encumbrance is removed for the same amount that it was established, and the expenditure is recorded at the actual amount.

Encumbrances can be very useful in controlling expenditures. Governments can choose to use an encumbrance system that is efficient and effective for their needs. For example, governments can require encumbrances for purchases only over a certain amount. Often, governments will not encumber salaries and other routine expenses such as utilities. Some governments do not use an encumbrance system at all.

Outstanding encumbrances at the end of the year are typically removed as part of the budgetary closing procedures. In a manual system, outstanding encumbrances can be removed by reversing the original entry. An outstanding encumbrance of $10,000 would be removed as follows:

	DR	CR
Budgetary fund balance		
Reserve for encumbrances	10,000	
Encumbrances		10,000

Governments establish various policies regarding outstanding commitments at year-end. Some consider all outstanding commitments to be canceled. Some intend to honor outstanding commitments but require that the appropriation for the next year include these items. Still others consider outstanding encumbrances to be an appropriate charge against current-year appropriations.

Prior to the issuance of GASB Statement No. 54, *Fund Balance Reporting and Governmental Fund Type Definitions*, in cases where encumbrances represented a charge against current-year appropriations, the government would reserve fund balance for the amount of outstanding encumbrances. With the advent of GASB Statement No. 54, amounts related to outstanding encumbrances at year-end are no longer reported as a separate line on the face of the balance sheet. Significant encumbrances are disclosed in the notes to the financial statements.

Knowledge check

3. Which statement is correct regarding the role of available appropriation?

    a. It represents the amount that can be spent in total for the year.
    b. It is computed by subtracting actual expenditures from estimated revenue.
    c. It is computed by subtracting actual expenditures and outstanding commitments from the appropriated amount.
    d. It represents the amount spent for the year.

Comparing budgeted amounts to actual amounts

Accountability requires governments to demonstrate their compliance with legally adopted annual budgets. To do this, governments must report budgetary comparison schedules for the general fund and for each major special revenue fund with a legally adopted annual budget.

Budgetary comparison schedules are schedules that are reported as part of required supplementary information (RSI). RSI is unaudited information included with governmental financial statements. However, governments may elect to include these schedules as part of the fund financial statements. In this case, the budgetary comparison schedule becomes subject to the same audit requirements as other fund-based statements. An example of a budgetary comparison schedule is in appendix B.

These schedules must contain at least three columns for each governmental fund reported:

a.   A column for the **original** budget, the first complete appropriated budget (amount may include adjustments made to the budget before the beginning of the fiscal year; also, actual appropriation amounts that automatically carry forward from prior years should be included)
b.   A column for the **final** budget (with all amendments and revisions)
c.   A column for **actual** amounts reported using the budgetary basis of accounting

A variance column may be included to facilitate the comparison of budget and actual amounts; however, this column is not required.

The budget may be prepared on a basis other than GAAP. In this case, the actual amount reported for revenues and expenditures is reported on the same basis as the budget. This does not change the requirement that the statement of revenues, expenditures, and changes in fund balance be prepared on a GAAP basis of accounting.

Any differences between the statement of revenues, expenditures, and changes in fund balance and the budgetary comparison schedule must be reconciled. This can be done on the face of the schedule or in the notes to RSI.

The budget comparison schedule can be prepared using the same format and terminology of the budget document or using the same format as the statement of revenues, expenditures, and changes in fund balances. If expenditures exceed budgeted amounts for an individual fund, this information must be disclosed.

Some governments have significant budgetary perspective differences that result in their inability to present budgetary comparisons for the general fund and each major special revenue fund. These governments are required to present budgetary comparison schedules as RSI based on the fund, organization, or program structure that the government uses for its legally adopted budget.

Summary

Budgets play a special role in governments. Once approved, budgets become legal contracts between a government and the citizens it serves. Elected officials formally pass an appropriation act, resolution, or ordinance, giving the government legal authority to spend money. Legally adopted budgets are used for the general fund and often for other governmental funds.

To ensure budgetary control, budgets are often recorded in the accounting system. Many governments also use encumbrances as a budgetary tool to record commitments against budgets. Governments are required to report a budgetary comparison schedule with their financial statements. This schedule is usually reported as part of RSI or can be reported as part of the fund financial statements.

Budgets can be prepared on some other basis than GAAP. The actual amount of revenue and expenditures in the budgetary comparison schedule is reported on the same basis of the budget. If the basis is other than a GAAP basis, a reconciliation of the two bases is required.

Key foundational points	
1	Matters related to the budget are some of the most important decisions that elected officials make.
2	Governments often use encumbrances to record outstanding commitments in the accounting system.
3	Governments are required to report budgetary comparison schedules for the general fund and each major special revenue fund with a legally adopted annual budget.

Practice questions

Please note that the following practice questions are not required reading material.

1. What is the legally adopted budget for expenditures called?

   a. Estimated expenditures.
   b. Appropriations.
   c. Allotments.
   d. Encumbrances.

2. A flexible budget would be typically used for which fund?

   a. General fund.
   b. Enterprise fund.
   c. Special revenue fund.
   d. All the above.

3. In recording the adoption of a budget for a general fund, a debit amount is recorded to budgetary fund balance. What does this entry indicate?

   a. Estimated revenues exceed appropriations.
   b. Appropriations exceed estimated revenues.
   c. The budget is balanced.
   d. Revenues exceed expenditures.

4. What should the entry to record adoption of a general fund budget include?

   a. A debit to estimated revenues.
   b. A credit to estimated revenues.
   c. A debit to appropriations.
   d. Both (*b*) and (*c*).

5. Entries to the appropriation account would be made when

   a. The expenditure budget is revised.
   b. The budget is recorded.
   c. The budget is closed.
   d. All the above.

6. To record an encumbrance, which account is debited?

   a. Expenditures.
   b. Appropriations.
   c. Encumbrances.
   d. Reserve for encumbrances.

---

7. A budgetary comparison schedule is required for which?

    a. All governmental funds with annual enacted budgets.
    b. The general fund.
    c. Each major special revenue fund with an annual enacted budget.
    d. Both (b) and (c).

8. A general fund ordered supplies with an expected cost of $3,000. This amount is encumbered. The supplies are received with an invoice of $3,100. The entries to record the receipt of the supplies should include a debit to what account?

    a. Encumbrances of $3,100.
    b. Expenditures of $3,100.
    c. Reserve for encumbrances of $3,000.
    d. Both (b) and (c).

9. A budgetary comparison schedule should be reported as part of which?

    a. Fund financial statements.
    b. Notes to the financial statements.
    c. RSI.
    d. Either (a) or (c).

10. Explain the difference between an expenditure and an encumbrance.

11. Where in the financial statements may the budgetary comparison schedules be presented? Explain the impact that placement will have on the audit.

12. A city approves an expenditure budget in the amount of $25,000. The city encumbers two items. The first item is an order for supplies in the amount of $6,000; the second item is an order for parts in the amount of $2,500. The first order is received at a cost of $5,800. What is the amount of available appropriation? What does this represent?

Chapter 4

Measurement Focus and Basis of Accounting

Learning objectives

- Differentiate the two measurement focuses used by governments.

- Differentiate the two bases of accounting used by governments.

- Recognize special terminology used to account for certain items and transactions.

Just what is it that you want to measure?

As it turns out, this is an important question in governmental accounting. The same transaction can be reported differently by different funds. *Which* transactions a fund records and *when* depend on the fund's operating objective. It all comes down to the measurement focus and basis of accounting (MFBOA) being used.

Governmental funds are used to account for the general activities of the government financed primarily by taxes and grants. Proprietary funds are used to account for the business-type activities financed primarily by user fees. The activities and operating objectives of these two fund categories are different and therefore their reporting objectives are different. The two types of fund categories use different measurement focuses and bases of accounting.

Measurement focus

A key to understanding governmental accounting is recognizing that financial statements can measure different things. For example, a cash flow statement will report all transactions that affect cash only. *Measurement focus* is concerned with *what* is being measured and reported in the financial statements. The financial statements for governmental and proprietary funds measure two different things.

Governmental funds

Governmental funds use a *flow of current financial resources* measurement focus. The financial statements measure whether financial resources that can be spent in the near future have increased or decreased for the accounting period.

Inflows of current financial resources are reported as *revenues or other financing sources* and outflows are reported as *expenditures or other financing uses*. The net change for the year indicates whether inflows of current financial resources were larger than outflows of such resources.

Another way to describe the measurement basis of accounting is by using the accounting equation. The accounting equation for a governmental fund follows:

Current assets + Deferred outflows of resources = Current liabilities + Deferred inflows of resources + Fund balance

There are three major differences between this accounting equation and that used by a business. The first is that the fund balance represents net financial resources that can be spent in the near future. It does not represent the difference between all the economic assets and liabilities of the organization.

The second major difference between the equations is the exclusion of capital assets. What happens when a capital asset is purchased? Cash and fund balance would both decrease (an expenditure would be recorded). There would be no need to record depreciation because the full cost of the assets would have been recorded as an expenditure when it was purchased.

The third major difference between the equations is the absence of long-term debt. Does this mean that governments do not issue long-term debt for governmental activities? No. When a government issues long-term debt for governmental activities, both cash and fund balance would increase (other financing sources would be recorded). The future repayment of the long-term debt would not need to come from current available financial resources but would be repaid from financial resources generated in the future. When debt is repaid from a governmental fund, cash and fund balance would decrease (an expenditure would be recorded).

Does this mean that capital assets and long-term debt are not reported in the financial statements? It depends. Because the governmental funds' financial statements are reporting the flow of current financial resources, they would not appear there. However, they would appear in the government-wide financial statements. The government-wide financial statements are reporting all economic resources and liabilities of the government.

Proprietary funds

Proprietary funds use a *flow of economic resources* measurement focus. The financial statements measure whether the economic resources have increased or decreased for the accounting period. This is the same measurement focus used by business organizations.

Inflows of economic resources are reported as *revenues or gains* and outflows are reported as *expenses or losses*. The net change in economic resources for a year is very similar to the net income measurement used in business.

The accounting equation for a proprietary fund follows:

Assets + Deferred outflows of resources − Liabilities − Deferred inflows of resources = Net position

Proprietary funds would account for both current and noncurrent assets and liabilities. For example, capital assets and long-term debt both would be reported as part of these funds.

The following table lists the key differences between governmental and proprietary funds that result from the measurement focus of accounting.

Key differences resulting from the measurement focus of accounting

Item	Fund balance governmental funds	Net position proprietary funds
Capital assets acquisition	Decrease	No effect
Depreciation	No effect	Decrease
Issuance of long-term debt	Increase	No effect
Payment of long-term debt principal	Decrease	No effect

Knowledge check

1. Which statement is correct regarding the measurement focus used for proprietary funds?

    a. Proprietary funds do not really have a measurement focus.
    b. Proprietary funds would account for only noncurrent assets and liabilities.
    c. The financial statements measure whether the economic resources have increased or decreased for the accounting period.
    d. Proprietary funds report inflow of resources as revenue and other financing sources.

Basis of accounting

Basis of accounting is concerned with *when* a transaction or event is recognized in the accounting system. For example, a cash basis of accounting would recognize transactions only when they affect cash. The basis of accounting used by governments is directly linked to the measurement focus.

Governmental funds recognize transactions using one basis of accounting; proprietary funds use another.

Knowledge check

2. Which statement is correct regarding bases of accounting?

   a. Both governmental funds and proprietary funds use the same basis of accounting.
   b. The basis of accounting used by governments is not linked to the measurement focus.
   c. The basis of accounting is concerned with when a transaction or event is recognized in the accounting system.
   d. The basis of accounting is concerned with what transaction or event is recognized in the accounting system.

Governmental funds

Governmental funds use the *modified accrual basis* of accounting. This basis of accounting requires a transaction that affects current financial resources to be measured as a revenue or expenditure. For example, an inflow of current financial resources will be recorded as revenue only if it is received in time to liquidate a current-period liability.

For an item to be measured as revenue it must meet two conditions: it must be measurable and it must be available to meet current obligations. To meet the availability criterion, revenue must be collected during the year or soon enough after year-end to pay liabilities of the current period.

Expenditures are recorded when incurred only if the transaction will require the use of current financial resources. For example, vacation leave earned by an employee will be recognized as an expenditure only to the extent that it will be paid out of current financial resources. There are certain exceptions to the expenditure recognition rule.

Proprietary funds

Proprietary funds use an *accrual basis* of accounting similar to that used by a business. This basis of accounting records transactions when they occur, regardless of the related cash flow. Revenues are recognized when they are both measurable and earned. Expenses are recorded when incurred. In contrast to the modified accrual basis of accounting, the full amount of vacation leave earned by an employee would be recognized as an expense.

Government-wide statements' MFBOA

The government-wide statements bring the financial activity together in one place and report accrual-based economic resources information. The government-wide statements organize information by whether it relates to governmental activities or business-type activities. The fiduciary funds (such as pension trusts and agency funds) are not included in the government-wide statements, because the

---

resources they account for do not belong to the government. The governmental and business-type activities combine to represent the total primary government. Additionally, discretely presented component units—legally separate entities for which the primary government is financially accountable—are shown on the face of the government-wide statements but are not included in the total for the primary government.

Fiduciary funds' MFBOA

Fiduciary funds generally use the same MFBOA as do proprietary funds and use the accrual basis of accounting.

GASB Statement No. 84, *Fiduciary Activities*, is effective for fiscal years beginning after December 15, 2018. Agency funds are replaced with custodial funds under this statement. Custodial funds will report a net position and have the same measurement focus as proprietary funds.

Terminology

Governments use several unique terms to describe their activities. Some of these terms relate to interfund transactions, some to transactions of all funds and activities, and some only to governmental funds transactions. Governments also use unique terms and classifications to describe fund balance and net position.

Interfund transactions

There are frequent transactions between different funds of a government. Activities among the funds are classified as either reciprocal interfund activity or nonreciprocal interfund activity.

Reciprocal interfund activity includes loans and services provided and used. Interfund loans should be reported separately in the financial statements as interfund receivables and payables. If repayment of a loan is not expected within a reasonable time, the amount recorded as a loan should be reduced and reported as a transfer.

Interfund services provided and used are treated as an internal exchange-like transaction. Revenue is recorded in the seller fund and expenditures or expenses are recorded in the purchaser fund.

Nonreciprocal interfund activity includes transfers and reimbursements. Interfund transfers represent a flow of assets from one fund to another that will not be repaid. In governmental funds, these transfers are reported as "other financing sources" (by the fund receiving the transfer) or "other financing uses" (by the fund making the transfer). Proprietary funds would report transfers after nonoperating revenues and expenses on the statement of revenues, expenses, and changes in fund net position.

Interfund reimbursements represent the repayment for a particular expenditure or expense by a fund responsible for the charge to the fund that initially paid for the item. The net effect of a reimbursement is that the expense or expenditure in one fund would be reduced; the expense or expenditure in another fund would be increased.

Special items and extraordinary items

Governments separately report transactions or events that meet the definition of special items and extraordinary items. These items are reported at the bottom of the fund financial operating statements for governmental and proprietary funds and at the bottom of the government-wide statement of activities.

A *special item* is a significant transaction or event **within** the control of management that is either unusual in nature or infrequent in occurrence.

An *extraordinary item* is a transaction or event that is both unusual in nature and infrequent in occurrence.

Deferred outflows of resources and deferred inflows of resources

GASB Statement No. 65, *Items Previously Reported as Assets and Liabilities,* lists several specific items that should now be reported as either deferred outflows of resources or deferred inflows of resources. In addition, GASB Statement No. 53, *Accounting and Financial Reporting for Derivative Instruments*; GASB Statement No. 60, *Accounting and Financial Reporting for Service Concession Arrangements*; GASB Statement No. 68, *Accounting and Financial Reporting for Pensions — An Amendment of GASB Statement No. 27*; GASB Statement No. 69, *Government Combinations and Disposals of Government Operations*; GASB Statement No. 73, *Accounting and Financial Reporting for Pensions and Related Assets That Are Not Within the Scope of GASB Statement 68, and Amendments to Certain Provisions of GASB Statements 67 and 68*; GASB Statement No. 75, *Accounting and Financial Reporting for Postemployment Benefits Other Than Pensions*; GASB Statement No. 81, *Irrevocable Split-Interest Agreements*; GASB Statement No. 83, *Certain Asset Retirement Obligations*; and GASB Statement No. 87, *Leases*, also identified items that should be reported as deferred outflows of resources or deferred inflows of resources.

A *deferred outflow of resources* is a consumption of net assets by the government that is applicable to a future reporting period. The following is a list of items that the GASB has identified that should be reported as deferred outflows of resources:

- Grant paid in advance of meeting timing requirement
- Deferred amounts from refunding of debt (debits)
- Cost to acquire rights to future revenues (intra-entity)
- Deferred loss from sale-leaseback
- Certain items related to pensions under GASB Statement No. 68
- Certain Items related to postemployment benefits other than pensions under GASB Statement No. 75
- Asset retirement obligation

A *deferred inflow of resources* is an acquisition of net assets by the government that is applicable to a future reporting period. The following is a list of items that GASB has identified that should be reported as deferred inflows of resources:

- Grants received in advance of meeting timing requirement
- Deferred amounts from refunding of debt (credits)
- Proceeds from sales of future revenues
- Deferred gain from sale-leaseback
- "Regulatory" credits
- Certain items related to pensions under GASB Statement No. 68
- Certain items related to postemployment benefits other than pensions under GASB Statement No. 75
- Net resources received pursuant to an irrevocable split-interest agreement
- The value of a lease receivable plus any payments received at or before the commencement of a lease term that relate to future periods by the lessor for the inception of a lease under GASB Statement No. 87

Governmental funds recognize revenue when it is measurable and available. When an asset is recorded in a governmental fund but the revenue is not available, a deferred inflow of resources should be reported.

Transactions reported by governmental funds

Governmental funds report certain transactions in a separate section of the statement of revenues, expenditures, and changes in fund balances; this section is called "Other financing sources and uses." These transactions either provide or use financial resources but are not considered revenues or expenditures.

Other financing sources and uses include the face value of debt issued, issuance premiums or discounts, certain payments to escrow agents for bond refundings, transfers, some insurance proceeds, and sales of capital assets (unless the sale meets the criteria to be reported as a special item).

Only items identified in the preceding paragraph can be reported as other financing sources and uses.

Fund balance

Governmental funds use the term *fund balance* to represent the difference between current financial assets and current financial liabilities. Under GASB Statement No. 54, *Fund Balance Reporting and Governmental Fund Type Definitions,* governments have five classifications.

Under GASB Statement No. 54, governmental fund balances should be reported in classifications arranged in a hierarchy. This hierarchy is built primarily on the extent to which a government is bound to honor constraints on the specific purposes for which amounts in those funds can be spent.

Nonspendable fund balance	The *nonspendable fund balance* classification includes amounts that cannot be spent because they are either (1) not in spendable form or (2) legally or contractually required to be maintained intact. *Not in spendable form* describes items that are not expected to be converted to cash (such as inventories and prepaid amounts). It also includes the long-term amount of loans and notes receivable as well as property acquired for resale. However, if the use of proceeds from the collection of those receivables or from the sale of those properties is restricted, committed, or assigned, then they should be included under the appropriate fund balance classification (restricted, committed, or assigned) rather than under the nonspendable fund balance classification.
Restricted fund balance	Fund balances should be reported as *restricted* when constraints placed on the use of the resources are either • externally imposed by creditors (such as through debt covenants), grantors, contributors, or laws or regulations of other governments; or • imposed by law through constitutional provisions or enabling legislation.

Committed fund balance	*Committed fund balances* describe amounts that can be used only for specific purposes pursuant to constraints imposed by formal action of the government's highest level of decision-making authority. Those committed amounts cannot be used for any other purpose unless the government removes or changes the specified use by taking the same type of action (such as legislation, resolution, or ordinance) it employed previously to commit those amounts.
Assigned fund balance	Amounts that are constrained by the government's intent to be used for specific purposes, but are neither restricted nor committed, should be reported as *assigned fund balances*; an exception is made for stabilization arrangements, as discussed in paragraph 21 of GASB Statement No. 54.
Unassigned fund balance	An *unassigned fund balance* is the residual classification for the general fund. This classification represents a fund balance that has not been assigned to other funds and that has not been restricted, committed, or assigned to specific purposes within the general fund.

GASB Statement No. 54 allows some flexibility in the level of detail presented. For example, the two components of nonspendable fund balances (not in spendable form and legally or contractually required to be maintained intact) may be presented separately or in the aggregate. However, if a nonspendable fund balance is displayed in the aggregate on the face of the balance sheet, amounts for the two nonspendable components should be disclosed in the notes to the financial statements.

GASB Statement No. 54 has several disclosure requirements. For example, governments should disclose the following about their fund balance classification policies and procedures:

 For committed fund balance: (1) the government's highest level of decision-making authority and (2) the formal action that is required to be taken to establish (and modify or rescind) a fund balance commitment

 For assigned fund balance: (1) the body or official authorized to assign amounts to a specific purpose and (2) the policy established by the governing body pursuant to which that authorization is given.

 For the classification of fund balances in accordance with paragraph 18 of GASB Statement No. 54: (1) whether the government considers restricted or unrestricted amounts to have been spent when an expenditure is incurred for purposes for which both restricted and unrestricted fund balance is available; and (2) whether committed, assigned, or unassigned amounts are considered to have been spent when an expenditure is incurred for purposes for which amounts in any of those unrestricted fund balance classifications could be used

Net position

The term *net position* is used to represent the difference between assets (+ deferred outflows of resources) and liabilities (+ deferred inflows of resources) for proprietary funds and in the government-wide statements. Net position is divided into the following three components:

1. The **net investment in capital assets** component of net position consists of capital assets and net of accumulated depreciation, reduced by the outstanding balances of bonds, mortgages, notes, or other borrowings that are attributable to the acquisition, construction, or improvement of those assets. Deferred outflows of resources and deferred inflows of resources that are attributable to the acquisition, construction, or improvement of those assets or related debt should also be included in this component of net position. If there are significant unspent related debt proceeds or deferred inflows of resources at the end of the reporting period, the portion of the debt or deferred inflows of resources attributable to the unspent amount should not be included in the calculation of net investment in capital assets. Instead, that portion of the debt or deferred inflows of resources should be included in the same net position component (restricted or unrestricted) as the unspent amount.
2. The **restricted** component of net position consists of restricted assets reduced by liabilities and deferred inflows of resources related to those assets. Generally, a liability relates to restricted assets if the assets result from a resource flow that also results in the recognition of a liability or if the liability will be liquidated with the restricted assets reported. Constraints can be either externally imposed (for example, debt covenants or grantor restrictions) or imposed by constitutional provisions or enabling legislation[1].
3. The **unrestricted** component of net position is the net amount of the assets, deferred outflows of resources, liabilities, and deferred inflows of resources that are not included in the determination of net investment in capital assets or the restricted component of net position. Unlike fund balance, designations of unrestricted net assets should not be reported on the face of the financial statements.

---

[1] GASB Statement No. 46, *Net Assets Restricted by Enabling Legislation – An Amendment of GASB Statement No. 34,* provides additional guidance in this area.

Summary

Government funds use different measurement focuses and bases of accounting: governmental funds use the flow of current financial resources measurement focus and the modified accrual basis of accounting; proprietary funds use the flow of economic resources measurement focus and the accrual basis of accounting. Because of these differences, governmental and proprietary funds report certain transactions differently. There are major differences in how the two fund categories report certain transactions related to capital assets and long-term debt.

Governments use unique terminology to describe their activities and balances. Interfund activities, special and extraordinary items, and other financing sources and uses are unique items reported by a government. Components of fund balance and net position also have unique classifications.

	Key foundational points
1	Governmental funds use a flow of current financial resources measurement focus. Proprietary funds use a flow of economic resources measurement focus.
2	Governmental funds use the modified accrual basis of accounting. Proprietary funds use an accrual basis of accounting like that used by businesses.
3	All activities in the government-wide statements use the flow of economic resources and accrual basis of accounting.
4	GASB Statement No. 65 lists several specific items that should now be reported as either deferred outflows of resources or deferred inflows of resources.
5	Under GASB Statement No. 54, governmental fund balances should be reported in classifications arranged in a hierarchy. This hierarchy is built primarily on the extent to which a government is bound to honor constraints on the specific purposes for which amounts in those funds can be spent.
6	Net position is divided into three components.
7	Trust funds generally follow the same MFBOA as do proprietary funds. Custodial funds report only assets and liabilities and are not considered to have a measurement focus. They follow the accrual basis of accounting.

Practice questions

Please note that the following practice questions are not required reading material.

1. Which fund type would use the flow of economic resources measurement focus?

    a. General fund.
    b. Debt service fund.
    c. Special revenue fund.
    d. None of the above.

2. Which fund type would use the flow of current financial resources measurement focus?

    a. Private-purpose trust fund.
    b. Enterprise fund.
    c. Capital project fund.
    d. Internal service fund.

3. Which funds would use the availability criterion for recognizing revenues?

    a. Capital projects funds.
    b. Debt service funds.
    c. General Fund.
    d. All the above.

4. A special revenue fund would use which basis of accounting?

    a. Accrual.
    b. Modified accrual.
    c. Cash.
    d. Modified cash.

5. Proprietary funds recognize

    a. Revenues and qains.
    b. Expenditures and losses.
    c. Expenses and losses.
    d. Both a. and c.

6. The general fund pays resources to a capital projects fund. These resources will not be repaid. This transaction is an example of an interfund

    a. Transfer.
    b. Services provided and used transaction.
    c. Reimbursement transaction.
    d. Loan.

7. Which would be classified as other financing sources (uses)?

    a. Purchase of capital assets.
    b. Sale of capital assets.
    c. Payment of long-term debt.
    d. All the above.

8. The criteria for a transaction to be classified as a special item are which?

    a. Unusual in nature or infrequent in occurrence.
    b. Unusual in nature and infrequent in occurrence.
    c. Under the control of management.
    d. Both a. and c. combined.

9. Which fund type would report fund balance?

    a. Custodial fund.
    b. Debt service fund.
    c. Internal service fund.
    d. Private-purpose trust fund.

10. Which would **not** be reported as a component of net position of an enterprise fund?

    a. Unrestricted net position.
    b. Restricted net position.
    c. Net investment in capital assets.
    d. Designated net position.

11. What is the difference between an expenditure and expense? Give an example of a transaction that would be both an expense and an expenditure. Give an example of a transaction that would be an expenditure but not an expense.

12. What is the difference between revenues accounted for under the accrual method of accounting and those accounted for under the modified accrual method of accounting?

Chapter 5

Governmental Funds: Revenues and Expenditures

Learning objectives

- Recognize how governmental fund revenues are reported.

- Determine how to measure and report revenue from nonexchange transactions.

- Determine how to measure and report governmental fund expenditures.

- Identify which liabilities are excluded from governmental funds.

Refer to appendix A of this course for a statement of revenues, expenditures, and changes in fund balance.

The exception to the exception

No, governmental fund revenues and expenditures are not as complex as the income tax code. The general rules for recognizing revenue and expenditures work most of the time. There are a few exceptions to the rules and, in a few rare cases, exceptions to the exceptions.

Governmental funds use a **flow of current financial resources** measurement focus and the **modified accrual** basis of accounting. Under the modified accrual basis of accounting, revenues are recognized when they meet two conditions: **measurable** and **available**. Expenditures are recorded when incurred only if the transaction will require the use of current financial resources. This chapter further explains how revenues and expenditures are recognized and recorded. We also will discuss certain exceptions to normal recognition rules.

Revenues

Governmental funds receive revenues from a variety of sources. Typical sources of revenue for a local government include various types of taxes, fees, and fines; licenses and permits; intergovernmental charges for services; and investment earnings. Governments report revenues by major source.

Normally, two of the largest revenue sources for governmental funds are taxes and intergovernmental revenue. Such revenues are not exchange-type transactions and thus require a different type of recognition criteria. The modified accrual method of accounting for revenues is concerned with when the inflow of financial resources is available to pay for expenditures of the current period.

Under the modified accrual basis, only those revenues susceptible to accrual are recognized before the cash is received. To be *susceptible to accrual*, revenues must be both objectively measurable and available to finance current-period expenditures. Revenues that do not meet these criteria are recorded on a cash basis.

For revenue to be *available*, it must meet the following criteria:

- It must be collected in the current period or soon enough thereafter to be used to pay liabilities of the current period; the length of time to be considered "soon enough" varies in practice. Generally accepted accounting principles requires that this period of time for property taxes not exceed 60 days, which is also commonly used for other types of revenues; other time periods can be used.
- It must be legally available to finance current-period expenditures.

Consider the following example:

A county levies property taxes of $100,000 for the current year. During the year, $92,000 is collected. During the first 60 days of the following year, another $5,000 is collected and the balance of $3,000 is collected during the remainder of the year. How should the revenue be recorded?

The county would recognize revenue of $97,000 (the $92,000 collected during the year and the $5,000 collected in the first 60 days of the following year). At the end of the current year, the county would report a receivable of $8,000 and deferred of $3,000 (the amount that did not meet the availability criteria). In the following year, the county would record the $3,000 as revenue as it is collected.

The availability criteria also affect how the allowance for uncollectible accounts is recorded. Because the amount of accounts receivable estimated to be uncollectible will never be available to finance current-period expenditures, it should not be recorded as revenue. For example, if taxes in the amount of $100,000 are levied and $2,000 is estimated as uncollectible, the following entry would be made (assume that the $98,000 will be collected during the year).

	DR	CR
Taxes receivable	100,000	
Allowance for uncollectible accounts		2,000
Revenue		98,000

In essence, revenues are recorded net of the amount estimated to be uncollectible. If the allowance account needs to be increased or decreased during the year, the adjustment is made to the related revenue.

Revenues of governments are classified as either exchange or exchange-like transactions and nonexchange transactions. Generally, the availability criteria apply to both types of transactions for governmental funds.

Knowledge check

1. Which is correct regarding governmental fund revenues?

    a. Governmental funds receive revenues from a variety of sources.
    b. Normally, two of the smallest revenue sources for governmental funds are taxes and intergovernmental revenue.
    c. Governments report revenues by minor source.
    d. The amount of revenue estimated to be uncollectible is recorded as bad debt expenditure.

Nonexchange transactions

GASB Statement No. 33, *Accounting and Financial Reporting for Nonexchange Transactions,* provides guidance on recognizing both receivables and revenues for nonexchange transactions. *Nonexchange transactions* are transactions that do not involve an exchange of value. Most taxes and grants fall into this category. The GASB has classified nonexchange transactions into the following four categories:

1. *Derived tax revenues* — Taxes assessed on exchange transactions (for example, sales tax imposed on sales transactions and income tax imposed on earnings)
2. *Imposed nonexchange transactions* — Taxes assessed on something other than exchange transactions (most commonly, property taxes and fines and forfeitures)
3. *Government-mandated nonexchange transactions* — Resources provided by a higher-level government with the requirement that they be used for a purpose established by the higher-level government
4. *Voluntary nonexchange transactions* — Resources provided by legislative or contractual agreements (other than exchange) entered into willingly by the parties (for example, certain government grants and entitlements and donations)[1]

GASB Statement No. 33 provides guidance on recording revenue for nonexchange transactions under both the accrual method (used by proprietary funds and for all activities reported in the government-wide statement) and for the modified accrual method (used by governmental funds).

---

[1] Determining whether a resource is either government-mandated or voluntary is not important for recognition purposes because both are recognized in the same manner.

The following table summarizes the guidance on reporting nonexchange transactions from GASB Statement No. 33:

Classes and timing of recognition of nonexchange transactions

Class	Recognition
Derived tax revenues Examples: sales taxes, income taxes, motor fuel taxes	**Assets** Period when underlying exchange has occurred or when resources are received, whichever is first. **Revenues** Period when underlying exchange has occurred. When modified accrual accounting is used, resources should also be "available."
Imposed nonexchange revenues Examples: property taxes, most fines and forfeitures	**Assets** Period when an enforceable claim has arisen or when resources are received, whichever is first. **Revenues** Period when resources are required to be used or first period that use is permitted. When modified accrual accounting is used, resources should also be "available."
Government-mandated nonexchange transactions Examples: federal government mandates on state and local governments **Voluntary nonexchange transactions** Examples: certain grants, entitlements, most donations	**Assets** Period when all eligibility requirements have been met or when resources are received, whichever is first. **Revenues** Period when all eligibility requirements have been met. Time requirements specify when resources are to be used and are considered an eligibility requirement. Purpose restrictions specify the purpose for which the resources must be used and are **not** considered an eligibility requirement. When modified accrual accounting is used, resources should also be "available."

Governments often share their own derived tax revenues or imposed nonexchange revenues with other governments. For example, a state may share a portion of its sales tax revenue with local governments. In this case, the local government would report this transaction using the guidance for government-mandated and voluntary nonexchange transactions.

Tax abatements are widely used by state and local governments to induce behavior by individuals and entities that is beneficial to the government or its citizens, such as in encouraging economic development. Financial statement users need information about certain limitations on a government's ability to raise resources. GASB Statement No. 77, *Tax Abatement Disclosures*, requires disclosure of tax abatement information about (1) a reporting government's own tax abatement agreements and (2) agreements entered into by other governments that reduce the reporting government's tax revenues.

Knowledge check

2. Which statement is correct regarding nonexchange transactions?

    a. GASB Statement No. 33 provides guidance on recognizing both receivables and revenues for nonexchange transactions.
    b. Sales taxes are a type of imposed nonexchange revenue.
    c. Nonexchange transactions are transactions that involve an exchange of value.
    d. Property taxes are a type of government-mandated nonexchange transaction.

Investments

GASB Statement No. 72, *Fair Value Measurement and Application*, defines an *investment* as a security or other asset held primarily for the purpose of income or profit. A government-held investment has a present service capacity based solely on its ability to generate cash or to be sold to generate cash. GASB Statement No. 72 generally requires investments to be reported at fair value. However, certain investments are excluded from being measured at fair value, such as money market investments, qualified external investment pools, investments in life insurance contracts, common stock meeting the criteria for applying the equity method, unallocated insurance contracts, and synthetic guaranteed investment contracts.

GASB Statement No. 72 defines *fair value* as an exit price — the price that would be received to sell an asset or paid to transfer a liability in an orderly transaction between market participants at the measurement date. This statement requires a government to use valuation techniques appropriate under the circumstances. These techniques should be consistent with at least one of the following approaches: the market approach, the cost approach, and the income approach.

Income on investments should be recorded as revenue when earned. The change in fair value should be reported as part of investment income. In addition, realized gain and losses should not be reported separately from unrealized gains and losses in the financial statements.

Derivative instruments

GASB Statement No. 53, *Accounting and Financial Reporting for Derivative Instruments,* requires governments to measure most derivative instruments at fair value as assets or liabilities in the financial statements for accrual-based, government-wide proprietary funds and fiduciary funds (but not in those for governmental funds). GASB Statement No. 53 does not address the issue of reporting derivative instruments at fair value in governmental fund statements. The GASB will reserve consideration of this issue for its conceptual framework project on recognition and measurement attributes.

Expenditures

Governmental funds expend resources for a variety of purposes. Expenditures are reported by character: current, debt service, and capital outlay. Typical current expenditures for a local government comprise, for example, general government, public safety, public works, health and sanitation, culture and recreation, and community development. Governments should report expenditures by function (general government and public safety) and character (current operations, capital outlay, and debt service). Because governmental funds use flow of financial resources as a measurement focus, purchase of capital assets and payment of debt principal are recorded as expenditures.

Generally, expenditures should be recognized in the period in which the fund liability is incurred. In other words, expenditures are recorded when the transaction requires the use of current financial resources. However, there are a few exceptions and modifications to this general rule for recognizing expenditures.

Debt service payments

The first exception deals with debt service payments on general long-term liabilities. Governmental entities typically budget resources to meet current-year principal and interest payment requirements. Recording accrued interest at year-end would not be consistent with how these costs are often budgeted. Therefore, expenditures for interest and principal payments should be recorded when they become due.

The exception to the exception: if a government provides resources during the current period to a debt service fund for a payment due early in the next fiscal year (but not more than one month), the government may record an expenditure for such interest and principal payment.

Inventories and prepaid items

A modification to the expenditures recognition is allowed for inventory of material and supplies. In general, purchases of material and supplies consume financial resources and should be recorded as an expenditure when purchased. This is known as the purchase method of accounting for inventories.

However, *significant* amounts of inventory should be reported as an asset even when the purchase method is used. A year-end adjusting entry for an inventory balance of $25,000 allows for significant amounts of inventory to be reported as both an expenditure and as an asset, as follows:

	DR	CR
Inventory	25,000	
Nonspendable fund balance		25,000

Because the entry does not adjust expenditures, the full amount of inventory purchased remains reported as an expenditure. Future year-end adjustments for inventory would be made to the same two accounts. For example, if inventory decreased by $3,000 the next year, a debit to nonspendable fund balance and a credit to inventory for $3,000 would be made.

Governments are also allowed to use the consumption method of accounting for inventories. This method is similar to the method businesses use. Expenditures would be reported when materials and supplies are used, not when purchased.

Governments also may use either the purchase or consumption method to report the prepayment of certain costs (such as insurance premiums). When the purchase method is used for prepaid items, however, there is no requirement to report significant amounts of prepaid items as an asset.

Leases

Issued in June 2017, GASB Statement No. 87, *Leases*, will be effective for reporting periods beginning after December 15, 2019. One of the principal changes this statement brings to accounting for leases is that it establishes a single model for lease accounting rather than the historical approach of classifying leases either as operating leases or as capital leases. In general, a lease asset and liability will be recorded for a contract that conveys the right-to-use another entity's nonfinancial asset (the underlying asset) for longer than 12 months. A lessee should recognize a lease liability and an intangible right-to-use the lease asset (a "capital asset" is hereinafter referred to as a "lease asset") measured at the present value of payments expected to be made during the lease term.

Governments may account for lease activities in the general fund or in a special revenue fund. They may also account for the inception of the lease in a capital project fund and the lease payments in a debt service fund.

For governmental funds, this transaction is viewed as long-term borrowing to purchase the right-to-use an asset. This borrowing would be reported as an "other financing source"; the purchase of the right-to-use an asset would be reported as an expenditure. Future lease payments would be reported as debt service expenditures.

Consider the following example:

A county enters into a 60-month lease agreement for equipment. The present value of payments expected to be made during the lease term is $300,000, which includes a $25,000 down payment made at the inception of the lease. The entry to record this transaction in a governmental fund is as follows:

	DR	CR
Expenditure	300,000	
Other financing source		275,000
Cash		25,000

For governmental funds, a lease asset and a lease liability are not reported.

Debt refunding

An example of a debt refunding occurs when new debt is issued to retire existing debt. Governments can use the proceeds of the new debt to immediately pay the old debt (*current refunding*) or place the proceeds with an escrow agent to invest until they are needed to pay the principal and interest of the old debt (*advanced refunding*).

In advanced refunding, the old debt is considered extinguished, or *defeased*, if it meets certain criteria. If the debt is considered defeased, the transaction is treated as a retirement of the old debt. If the criteria are not met, then both the old debt and new debt are reported by the government.

GASB Statement No. 86, *Certain Debt Extinguishment Issues*, addresses when a government places cash and other monetary assets acquired with only existing resources in an irrevocable trust to extinguish the debt. In such cases, a governmental fund should report a debt service expenditure for the payment into the trust.

For governmental funds, when the proceeds of refunding bonds are either used to redeem existing debt or placed with an escrow agent for the advanced refunding of existent debt, the payment should be reported as an "other financing use." Debt repayment normally is reported as an expenditure; however, a debt refunding may distort the normal amount reported for debt service and is therefore reported separately as an other financing use. Consider the following example:

A county issues new bonds in the amount of $700,000 to advance-refund existing debt. The county is required to place $800,000 in escrow trust to service future debt payments of the existing debt. Entries to record this would be as follows:

Sale of bonds

	DR	CR
Cash	700,000	
Other financing source — refunding bonds		700,000

Payment to escrow agent

	DR	CR
Expenditure	100,000	
Other financing use — payment to refunded bond escrow agent	700,000	
Cash		800,000

Certain accrued liabilities not reported in governmental funds

Accrued liabilities for such things as salaries payable are recorded in governmental funds. These liabilities will be paid from available current financial resources of governmental funds. However, certain long-term liabilities will not require the use of currently available fund resources. These types of liabilities will not be recorded in the governmental funds until they become due, at which time an expenditure will be recorded.

This treatment applies to the following liabilities:

1. **Claims, judgments, and compensated absences**. The number of claims, judgments, and compensated absences recorded as expenditures in governmental funds shall be the amount accrued during the year that would normally be liquidated with expendable available financial resources. Because governmental fund balance sheets reflect current liabilities, only the current portion of the liability should be reported in the fund. The *current portion* is the amount left unpaid at the end of the reporting period that normally would be liquidated with expendable available financial resources. Governments, in general, are normally expected to liquidate liabilities with expendable available financial resources to the extent that the liabilities *mature* (come due for payment) each period. For example, compensated-absence liabilities are normally liquidated with expendable available financial resources; a governmental fund liability and expenditure should be recognized because payments come due each period on the occurrence of relevant events, such as employee resignations and retirements. The remainder of the liability should not be reported as liabilities in governmental funds but should be reported in the governmental activities column in the government-wide statement of net position.

2. **Landfill closure and postclosure costs**. For municipal solid waste landfills (MSWLFs) reported in governmental fund financial statements, the measurement of the liability for MSWLF closure and postclosure care should be consistent with proprietary funds. MSWLF expenditures and liabilities should be recognized in governmental funds using the modified accrual basis of accounting. Liabilities for MSWLF closure and postclosure care are normally liquidated with expendable available financial resources; a governmental fund liability and expenditure should be recognized because payments come due each period on receipt of goods and services used in the closure and postclosure care processes. The accumulation of earmarked net assets in a governmental fund for eventual payment of unmatured general long-term indebtedness, including landfill closure and postclosure care costs, does not constitute an outflow of current financial resources and should not result in the recognition of an additional governmental fund liability or expenditure. Long-term liabilities for MSWLF closure and postclosure care reported in governmental funds are general long-term liabilities and should be reported in the governmental activities column in the government-wide statement of net position. In the statement of revenues, expenditures, and changes in fund balances, facilities and equipment acquisitions included in estimated total current cost should be reported as closure and postclosure care expenditures.

3. **Pension activities**. Pension expenditures from governmental funds should be recognized on the modified accrual basis; that is, the amount recognized should be equal to the amount contributed to the plan or expected to be liquidated with expendable available financial resources. GASB Statement No. 68, *Accounting and Financial Reporting for Pensions — An Amendment of GASB Statement No. 27*, provides guidance for this type of cost.

   GASB Statement No. 68 requires that the liability of employers to employees for defined benefit pensions (net pension liability) be measured as the portion of the present value of projected benefit payments to be provided through the pension plan to current active and inactive employees attributed to those employees' past periods of service (total pension liability) **less** the amount of the pension plan's fiduciary net position. This liability is reported in the government-wide statements but not in governmental funds statements.

4. **Postemployment benefits other than pensions (OPEB)**. Governments may offer postemployment benefits other than pension benefits, including postemployment healthcare and other nonpension benefits. In June 2015, the GASB issued Statement No. 75, *Accounting and Financial Reporting for Postemployment Benefits Other Than Pensions*. This statement replaces the requirements of Statement No. 45, *Accounting and Financial Reporting by Employers for Postemployment Benefits Other Than Pensions*, as amended, and Statement No. 57, *OPEB Measurements by Agent Employers and Agent Multiple-Employer Plans*, for OPEB.

   GASB Statement No. 75 requires that OPEB follow accounting and reporting requirements for pensions similar to those found under GASB Statement No. 68. It establishes standards for recognizing and measuring liabilities, deferred outflows and deferred inflows of resources, and expenses and expenditures. In governmental fund financial statements, a net OPEB liability is required to be recognized to the extent the liability is normally expected to be liquidated with expendable available financial resources.[2]

5. **Termination benefits**. Governments may provide benefits to hasten employees' voluntary termination of services (such as early-retirement incentives). Governments also may provide benefits following involuntary terminations (such as severance benefits). GASB Statement No. 47, *Accounting for Termination Benefits*, provides guidance on these types of costs.

   GASB Statement No. 47 generally requires governments to recognize a liability and expense for voluntary termination benefits when an offer is accepted and the amount can be estimated. A liability and expense should be recognized for involuntary termination benefits when the plan for termination has been approved by those with the authority to commit a government to the plan, the plan has been communicated to the employees, and the amount can be estimated. If a plan of involuntary termination requires that employees render future service to receive benefits, the employer should recognize a liability and expense for the portion of involuntary termination benefits that will be provided after completion of future service ratably over the employees' future service period, beginning when the plan otherwise meets the recognition criteria.

   In financial statements prepared on the modified accrual basis of accounting, liabilities and expenditures for termination benefits should be recognized to the extent the liabilities are normally expected to be liquidated with expendable available financial resources.

6. **Pollution remediation obligations**. Governments may have obligations to address the effects of existing pollution by participating in pollution remediation activities. GASB Statement No. 49,

---

[2] An online toolkit designed to help preparers and auditors of state and local government pension plans implement new accounting and financial reporting standards was released by the GASB. The toolkit is available at no cost at the GASB website. To download a copy of the toolkit, go to https://gasb.org/jsp/GASB/Page/GASBSection Page&cid=1176163527940.

Accounting and Financial Reporting for Pollution Remediation Obligations, provides guidance for these types of costs.

GASB Statement No. 49 excludes pollution prevention or control obligations with respect to current operations. The statement identifies five specific obligating events that would require a government to estimate the expected pollution remediation costs and to determine whether outlays for those components should be accrued as a liability or, if appropriate, capitalized when goods and services are acquired. These obligating events follow:

a. The government is compelled to take pollution remediation action because of an imminent endangerment.
b. The government violates a pollution prevention-related permit or license.
c. The government is named, or evidence indicates that it will be named, by a regulator as a responsible party or potentially responsible party for remediation, or as a government responsible for sharing costs.
d. The government is named, or evidence indicates that it will be named, in a lawsuit to compel participation in pollution remediation.
e. The government commences or legally obligates itself to commence pollution remediation.

GASB Statement No. 49 also provides guidance on how and when to measure the liability for pollution remediation costs.

Regarding the display of goods and services used for pollution remediation activities in the governmental fund financial statements, amounts that are normally expected to be liquidated with expendable available financial resources should be recognized as liabilities on receipt of those goods and services. In the statement of revenues, expenditures, and changes in fund balances, any facilities and equipment acquisitions for pollution remediation activities should be reported as expenditures.

7. **Nonexchange financial guarantees**. Some governments extend financial guarantees for the obligations of another organization without directly receiving equal (or approximately equal) value in exchange (in other words, a nonexchange transaction). GASB Statement No. 70, *Accounting and Financial Reporting for Nonexchange Financial Guarantees*, issued in April 2013, provides guidance for these types of costs.

GASB Statement No. 70 requires a government that extends a nonexchange financial guarantee to recognize a liability when qualitative factors and historical data, if any, indicate that it is more likely than not that the government will be required to make a payment on the guarantee. The amount of the liability to be recognized should be the discounted present value of the best estimate of the future outflows related to the guarantee expected to be incurred. When there is no best estimate, but a range of the estimated future outflows can be established, the amount of the liability to be recognized should be the discounted present value of the minimum amount within that range.

Regarding their display in the governmental fund financial statements, liabilities and expenditures should be recognized for the amounts normally expected to be liquidated with expendable available financial resources when it is more likely than not that the government will be required to make a payment on the guarantee.

8. **Asset retirement obligations**. Governments may have obligations related to the legally enforceable liability associated with the retirement of a tangible asset. GASB Statement No. 83, *Certain Asset Retirement Obligations,* issued in November 2016, provides guidance for these types of costs.

GASB Statement No. 83, which is effective for periods beginning after June 15, 2018, requires a government to recognize an asset retirement obligation (ARO) when the liability is incurred and reasonably estimable. A liability is incurred by the occurrence of both an external obligating event and an internal obligating event resulting from normal operations.

An *obligating event* refers to an event whose occurrence determines the timing for recognition of an ARO. An external obligating event includes one of the following:

a. Approval of a federal, state, or local laws or regulations
b. Creation of a legally binding contract
c. Issuance of a court judgment

An internal obligating event includes one of the following:

a. For contamination-related AROs, the occurrence of contamination
b. For noncontamination-related AROs, the event could be placing the asset into use, using the asset, or permanently abandoning the asset before it is placed into use
c. For AROs related to acquired tangible capital assets, the event is the acquisition of the tangible capital asset

The measurement of an ARO should be based on the best estimate of the current value of outlays expected to be incurred. When an ARO is recognized, a government should also recognize a corresponding deferred outflow of resources. A government should recognize a reduction of the deferred outflow of resources as an outflow of resources (for example, expense) in a systematic and rational manner over a period of time.

Regarding their display in the governmental fund financial statements, liabilities and expenditures should be recognized for the amounts normally expected to be liquidated with expendable available financial resources.

Knowledge check

3. Which statement is correct regarding governmental fund expenditures?

    a. The purchase of capital assets and payment of debt principal are recorded as investments.
    b. Expenditures are recognized in the period in which the fund liability is incurred.
    c. Governments report expenditures by minor source.
    d. The consumption method must be used for reporting the purchase of inventories.

Governmental funds revenues and expenditures

Governmental funds use the modified accrual basis of accounting. Revenues are recognized when they are measurable and available to finance the current period. To be available, revenues must be collected in the current period or soon enough thereafter to be used to pay liabilities of the current period; they also must be legally available to finance current-period expenditures. Investments in debt and equity securities are reported at fair value unless they fall into one of two categories that use the amortized cost method.

Generally, expenditures should be recognized in the period in which the fund liability is incurred. However, there are a few exceptions and modifications to the general rule for recognizing expenditures, such as interest on long-term debt and the reporting on inventories and prepaid items. Certain long-term accrued liabilities are not reported in governmental funds.

	Key foundational points
1	The modified accrual method of accounting for revenues is concerned with when the inflow of financial resources is available to pay for expenditures of the current period.
2	Revenues are recorded net of the amount estimated to be uncollectible.
3	GASB Statement No. 33 provides guidance on recording revenue for nonexchange transactions.
4	Expenditures should be recognized in the period in which the fund liability is incurred.
5	There are certain exceptions to the expenditures recognition rule for inventories, prepaid items, and interest on long-term debt.
6	Certain long-term accrued liabilities are not reported in governmental funds.

Practice questions

Please note that the following practice questions are not required reading material.

1. Income taxes are an example of which category of nonexchange transactions?

    a. Derived tax revenue.
    b. Imposed nonexchange revenue.
    c. Government-mandated nonexchange revenue.
    d. Voluntary nonexchange revenue.

2. Fines and forfeitures are an example of which category of nonexchange transactions?

    a. Derived tax revenue.
    b. Imposed nonexchange revenue.
    c. Government-mandated nonexchange revenue.
    d. Voluntary nonexchange revenue.

3. Under the modified accrual basis of accounting, revenues are considered susceptible to accrual if they are

    a. Measurable.
    b. Available.
    c. Earned.
    d. Both (*a*) and (*b*).

4. A city levies property taxes of $100,000, 1% of which is expected to prove uncollectible. How should the city record this transaction?

    a. Revenues of $99,000 and no expenditures or other financing uses.
    b. Revenues of $99,000 and expenditures of $1,000.
    c. Revenues of $99,000 and other financing uses of $1,000.
    d. None of the above.

5. The county received a restricted grant from the state government to be used to train police officers. The county has met all eligibility requirements of the grant but will not expend the money until next fiscal year. In the current year, how should this grant be reported?

    a. Other financing sources.
    b. Deferred revenues.
    c. Revenues.
    d. None of the above.

6. A county debt service fund made principal payments of $200,000 and interest payments of $150,000 during the year. The accrued interest on the long-term debt was $10,000 at the beginning of the year and $12,000 at the end of the year. What should be reported by the debt service fund as expenditures for debt service for the year?

    a. $150,000.
    b. $152,000.
    c. $350,000.
    d. $352,000.

7. The purchases method of accounting is permitted for

    a. Materials and supplies.
    b. Prepaid insurance.
    c. Leases.
    d. Both a. and b.

8. The special revenue fund purchased $500,000 of material and supplies during the year. At the beginning of the year, there was an inventory of materials and supplies on hand of $100,000. The ending balance of material and supplies was $150,000. The county uses the purchase method to report inventory. How much in expenditures should the special revenue fund report for material and supplies?

    a. $450,000.
    b. $500,000.
    c. $550,000.
    d. None of the above.

9. A city reports property tax revenue of $2 million for the year. What is included in this amount and does it include only taxes levied this year?

10. A county reports investment income of $500,000 for the year. What is included in this amount?

11. Explain the difference between the purchase method and the consumption method of accounting. For which items can the two methods be used?

Chapter 6

Proprietary Funds

Learning objectives

- Determine when the use of proprietary funds is allowed and when their use is required.

- Determine how certain transactions are reported in proprietary funds.

- Identify some of the unique reporting practices of proprietary funds.

Back in familiar territory with proprietary funds

Proprietary funds use businesslike accounting. But where is net income? There are some differences in how information is displayed in governmental financial statements. In addition, the GASB has adopted a few accounting standards different from those used in business. This chapter will focus on those areas where GASB guidance differs from normal business practice.

Proprietary funds use a **flow of economic resources measurement focus** and **accrual basis of accounting**; they are used to account for a government's business-type activities and use businesslike accounting.

Use of proprietary funds

There are two types of proprietary funds: internal service funds and enterprise funds. The basic difference between them derives from who the primary customer is. Enterprise funds provide goods and services to customers outside the reporting entity; internal service funds provide goods and services to internal customers. The two fund types and their uses are defined as follows:

1. *Enterprise fund* — This type of fund may be used to report any activity for which a fee is charged to external users for goods or services. An enterprise fund **must** be used when any of the following occurs:
   a. The activity is financed with debt secured solely by a pledge of the net revenues from fees and charges of the activity.
   b. Laws or regulations require that the activity's costs, including capital costs, be recovered from fees and charges.
   c. The pricing policy is designed to recover an activity's costs, including capital costs.
2. *Internal service fund* — This type of fund may be used to report any activity that provides goods or services to other funds, departments, or agencies of the primary government and its component units on a cost-reimbursement basis **or** any activity that provides goods or services to other governments on a cost-reimbursement basis. Internal service funds should be used **only** when the reporting government is the predominant participant in the activity; otherwise, the activity should be reported as an enterprise fund.

Either type of fund can be used any time there is a fee charged for goods and services. Using a proprietary fund allows the government to measure the cost of providing such goods and services using a business model.

An activity need not be self-supporting to be reported as an enterprise fund. In such cases, using a business reporting model will enable a government to determine to what extent the activity needs to be subsidized.

Internal service funds should generally operate on a cost-reimbursement basis. Because customers of internal service funds usually are internal, significant long-term deficits or surpluses indicate that other parts of the government are not being properly charged for goods and services. For example, an internal service print shop's charges for services should be based on the cost of operating that print shop.

Knowledge check

1. Which statement is correct regarding proprietary funds?

   a. Either an enterprise or an internal service fund can be used any time there is a fee charged for goods and services.
   b. Internal service funds may not be used to report an activity that provides goods or services to the general fund.
   c. Using a proprietary fund prohibits the government from measuring the cost of providing such goods and services.
   d. Governments are never required to use an enterprise fund.

2. Which statement is **not** correct regarding internal service funds?

    a. Internal service funds generally operate on a cost-reimbursement basis.

    b. Internal service funds should be used only when the reporting government is the predominant participant in the activity.

    c. Internal service funds are used to account for the general operations of a government.

    d. Internal service funds usually provide services to internal customers.

Accounting differences

Proprietary funds use most of the accounting rules used by businesses. There are, however, a few areas where the GASB has issued different guidance for governments and a few areas unique to governments. These are discussed in the following section.

Debt refunding

Proprietary funds report debt refunding differently than do governmental funds. The reporting also differs from how a business reports such transactions. This is one case where GASB guidance (GASB Statement No. 23, *Accounting and Financial Reporting for Refundings of Debt Reported by Proprietary Activities*) differs from FASB guidance for business-type activities.

In a debt refunding, new debt is issued to retire existing debt. The old debt can either be redeemed or be considered defeased. Often the cost of retiring the old debt (either through redemption or defeasance) will be different than the carrying value of the old debt. The GASB requires that this difference be initially deferred as either a deferred inflow of resources or a deferred outflow of resources. The difference is then amortized over the remaining life of the old debt or the life of the new debt, whichever is shorter. The unamortized portion of the deferred amount is reported as an adjustment to the carrying value of the new debt. In contrast, the FASB requires that this difference be reported in the current-period income statement.

For example, a county water enterprise fund issues new bonds in the amount of $700,000 to advance-refund existing debt. The existing debt has a carrying value of $750,000. The county is required to place $800,000 in escrow trust to service the future debt payments of the existing debt. Journal entries follow.

Entry for sale of bonds:

	DR	CR
Cash	700,000	
New bonds payable		700,000

Entry for payment to escrow agent:

	DR	CR
Old bonds payable	750,000	
Deferred inflow amount on refunding	50,000	
Cash		800,000

GASB Statement No. 86, *Certain Debt Extinguishment Issues*, addresses when a government places cash and other monetary assets acquired with only existing resources in an irrevocable trust to extinguish the debt. The cost of retiring the old debt (either through redemption or defeasance) will often be different than the carrying value of the old debt. For financial statements using the economic resources measurement focus, GASB Statement No. 86 requires that this difference be reported separately as a gain or loss.

Pension cost

Pension cost is another area for which the GASB has issued separate guidance for governments. GASB Statement No. 68, *Accounting and Financial Reporting for Pensions — An Amendment of GASB Statement No. 27*, brought significant changes to how pension expense is measured and reported in proprietary funds and in government-wide statements. This statement uses an accounting approach instead of a funding approach to report pension costs.

GASB Statement No. 68 requires that the difference between a plan's assets (plan net position) and the present value of projected benefits for past service (total pension liability) be reported as a net pension liability in the proprietary funds' financial statements. In addition, this statement provides guidance on how to measure the plan's assets, total pension liability, and pension expense.

GASB Statement No. 68 replaced the requirements of GASB Statement No. 27, *Accounting for Pensions by State and Local Governmental Employers*, as well as the requirements of GASB Statement No. 50, *Pension Disclosures — An Amendment of GASB Statements No. 25 and No. 27*, as they relate to pensions that are provided through pension plans administered as trusts or equivalent arrangements (hereafter jointly referred to as "trusts") that meet certain criteria. GASB Statement No. 73, *Accounting and Financial Reporting for Pensions and Related Assets That Are Not Within the Scope of GASB Statement 68, and Amendments to Certain Provisions of GASB Statements 67 and 68*, provides guidance for pensions that are not covered by the scope of GASB Statement No. 68.

In addition, GASB Statement No. 71, *Pension Transition for Contributions Made Subsequent to the Measurement Date — An Amendment of GASB Statement No. 68*, provides transition guidance as governments implement GASB Statement No. 68. It corrects a potential understatement of beginning net position and pension expense in the year of implementation.

GASB Statement No. 71 requires governments to recognize a beginning deferred outflow of resources for its pension contributions made during the time between the measurement date of the beginning net pension liability and the beginning of the initial fiscal year of implementation.

GASB Statement No. 82, *Pension Issues — An Amendment of GASB Statements No. 67, No. 68, and No. 73*, addresses issues regarding the presentation of payroll-related measures in required supplementary information, the selection of assumptions and treatment of deviations from the guidance in an actuarial standard of practice (ASOP) for financial reporting purposes, and the classification of payments made by employers to satisfy employee (plan member) contribution requirements. GASB Statement No. 82

clarifies that a deviation from the ASOPs is also a deviation from generally accepted accounting principles.

GASB Statement No. 78, *Accounting and Financial Reporting for Pensions,* excludes certain pension plans from the scope of GASB Statement No. 68. It excludes pensions provided to employees of state or local governmental employers through a cost-sharing, multiple-employer defined benefit pension plan that (1) is not a state or local governmental pension plan, (2) is used to provide defined benefit pensions both to employees of state or local governmental employers and to employees of employers that are not state or local governmental employers, and (3) has no predominant state or local governmental employer (either individually or collectively with other state or local governmental employers that provide pensions through the pension plan).

Postemployment benefits other than pensions

Governments may offer postemployment benefits other than pension (OPEB) benefits, including postemployment healthcare and other non-pension benefits. GASB Statement No. 75, *Accounting and Financial Reporting for Postemployment Benefits Other Than Pensions*, requires that OPEB follow similar accounting and reporting requirements for pensions under GASB Statement No. 68.

GASB Statement No. 75 requires that the difference between a plan's assets (plan net position) and the present value of projected benefits for past service (total OPEB liability) be reported as a net OPEB liability in the proprietary funds' financial statements. In addition, GASB Statement No. 75 provides guidance on how to measure the plan's assets, total OPEB liability, and OPEB expense.

This statement replaced the requirements of GASB Statement No. 45, *Accounting and Financial Reporting by Employers for Postemployment Benefits Other Than Pensions*.

Termination benefits

Governments may provide benefits to hasten employees' voluntary termination of services (for example, early-retirement incentives). In addition, governments may provide benefits following involuntary terminations (such as severance benefits). GASB Statement No. 47, *Accounting for Termination Benefits,* provides guidance on these types of costs.

GASB Statement No. 47 generally requires governments to recognize a liability and expense for voluntary termination benefits when an offer is accepted and the amount can be estimated. A liability and expense should be recognized for involuntary termination benefits when the plan for termination has been approved by those with the authority to commit a government to the plan, the plan has been communicated to the employees, and the amount can be estimated. If a plan of involuntary termination requires that employees render future service to receive benefits, the employer should recognize a liability and expense for the portion of involuntary termination benefits that will be provided after completion of future service ratably over the employees' future service period, beginning when the plan otherwise meets the recognition criteria.

Landfill

Governments often account for solid waste landfills in an enterprise fund. There are certain significant costs related to closing a landfill and monitoring the closed landfill. These costs are *landfill closure* and *postclosure care* costs and are accrued over the life of the landfill.

Closure and postclosure care costs should be estimated using current costs. The amount of expense recognized each period should be based on updated current cost data multiplied by the current estimate of the portion of the landfill capacity used, less the amount previously recorded. The following example reflects how the expense is determined:

Estimated landfill closure costs based on current cost	$100,000
Current estimate of landfill capacity used	60%
Expense previously recorded	$50,000
Current year expense ($100,000 × 60% - $50,000) = $10,000	

This approach allows for any changes in estimates to be recorded in the current-period expense.

Risk financing

Governments often pool some of or all their risk financing activities. For example, governments may self-insure for worker compensation; they can account for this activity as part of the general fund or in a separate internal service fund. The accounting issue is how to account for the charges that an internal service fund collects for risk financing activities from other funds. Generally, internal service funds should record the amount charged to other funds as revenue.

However, the internal service fund should recognize revenue only to the extent that the amount charged to other funds is based on

1. probable and measurable losses for the period; or
2. charges based on some actuarial funding method; and
3. in addition to item 2 above, reasonable provision for anticipated catastrophic losses.

Any amount charged in excess of this should be reported as a transfer, not as revenue.

Payments in lieu of taxes

Because enterprise funds are part of the government, they usually do not pay taxes to that government. However, some governments charge enterprise funds an amount "in lieu of taxes." If these payments represent charges for services received by the enterprise fund, they should be reported as an expense by the enterprise fund. Typically, no clear relationship exists between the amount charged in lieu of taxes and the services received. In this case, the payment should be reported as a transfer, not as an expense.

Payments in lieu of taxes should be evaluated to determine if they are, in substance, a tax abatement that should be disclosed in accordance with GASB Statement No. 77, *Tax Abatement Disclosures*.

Interest capitalization

Proprietary funds often finance the construction of capital assets with tax-exempt debt or grants.

The amount of interest that should be capitalized when tax-exempt debt is used is limited to the difference between the interest costs incurred during construction and any interest earned on the proceeds of the debt issued. In the case of projects financed with capital grants, no interest should be capitalized.

For example, a county water enterprise fund has a major capital project underway funded by $1 million in grants and $4 million in tax-exempt bonds. During the year, the county spent $2.5 million on the project. The bonds were issued at the beginning of the year and interest on the bonds for the year totaled $160,000. The proceeds from the bonds were invested and earned interest income of $110,000.

The water enterprise fund should capitalize $50,000. This is the difference between the interest costs of $160,000 and the interest earned of $110,000. No interest should be capitalized related to the grant.

GASB Statement No. 89, *Accounting for Interest Cost Incurred before the End of a Construction Period*, removes the requirement to capitalize interest costs incurred before the end of a construction period; such costs are expensed. The requirements of this statement are effective for reporting periods beginning after December 15, 2019; earlier application is encouraged. The requirements of this statement should be applied prospectively.

Leases

GASB Statement No. 87, *Leases*, was issued in June 2017 and is effective for reporting periods beginning after December 15, 2019. One of the principal changes this statement brings to accounting for leases its establishment of a single model for lease accounting rather than the historical approach of classifying leases as either operating or capital leases. In general, a lease asset and liability will be recorded for a contract that conveys control of the right to use another entity's nonfinancial asset (the underlying asset) for longer than 12 months. A lessee should recognize a lease liability and an intangible right-to-use the lease asset (a capital asset, hereinafter referred to as the "lease asset") measured at the present value of payments expected to be made during the lease terms.

A lessee should reduce the lease liability as payments are made and recognize an expense for interest on the liability. The lessee should amortize the lease asset in a systematic and rational manner over the shorter of the lease term or the useful life of the underlying asset.

Contributed capital and special items

Proprietary funds often receive grants to purchase capital assets. This type of revenue should be displayed separately as "capital contribution" and reported after nonoperating revenue and expenses in the statement of revenues, expenses, and changes in net position. Proprietary funds also report "special items" in a manner similar to capital contributions.

Pollution remediation obligations

GASB Statement No. 49, *Accounting and Financial Reporting for Pollution Remediation Obligations*, sets forth the key circumstances under which a government would be required to report a liability related to pollution remediation. According to the statement, a government would have to determine whether one or more components of a pollution remediation liability are recognizable.

GASB Statement No. 49 indicates that pollution remediation liabilities should be measured at their current value using the expected cash flow technique, which measures the liability as a sum of probability-weighted amounts in a range of possible estimated amounts. Expected recoveries from other responsible parties and from insurers reduce the amount of remediation expense. GASB Statement No. 49 also specifies criteria for capitalization of some pollution remediation outlays.

Asset retirement obligations

GASB Statement No. 83, *Certain Asset Retirement Obligations*, sets forth the key circumstances under which a government would be required to report a liability related to an asset retirement. According to the statement, a government would recognize an asset retirement obligation (ARO) when the liability is incurred and reasonably estimable. A liability is incurred by the occurrence of both an external obligating event and an internal obligating event resulting from normal operations.

The measurement of an ARO should be based on the best estimate of the current value of outlays expected to be incurred. When an ARO is recognized, a government also should recognize a corresponding deferred outflow of resources. A government should recognize a reduction of the deferred outflow of resources as an outflow of resources (for example, expense) in a systematic and rational manner over a period of time.

GASB Statement No. 83 is effective for periods beginning after June 15, 2018.

Intangible assets

GASB Statement No. 51, *Accounting and Financial Reporting for Intangible Assets*, provides guidance regarding how to identify, account for, and report intangible assets. GASB Statement No. 51 requires that all intangible assets not specifically excluded by its scope provisions (see following chart) be classified as capital assets.

Accounting for intangible assets in state and local governments	
Intangible assets within the scope of GASB Statement No. 51 possess all the following characteristics:	Intangible assets excluded from the scope of GASB Statement No. 51:
1. *Lack of physical substance.* An asset may be contained in or on an item with physical substance (such as a compact disc in the case of computer software). An asset also may be closely associated with another item that has physical substance (for example, the underlying land in the case of a right-of-way easement). These modes of containment and associated items should not be considered when determining whether an asset lacks physical substance.	1. Assets that meet the description in the left column but are acquired or created primarily for the purpose of directly obtaining income or profit (these assets generally should follow guidance for investments).
2. *Nonfinancial nature.* In the context of GASB Statement No. 51, an asset with a nonfinancial nature is one that is not in a monetary form similar to cash and investment securities and that represents neither a claim or right to assets in a monetary form similar to receivables nor a prepayment for goods or services.	2. Assets resulting from capital lease transactions reported by lessees (these assets are addressed in National Council on Governmental Accounting Statement No. 5, as amended).[1]
3. *Initial useful life extending beyond a single reporting period.*	3. Goodwill created through the combination of a government and another entity.

Accordingly, existing authoritative guidance related to accounting and financial reporting for capital assets should be applied to intangible assets covered by GASB Statement No. 51, as applicable. GASB Statement No. 51 provides authoritative guidance that specifically addresses the nature of these intangible assets. Such guidance should be applied in addition to existing authoritative guidance for capital assets.

---

[1] See chapter 5 for updates related to GASB Statement No. 87, *Leases.*

GASB Statement No. 51 requires that an intangible asset be recognized in the statement of net position only if it is considered identifiable. An intangible asset is considered identifiable when either of the following conditions is met:

- The asset is separable; that is, the asset is capable of being separated or divided from the government and sold, transferred, licensed, rented, or exchanged, either individually or together with a related contract, asset, or liability.
- The asset arises from contractual or other legal rights, regardless of whether those rights are transferable or separable from the entity or from other rights and obligations.

GASB Statement No. 51 establishes a specified-conditions approach to recognizing intangible assets that are internally generated. Effectively, outlays associated with the development of such assets should not begin to be capitalized until certain criteria are met. Outlays incurred prior to meeting these criteria should be expensed as incurred. GASB Statement No. 51 also provides guidance on recognizing internally generated computer software as an intangible asset.

GASB Statement No. 51 establishes guidance specific to intangible assets related to amortization and discusses issues related to impairment.

Derivative instruments

GASB Statement No. 53, *Accounting and Financial Reporting for Derivative Instruments*, requires governments to measure most derivative instruments at fair value as assets or liabilities in their accrual-based, government-wide, proprietary fund and fiduciary fund financial statements (but not in the governmental fund financial statements). The fair value of a derivative instrument is either the value of its future cash flows in today's dollars or the price it would bring if it could be sold on an open market.

In general, the fair value of a derivative instrument as of the end of the period covered by the financial statements will be reported in the statement of net position (balance sheets). Changes in fair value should be reported in the resource flows statements (such as the statement of activities) as investment gains or losses. However, annual changes in the fair value of a hedging derivative instrument should be reported as deferred inflows or deferred outflows on the statements of net position.

Service concession arrangement

GASB Statement No. 60, *Accounting and Financial Reporting for Service Concession Arrangements*, provides guidance on certain public-private or public-public partnerships. A service concession arrangement (SCA) is an arrangement that meets all the following criteria:

- The transferor conveys to the operator the right and related obligation to provide public services through the operation of a capital asset in exchange for significant consideration, such as an up-front payment, installment payments, a new facility, or improvements to an existing facility.
- The operator collects and is compensated from fees from third parties.

- The transferor determines or has the ability to modify or approve what services the operator is required to provide, to whom the operator is required to provide the services, and the prices or rates that can be charged for the services.
- The transferor is entitled to significant residual interest in the service utility of the facility at the end of the arrangement.

The transferor would continue to report any capital asset transfer to the operator. If the facility associated with an SCA is a new facility purchased or constructed by the operator or an existing facility that has been improved by the operator, then the transferor should report the new facility or the improvement as a capital asset at fair value when it is placed in operation.

The transferor should report the up-front payment or the present value of installment payments as an asset and any contractual obligations recorded as liabilities along with a related deferred inflow of resources. Revenue should be recognized as the deferred inflow of resources is reduced. This revenue should be recognized in a systematic and rational manner over the term of the arrangement, beginning when the facility is placed into operation.

Nonexchange financial guarantees

Some governments extend financial guarantees for the obligations of another organization without directly receiving equal or approximately equal value in exchange (a nonexchange transaction). GASB Statement No. 70, *Accounting and Financial Reporting for Nonexchange Financial Guarantees*, provides guidance for these types of costs.

This statement requires a government that extends a nonexchange financial guarantee to recognize a liability when qualitative factors and historical data, if any, indicate that it is more likely than not that the government will be required to make a payment on the guarantee. The amount of the liability to be recognized should be the discounted present value of the best estimate of the future outflows related to the guarantee expected to be incurred. When there is no best estimate, but a range of the estimated future outflows can be established, the amount of the liability to be recognized should be the discounted present value of the minimum amount within the range.

Certain accrued liabilities

Governmental funds do not accrue certain long-term liabilities. Unlike governmental funds, proprietary funds should report all accrued liabilities. This includes liabilities for claims and judgments, compensated absences, landfill closure and postclosure costs, net pension liabilities, OPEB, termination benefits, pollution remediation obligations, and asset retirement obligations.

Reporting differences

Although proprietary funds generally follow business reporting practices, there are several important differences in how they report information in the financial statements. Key differences are described here.

Proprietary funds report a balance sheet or statement of net position (see appendix A). The key difference between a business and a proprietary fund is how net position is classified. Proprietary funds are concerned with the limitations placed on net position; they report net position in three categories: **net investment in capital assets**, **restricted net position**, and **unrestricted net position**.

Proprietary funds report a statement of revenues, expenses, and changes in net position (see appendix A). The classification of operating and nonoperating revenues and expenses is different than that for a business. Also, change in net position — as opposed to net income — is reported. Proprietary funds may also report transfers, special items, and contributed capital in this operating statement.

Proprietary funds report a statement of cash flows (see appendix A). A government's cash flow statement is, again, different from that of a business. The GASB defines four types of cash flows: **operating activities**, **noncapital financing activities**, **capital and related financing activities**, and **investing activities**. In addition, interest income and interest expenses are not considered cash flow from operating activities; instead, cash flow from interest is considered as part of one of the other types of cash flow, depending on the nature of the interest. Finally, the statement of cash flows must be done using the direct method.

Summary

Proprietary funds are used to account for a government's business-type activities. There are two types of proprietary funds: enterprise funds (customers are primarily external to the government) and internal service funds (customers are primarily internal). Proprietary funds follow business-type accounting and reporting. There are, however, instances where governments follow accounting and reporting practices that differ from those followed by businesses.

There are also key differences in the financial statements of proprietary funds and business organizations. Governments have a unique way of classifying net position, classifying operating and nonoperating income and expenses, and classifying cash flows.

Knowledge check

3. Which is **not** one of the three categories in which proprietary funds report net position on a balance sheet or a statement of net position?

   a. Net income.
   b. Restricted net position.
   c. Net investment in capital assets.
   d. Unrestricted net position.

Key foundational points

1	Proprietary funds use a flow of economic resources measurement focus and the accrual basis of accounting.
2	There are two types of proprietary funds: internal service funds and enterprise funds. The basic difference between the two fund types derives from who the primary customer is.
3	There are a number of areas in which the accounting used by proprietary funds is different from that used by a business.
4	Proprietary funds report net position in three categories.
5	For proprietary funds, the statement of cash flows uses four categories and must be done using the direct method.

Practice questions

Please note that the following practice questions are not required reading material.

1. Which would be reported as a component of net position of a proprietary fund?

    a. Retained earnings.
    b. Contributed capital.
    c. Net investment in capital assets.
    d. Permanently restricted net position.

2. Payments in lieu of taxes that are not payments for services from a government should be reported by an enterprise fund as which of the following?

    a. Transfers.
    b. Operating expenses.
    c. Nonoperating expenses.
    d. A special item.

3. An enterprise fund advance-refunds $3.2 million of old enterprise fund bonds by issuing new bonds for $3 million and paying that amount into a qualifying trust for that purpose. What should the enterprise fund report from this transaction?

    a. Gain of $200,000.
    b. Special item of $200,000.
    c. Deferred inflow of resources of $200,000.
    d. Deferred outflow of resources of $200,000.

4. An enterprise fund issues $2 million of 6%, 10-year tax-exempt bonds at the beginning of the year to finance the construction of a new water treatment plant. During the year, the enterprise fund earned $80,000 of interest income on the bond proceeds and incurred $120,000 of interest cost. The average construction cost for the year was $1 million. What amount of interest should be capitalized for the year under GASB Statement No. 89?

    a. $0.
    b. $40,000.
    c. $60,000.
    d. $120,000.

5. Which is a cash flow classification used in a proprietary fund statement of cash flows?

    a. Cash flow from capital and related financing activities.
    b. Cash flow from investing activities.
    c. Cash flow from noncapital financing activities.
    d. All the above.

6. The enterprise fund receives a capital grant from the federal government. How would this transaction be reported?

    a. Revenues.
    b. Other financing sources.
    c. Nonoperating revenues.
    d. Capital contributions.

7. An internal service fund used to account for risk financing activities would not include which in revenue?

    a. A reasonable provision for profit.
    b. Charges based on actuarial or other acceptable estimates of costs.
    c. A reasonable provision for expected future catastrophic losses.
    d. Actual losses incurred during the year.

8. An enterprise landfill fund estimates that its closure and postclosure costs are $300,000 at the end of the year. It also estimates that the landfill has 30% of its capacity left. The amount of liability for closing the landfill was $200,000 at the beginning of the year. What amount should be reported as closure costs for the year?

    a. $0.
    b. $10,000.
    c. $210,000.
    d. $290,000.

9. Explain how the reporting of an enterprise debt refunding differs from that of a business.

10. Explain some of the key differences between the statement of cash flows for a proprietary fund and that for a business.

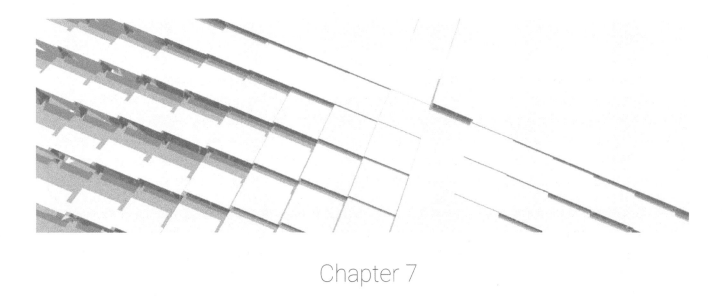

Chapter 7

Fiduciary Funds

Learning objectives

- Identify the four types of fiduciary funds.

- Identify how certain transactions are reported in fiduciary funds.

- Identify some of the unique reporting practices of fiduciary funds.

Reporting assets held by a government for others

How should governments report assets they hold that belong to others, such as private organizations or other governments? Governments use *fiduciary funds* — comprising trust funds and custodial funds, among others — to report the activities of assets held for others.

The use of fiduciary funds

Governments are sometimes asked to act as fiscal agents or custodians of resources for other organizations or individuals. In addition, large governments sometimes offer programs to other governments in which the other governments' resources will be held in, for example, an external investment pool. In these cases, resources belonging to others are held by the custodian government, which may not use them for its own programs. Fiduciary funds are used to report the activity of these resources. The custodian government has a fiduciary responsibility for these funds.

GASB Statement No. 84, *Fiduciary Activities*, is effective for fiscal years beginning after December 15, 2018, and establishes criteria for identifying and reporting fiduciary activities. The criteria for identifying fiduciary activities primarily focuses on (*a*) whether a government controls the assets of the fiduciary activity and (*b*) on the beneficiaries with whom a fiduciary relationship exists.

Accounting and financial reporting for fiduciary funds reflect the fact that these funds are held for others and are not to be used to support the government's own programs. Fiduciary funds are reported only in the fund statements; they are not included in the government-wide statements. Funds are reported by fund type and —rather than revenue and expenses — additions and deductions are reported.

Pension (and other employee benefit) trust funds do not report any actuarial liabilities in the fund financial statements. Actuarial information is included in separate schedules as part of required supplementary information.

There are four classifications of fiduciary funds: pension (and other employee benefit) trust funds, investment trust funds, private purpose trust funds, and custodial funds. Each type of fiduciary fund is described in the forthcoming sections.

Knowledge check

1. Which statement is correct regarding fiduciary funds?

    a. There are four classifications of fiduciary funds.
    b. Governments are never asked to act as fiscal agents or custodians of resources for other organizations or individuals.
    c. There are five categories of fiduciary funds.
    d. Custodial funds are usually used to report agreements defined in trust agreements or other long-term relationships.

Pension (and other employee benefit) trust funds

A government may hold in trust resources for members and beneficiaries of defined benefit pension trust funds, defined contribution plans, or postemployment benefit plans other than pensions (OPEB) plans. These resources should be reported in pension (and other employee benefit) trust funds.

A key point: **the government must control the resources in trust**. Many local governments offer pension benefits to employees through state-sponsored pension plans. In this case, the state, not the local government, would report the pension trust fund. The same treatment may apply for deferred compensation plans where other organizations hold the resources in trust for employees.

Investment trust funds

Larger governments sometimes offer to include funds from smaller governments as part of their investment program. The larger government may combine the investments into one pool or use a separate pool for the investments from other governments. GASB Statement No. 31, *Accounting and Financial Reporting for Certain Investments and for External Investment Pools,* provides guidance on reporting external investment pools and the external portion of investment pools where resources are combined with the sponsoring government. Generally accepted accounting principles require that these resources be reported in an investment trust fund.

Private-purpose trust funds

Other trust arrangements, in which the income or principal benefits individuals, private organizations, or other governments, should be reported as private-purpose trust funds. (Remember, if the purpose of the trust is to benefit government programs or the citizenry, the resources are reported as either a permanent fund or a special revenue fund.) A county government holding an endowment fund for scholarships for area high school students is an example of a private-purpose trust fund.

Custodial funds

Custodial funds are often used to report less formal arrangements in which the government is holding resources for others in a purely custodial capacity. Typically, the government is responsible for the receipt, temporary investment, and remittance of resources for individuals, private organizations, or other governments. For example, a county may have responsibility for billing and collecting taxes for a town and a separate school district within its borders. The county would use a tax custodial fund to bill, collect, and remit taxes for these other governments.

Custodial funds should report fiduciary activities that are not held in a trust or equivalent arrangement that meets specific criteria. Custodial funds are used if the government controls the assets and the assets are for the benefit of individuals. The government should not have administrative involvement with the assets or direct financial involvement with the assets.

Prior to the implementation of GASB Statement No. 84, agency funds were reported as part of fiduciary funds. Agency funds are no longer reported; most of this activity is now reported as custodial funds.

Accounting differences

GASB Statement No. 67, *Financial Reporting for Pension Plans — An Amendment of GASB Statement No. 25*, provides detailed guidance on reporting certain defined benefit pension plans. In addition, GASB Statement No. 74, *Financial Reporting for Postemployment Benefit Plans Other Than Pension Plans*, provides detailed guidance on reporting for OPEB plans.

GASB Statement No. 72 defines an *investment* as a security or other asset that a government holds primarily for the purpose of income or profit and has a present service capacity based solely on its ability to generate cash or to be sold to generate cash. GASB Statement No. 72 generally requires that investments be reported at fair-value. However, certain investments are excluded from being measured at fair value, including money market investments, qualified external investment pools, investments in life insurance contracts, common stock meeting the criteria for applying the equity method, unallocated insurance contracts, and synthetic guaranteed investment contracts.

In general, fiduciary funds report using the economic resources measurement focus and accrual basis of accounting. However, it is important to remember that these resources belong to another party (or parties). Accordingly, the accounting should reflect this fiduciary relationship, such as that best illustrated by the pension (and other employee benefit) trust fund. The pension (and other employee benefit) trust fund would not report any actuarial accrued liabilities or net pension liability in the financial statements for pension benefits. Instead, the pension (and other employee benefit) trust fund reports the assets, deferred outflows of resources, liabilities (such as benefit payments due to plan members), deferred inflows of resources, and the difference as net position held for others.

Fiduciary funds also report additions and deductions to net position instead of revenues and expenses. Again, these resources are held for others; changes in these resources are not revenues and expenses of the government.

Fiduciary funds generally report net positions simply as net positions held in trust for others. The requirement to report net position in three separate classes for proprietary funds does not apply to fiduciary funds.

Reporting differences

Fiduciary funds are reported only as part of the fund financial statements. Because these resources belong to others, they are excluded from the government-wide financial statements. The fiduciary financial statements should report all fiduciary funds of the primary government and any fiduciary component units.

Fiduciary funds report the following two financial statements (for sample statements, see appendix A):

- Statement of fiduciary net position
- Statement of changes in fiduciary net position

Unlike governmental and proprietary funds, fiduciary funds' financial statements are presented by fund type. For example, if a government has several private-purpose trust funds, only one column should be presented in the financial statements for this fund type.

Sometimes a fiduciary fund will hold financial resources that belong to other funds of the primary government. For reporting purposes, these resources should be included in the balances reported by these other funds; they should not be reported as part of the fiduciary fund. Therefore, the amounts reported in a fiduciary fund should reflect the amounts held for individuals and organizations outside the primary government.

For pension (and other employee benefit) trust funds, there are additional required supplementary information (RSI) requirements. RSI is reported after the notes to the financial statements and is part of the minimum requirements for general-purpose external financial statements. However, auditors do not opine on RSI.

GASB Statement No. 82, *Pension Issues — An Amendment of GASB Statements No. 67, No. 68, and No. 73*, was issued partially to address the way payroll-related measures are presented in required supplementary information.

GASB Statements No. 67 and No. 82 significantly changed the way certain information is measured and reported in RSI.

Knowledge check

2. Choose the correct statement regarding fiduciary funds.

   a. They report additions and deductions to net position.
   b. The fund financial statements are reported by net position class.
   c. They report revenues and expenses in the statement of changes in fiduciary net position.
   d. They report amounts that belong to other funds of the primary government.

Key foundational points

1	Governments are sometimes asked to act as fiscal agents or as custodian of resources for other organizations or individuals.
2	There are four classifications of fiduciary funds: pension (and other employee benefit) trust funds, investment trust funds, private-purpose trust funds, and custodial funds.
3	Fiduciary funds are reported only as part of the fund financial statements. Because these resources belong to others, they are excluded from the government-wide financial statements.
4	Fiduciary funds report a statement of fiduciary net position and a statement of changes in fiduciary net position.
5	The statement of changes in fiduciary net position reports additions and deductions.

Practice questions

Please note that the following practice questions are not required reading material.

1. A citizen establishes a $100,000 endowment fund with a county government. The earnings from the endowment are to be used to support study abroad for local high school students. Which type of fund should the government use to report this activity?

    a. Permanent fund.
    b. Private-purpose trust fund.
    c. Investment trust fund.
    d. Custodial fund.

2. During the year, a government receives a $500,000 contribution to a private-purpose trust fund. The contribution should be reported in the statement of changes in net position as what?

    a. Revenues.
    b. Other financing sources.
    c. Additions.
    d. Special item.

3. A pension (and other employee benefit) trust fund would report

    a. Expenditures.
    b. Expenses.
    c. Deductions.
    d. Revenue.

4. Which financial statement is required for a private-purpose trust fund?

    a. Statement of revenues, expenses, and changes in net position.
    b. Statement of net position.
    c. Statement of cash flows.
    d. All the above.

5. Which statement is required for a custodial fund?

    a. Statement of activities.
    b. Statement of changes in fiduciary net position.
    c. Statement of cash flows.
    d. None of the above.

6. A city government participates in a statewide pension trust fund. Which financial statement should the city report for its participation in the statewide pension trust fund?

    a. Statement of net position.
    b. Statement of revenue, expenses, and changes in net position.
    c. Statement of cash flows.
    d. None of the above.

7. A city tax custodial fund holds $700,000 in cash at year-end. The cash belongs to the following entities:

> City general fund — $300,000
> City special revenue fund — $100,000
> School district — $250,000
> Fire district — $50,000

In the statement of net position, what amount of cash should the tax custodial fund report?

a. $50,000.
b. $300,000.
c. $400,000.
d. $700,000.

8. Explain what items are reported in the statement of changes in fiduciary net position for trust funds.

9. What financial information should be reported for a pension (and other employee benefit) trust fund?

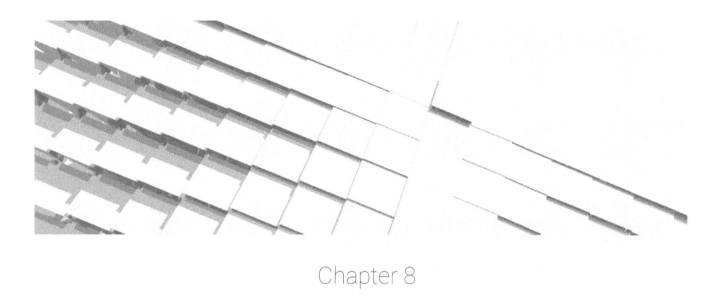

Chapter 8

Fund Financial Statements

Learning objectives

- Identify major funds for reporting purposes.

- Recognize the format and requirements of governmental fund financial statements.

- Recognize the format and requirements of proprietary fund financial statements.

- Identify fiduciary fund financial statements.

Refer to appendix A for financial statement samples.

Reviewing fund performance

Fund financial statements provide important information on how the separate components (funds) of a government performed for the year. How much was received, spent, and what remains for a certain purpose can best be determined with fund financial statements. These statements are also used to determine compliance with finance-related laws, rules, and regulations. Through the budget process, governments often make resource-allocation decisions on a fund-by-fund basis. To demonstrate accountability, governments must likewise provide financial information on a fund-by-fund basis.

General-purpose financial statements

The financial statements for governments include both fund-based and government-wide statements. Generally accepted accounting principles (GAAP) require that the general-purpose external financial statements contain, at minimum, the following elements:

- Management's discussion and analysis (MD&A)
- Basic financial statements
    - Government-wide financial statements
    - Fund financial statements
    - Notes to the financial statements
- Required supplementary information (RSI) (other than MD&A)

The relationship among the different elements required for general-purpose financial statements can be seen in the following chart. This chapter focuses on fund financial statements.

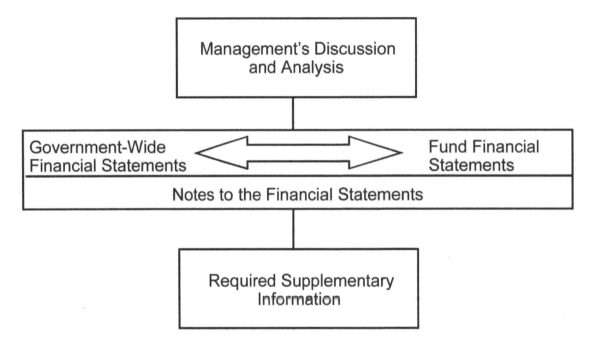

A government may have three different types of funds: governmental, proprietary, and fiduciary. These fund types have different operating objectives and use different measurement focuses and bases of accounting; they measure and report financial activities differently. Because of this, each fund type will have its own set of financial statements.

Reporting by major funds

The number of individual funds a government has can vary from just a few to several dozen. Generally, a government should have the minimum number of funds necessary for sound financial management and to meet legal and accounting requirements. Some governments need more funds than do others to meet this requirement.

Can information for each fund be reported in the basic financial statements? Yes, but the reports may become quite long. One alternative might be to report information by fund type; however, information about individual funds would be lost. The best alternative — and the one to use — is to present information about the largest, most important funds separately and combine information about the other funds into a single column. This is the *major fund* approach; it enables financial statement users to focus on the government's most important funds.

Reporting by major funds applies only to governmental funds and enterprise funds. It does not apply to internal service funds or fiduciary funds, which are reported in columns by fund type.

In governmental and proprietary fund financial statements, governments report each major fund in a separate column. Nonmajor funds and internal service funds are combined and reported in single columns.

Now that we understand that reporting is done by major funds, how do we determine which funds qualify as major funds? There are three ways that a fund can be designated as major.

1. The general fund is always major.
2. Apart from the general fund, governments must annually test all governmental and enterprise funds to determine whether they are major and must therefore be reported in a separate column.
3. A government can present any governmental or enterprise fund as "major" if the government believes the fund is important to financial statement users.

When performing the annual test, a fund is a major fund when it meets both of the following criteria:

- Total assets plus deferred outflows of resources and liabilities plus deferred inflows of resources, revenues, or expenditures divided by expenses of a fund equal at least 10% of the corresponding total for those items for all funds of that category (governmental or enterprise).
- Total assets plus deferred outflows of resources and liabilities plus deferred inflows of resources, revenues, or expenditures divided by expenses of a fund equal at least 5% of the corresponding total for all governmental and enterprise funds combined.

Only when a fund item (total revenues, for example) passes the first test is the second test done. Furthermore, the same item (total revenues, in this example) must meet both criteria. It should be noted that only one item in a given fund needs to pass both tests for that fund to be considered major.

For example, the first test would compare a special revenue fund's total assets plus deferred outflows of resources and liabilities plus deferred inflows of resources, revenues, and expenditures with the total for these same items for all governmental funds. If none of these listed items for the special revenue fund

---

exceeds 10% of the total for all governmental funds, the fund would not be considered major and the second test would not be done.

However, if total revenue for the special revenue fund was the only item that passed the 10% test, then total revenue of the special revenues fund would be tested to determine whether that amount was at least 5% of the total revenue of governmental and enterprise funds combined. If so, the special revenue fund would be determined to be major. The same item must pass both tests.

The major-fund tests need to be done annually. A fund that meets the criteria to be major in one year might not do so in the next year. It is therefore possible that, year to year, the major funds reported in separate columns in the fund financial statements will be different.

For example, a government may have a large capital project one year and none the next year. During the period where there is much activity, the fund could meet the major fund criteria and be reported in a separate column in the fund financial statements. In periods where there is little activity, the fund can be combined and reported with other nonmajor funds. However, it is important to remember that a government has the option of continuing to report the fund as major if the government believes the fund is important to financial statement users.

The table that follows is a sample major-fund calculation for a special revenue fund.

Consider the following example for Special Revenue Fund A					
	Special Revenue Fund A	All governmental funds	All governmental & enterprise funds	10% test	5% test
Total assets + deferred outflows of resources	$640,000	$3,200,000	$5,200,000	Passed	Passed
Total liabilities + deferred inflows of resources	$220,000	$3,000,000	$3,500,000	Failed	Not applicable
Total revenues	$270,000	$2,500,000	$6,500,000	Passed	Failed
Total expenditures	$180,000	$2,400,000	$4,500,000	Failed	Not applicable

Result: Two items (total assets and total revenues) passed the 10% test. Only these two items would be used for the 5% test. Because total assets passed both tests, special Revenue Fund A would be reported as a major fund.

Knowledge check

1. Which statement is correct regarding fund reporting?

    a. Generally, a government should have the minimum number of funds necessary for sound financial management and to meet legal and accounting requirements.
    b. A government has six different types of funds.
    c. The number of individual funds a government may have cannot vary.
    d. There are no differences in how things are reported and measured in the financial statements of the different fund types.

2. Which statement is correct regarding major fund reporting?

    a. Reporting by major funds applies only to governmental funds and enterprise funds.
    b. Major fund reporting applies to internal service funds.
    c. The major fund approach prevents the user from focusing on the most important funds of a government.
    d. Governments report information by fund type.

Governmental funds

Governmental funds are used to report what financial resources were received during the year, how they were spent, and what amounts remain at year-end. These funds follow the flow of financial resources measurement focus and the modified accrual basis of accounting. Capital assets and long-term liabilities are not reported in governmental fund financial statements.

Governmental funds report the following two financial statements:

- Balance sheet
- Statement of revenues, expenditures, and changes in fund balance

A governmental fund balance sheet reports current financial assets, current liabilities, and fund balances. Each major fund is reported in a separate column; nonmajor funds are aggregated and reported in a single column. A total column for all governmental funds is also required.

Governments are required to provide a summary reconciliation of the amount reported in the balance for total governmental fund balance to the amount reported as net position for governmental activities in the statement of net position. The summary reconciliation may be reported at the bottom of the balance sheet or in an accompanying schedule.

The governmental funds' statement of revenues, expenditures, and changes in fund balances reports inflows, outflows, and ending balances of current financial resources. Again, separate columns are used to report each major fund and one column is used to report nonmajor funds in the aggregate. A total column for all governmental funds is also required.

Governments are required to use the following format in the statement of revenues, expenditures, and changes in fund balances:

Format of the Statement of Revenues, Expenditures, and Changes in Fund Balances

Revenues (detailed)	XX
Expenditures (detailed)	XX
Excess (deficiency) of revenues over expenditures	X
Other financing sources and uses including transfers (detailed)	X
Special and extraordinary items (detailed)	X
Net change in fund balances	X
Fund balances — Beginning of period	X
Fund balances — End of period	X

A summary reconciliation is also required for the amount reported as change in governmental fund balances to the amount reported as change in net position for governmental activities in the statement of activities. The summary reconciliation may be reported at the bottom of the statement of revenues, expenditures, and changes in fund balances or in an accompanying schedule.

Governments are also required to report budgetary comparison schedules for the general fund and for each major special revenue fund with a legally adopted annual budget. These schedules are normally reported as part of RSI. However, governments may elect to report these schedules as budgetary comparison statements as part of the fund financial statements.

Knowledge check

3. Which statement is correct regarding governmental financial reporting?

    a. Each fund type uses the same set of fund financial statements.
    b. Only the governmental funds require a balance sheet.
    c. Financial statements for governments include both fund-based and government-wide statements.
    d. Capital assets are included in the financial statements of governmental funds.

4. Governmental funds are used to report

    a. What financial resources were received during the year.
    b. How financial resources were spent during the year.
    c. What financial resources remain at year-end.
    d. All the above.

Proprietary funds

Proprietary funds are used to report a government's business-type activities and follow business-type accounting. These funds follow the flow of economic resources measurement focus and the accrual basis of accounting. Their financial statements report all assets and liabilities belonging to the funds.

Proprietary funds report the following three financial statements:

- Statement of net position or balance sheet
- Statement of revenues, expenses, and changes in net position
- Statement of cash flows

The financial statements report each major enterprise fund in a separate column; nonmajor enterprise funds aggregated into a single column; and all enterprise funds in a combined total column, followed by a column for the combined total for all internal service funds. Internal service funds are reported as a fund type; they are not combined with enterprise funds.

Normally, a reconciliation of the proprietary funds' financial statements to the government-wide financial statements is not needed. The totals for net position and changes in net position for the enterprise funds are often the same for net position and changes in net position reported for business-type activities in the government-wide statements. When differences do exist, reconciliations should be presented in the fund financial statements or in an accompanying schedule.

Proprietary funds may present either a statement of net position (assets + deferred outflows of resources − liabilities − deferred inflows of resources = net position) or a balance sheet (assets + deferred outflows of resources = liabilities + deferred inflows of resources + net position). Although presentation of either the statement of net position or the balance sheet is permitted, the statement of net position format is encouraged. The statement should be presented in a classified format, separating current assets (and the current portion of deferrals) and liabilities (and the current portion of deferrals) from long-term assets and liabilities. Net position is reported in three broad categories: net investment in capital assets, restricted, and unrestricted. Any designations of net position are not reported on the face of the financial statements.

The proprietary fund financial statement — as in, the statement of revenues, expenses, and changes in net position — is analogous to the operating statement in for-profit reporting. The statement separates operating revenues and expenses from nonoperating revenues and expenses and other items. This format allows the fund to report an amount for operating income (or loss).

Governments should adopt a policy that defines operating revenues and expenses in a manner appropriate for a given activity. GAAP does not directly define what should be classified as "operating" but states that how items are classified in a cash flow statement should be considered. The classifications used for cash flow statements are discussed shortly.

The following table shows the format of a statement of revenues, expenses, and changes in net position.

Format of the Statement of Revenues, Expenses, and Changes in Net Position	
Operating revenues (detailed)	XX
Operating expenses (detailed)	XX
Operating income (loss)	X
Nonoperating revenues and expenses (detailed)	X
Income before other revenues, expenses, gains, losses, and transfers	X
Capital contributions, additions to permanent and term endowments, special and extraordinary items and transfers	X
Increase (decrease) in net position	X
Net position — Beginning of period	X
Net position — End of period	X

Proprietary funds report a statement of cash flows. The purpose of a statement of cash flows is to provide relevant information about cash receipts and disbursements for the period. This information should assist users in determining the following:

- The entity's ability to generate future cash flows
- Its ability to meet obligations when they become due
- Its needs for external financing
- The reasons for differences between operating income and cash flows from operating activities
- The effects on the entity's financial position on its cash and its noncash investing, capital, and financing transactions during the period

The GASB defines four types of cash flows: operating activities, noncapital financing activities, capital and related financing activities, and investing activities. The following table describes what should be included in each category of cash flow.

Cash flow categories

Cash flows from operating activities

Cash flows from providing goods and services and, generally, all cash flows not explained in the other three categories fall into this category. It includes cash flows from the following activities:

- Providing goods and services
- Executing quasi-external operating transactions with other funds
- Executing certain loan transactions when they are part of a fund's program and not classified as investing activity

Cash flows from investing activities

This category of cash flows primarily includes investment activities that are not part of a fund's program and involves investments that are not considered cash equivalents. It includes cash flows from the following activities:

- Making or collecting loans
- Buying and selling debt and equity investments
- Receiving interest and dividends on such loans or investments

Cash flows from noncapital financing activities

Noncapital financing activities primarily include borrowing activities not related to capital assets and certain interfund and intergovernmental activities not related to capital assets and operating purposes. It includes cash flows from the following activities:

- Borrowing or repaying on a short- or long-term basis that is not related to the acquisition, construction, or improvements of capital assets
- Making interest payments related to such borrowing
- Executing interfund transfers not related to capital assets
- Participating in intergovernmental activities not related to capital purposes
- Receiving cash from taxes collected not related to capital purposes

Cash flows from capital and related financing activities

Capital and related financing activities primarily include acquiring and disposing of capital assets. It includes borrowing activities and certain interfund and intergovernmental activities related to capital assets. It includes cash flows from the following activities:

- Making cash payments for the acquisition, construction, or improvements of capital assets
- Receiving cash from the sale of capital assets
- Borrowing or repaying on a short- or long-term basis that is related to the acquisition, construction, or improvements of capital assets
- Making interest payments related to such borrowing
- Executing interfund transfers related to capital assets;
- Participating in intergovernmental activities related to capital assets
- Receiving cash from taxes (including special assessments) collected related to capital assets

Cash flows from operating activities are reported under the **direct method** using the following minimum classes of receipts and payments:

- Cash receipts from customers
- Cash receipts from quasi-external operating transactions with other funds
- Other operating cash receipts, if any
- Cash payments to employees for services
- Cash payments to other suppliers of goods or services
- Cash payments for quasi-external operating transactions with other funds
- Other operating cash payments, if any

Proprietary funds must also report a schedule that reconciles cash flows from operating activities to the amount reported as operating income (loss) in the statement of revenues, expenses, and changes in net position. This schedule should be presented on the same page as the statement of cash flows, if space permits.

Governments may acquire assets by directly assuming a liability. For example, a building may be acquired by entering into a mortgage agreement. A separate schedule should be presented describing such noncash transactions. The schedule can be in either a narrative or a tabular format. Again, this schedule should be presented on the same page as the statement of cash flows, if space permits.

Fiduciary funds

Fiduciary funds (trust and custodial funds) are used to account for resources held by a government for other individuals or organizations. Like proprietary funds, fiduciary funds report using the flow of economic resources measurement focus and the accrual basis of accounting. The fiduciary financial statements should report all fiduciary funds of the primary government and any fiduciary component.

Fiduciary funds report the following two financial statements:

- Statement of fiduciary net position
- Statement of changes in fiduciary net position

Unlike governmental and proprietary funds, fiduciary fund financial statements are presented by fund type. For example, if a government has several private-purpose trust funds, only one column should be presented in the financial statements for this fund type. Also, total columns are not used in the financial statements.

The statement of fiduciary net position reports the assets, liabilities, and net position for each type of fiduciary fund. The statement does not include certain actuarial liabilities of defined benefit pension plans and other similar defined benefit plans. In most cases, a liability should be recognized in a fiduciary fund when an event has occurred that compels the government to disburse fiduciary resources. Fiduciary funds generally report net position simply as net position held in trust for others. The requirement to report net position in three separate classes does not apply to fiduciary funds.

The statement of changes in fiduciary net position reports additions to and deductions from net position for each fiduciary fund type. Revenues and expenses are not reported. A government that reports a pension plan or postemployment benefit plan other than pension plan in a pension (or other employee benefit) trust fund should report the plan's assets, deferred outflows of resources, liabilities, deferred inflow of resources, and fiduciary net position.

GASB Statement No. 84, *Fiduciary Activities*, issued in January 2017 and effective for fiscal years beginning after December 15, 2018, sets forth that agency funds are no longer to be reported upon the application of this statement.

Summary

Financial statements for governments include both fund-based and government-wide statements. There are separate sets of fund financial statements for each fund type: governmental, proprietary, and fiduciary. Fund financial statements focus on major funds. Each major fund is reported in separate columns; nonmajor funds are combined and reported as a separate column. Major fund reporting applies only to governmental and enterprise funds. Internal service funds and fiduciary funds report separate columns for each fund type.

The required financial statements for each fund type are different. Governmental funds report a balance sheet and a statement of revenues, expenditures, and changes in fund balances. Proprietary funds report a statement of net position (or balance sheet); a statement of revenues, expenses, and changes in net position; and a statement of cash flows. Fiduciary funds report a statement of fiduciary net position and a statement of changes in fiduciary net position.

	Key foundational points
1	In governmental and proprietary fund financial statements, governments report separate columns for each major fund. Nonmajor funds, as well as internal service funds, are combined and reported in a single column.
2	There are separate sets of financial statements for governmental funds, proprietary funds, and fiduciary funds.
3	Governments are required to report budgetary comparison schedules for the general fund and each major special revenue fund with a legally adopted annual budget.
4	A proprietary fund statement of cash flows uses four categories and must be done using the direct method.
5	Unlike governmental and proprietary funds, fiduciary fund financial statements are presented by fund type.

Practice questions

Please note that the following practice questions are not required reading material.

1. Separate sets of fund financial statements are prepared for which fund category?

   a. Fiduciary.
   b. Governmental.
   c. Proprietary.
   d. All the above.

2. In the fund financial statements, a government should include a separate column for each of these **except**

   a. Each major enterprise fund.
   b. Each major internal service fund.
   c. Each major capital projects fund.
   d. Each major special revenue fund.

3. Which funds must always be reported in a separate column in the fund financial statements?

   a. Capital projects fund.
   b. Debt service fund.
   c. General fund.
   d. Enterprise fund.

4. Which is **not** correct?

   a. Major fund reporting is required for all proprietary funds.
   b. The general fund is always major.
   c. Major fund reporting is required for all governmental funds.
   d. A government can report any fund as major.

5. Which column would **not** appear in a proprietary fund financial statement?

   a. Each major enterprise fund.
   b. Total for all enterprise funds.
   c. The internal service fund type.
   d. Total for all proprietary funds.

6. Which fund financial statements are required for governmental funds?

   a. Balance sheet.
   b. Statement of revenues, expenditures, and changes in fund balances.
   c. Budgetary comparison statement for all funds with annual budgets.
   d. Both (*a*) and (*b*).

7. Which set of fund financial statements would normally contain a reconciliation of the fund financial statement information to the government-wide financial statements?

    a. Governmental.
    b. Proprietary.
    c. Fiduciary.
    d. All the above.

8. Which fund type would report additions and deductions in the fund financial statements?

    a. Enterprise funds.
    b. Internal service funds.
    c. Permanent funds.
    d. Pension (and other employee benefit) trust funds.

9. Which is **not** a cash flow category used by an enterprise fund in the statement of cash flows?

    a. Financing activities.
    b. Capital and related financing activities.
    c. Operating activities.
    d. Noncapital financing activities.

10. Explain when a fund must be reported in a separate column in the fund financial statements.

11. What statements are included in the fund financial statements?

12. How would the following items be reported in the statement of cash flows for a proprietary fund? Operating activities (OA), noncapital financing activities (NC), capital and related financing activities (CA), investing activities (IA), or not reported (NR).

- Cash paid for supplies
- Cash received from sale of equipment
- Cash transferred from the general fund (noncapital)
- Cash received from state grant (noncapital)
- Cash paid for investments
- Cash received from short-term borrowing
- Cash paid for interest on capital-related debt
- Cash received from customers
- Cash received for interest from investment

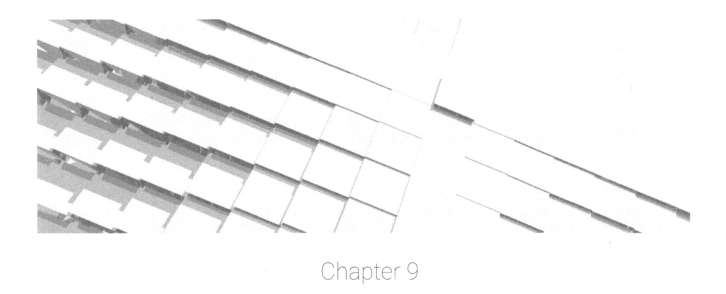

Chapter 9

Reporting Entity

Learning objectives

- Identify the reporting entity of a government.

- Distinguish what qualifies as a primary government.

- Distinguish what qualifies as a component unit.

- Recognize how component units are reported in the financial statements of a primary government.

What entities should be included in the financial statements?

In business, it is often easy to determine what separate legal entities should be included in the financial statements of a corporation. It is based on ownership. Often there is no ownership for governments, making it difficult to determine what entities to include. Governments come in all shapes and sizes. Some general-purpose governments provide a full range of services; others provide only limited services. Additional services often are provided by separate special-purpose entities. Under what circumstances should these separate legal entities be included in the financial statements of the general-purpose government? This chapter will try to answer that question.

The reporting entity

Governments can provide a range of services in different ways to meet the needs of its citizens. Sometimes, governments establish separate legal entities to provide services that meet certain needs. Alternatively, they may financially support extant separate organizations or may join with other governments in providing a regional approach to providing services. Examples include jails, airports, housing, and building authorities.

Should these separate legal entities be included in the government's financial reports? If so, how? Traditionally, accountants look to substance over legal form in financial reporting requirements. GASB Statement No. 39, *Determining Whether Certain Organizations Are Component Units*, relies on a **financially accountable** criterion to determine which entities should be included in the financial statements of a government.

The *reporting entity* for a government is defined as the primary government and its component units. To better understand this concept, it is important to clearly understand what a primary government is and what component units of a primary government are.

The primary government

The primary government is at the core of the financial reporting entity. All state and general-purpose local governments meet the definition of a *primary government*. Other governmental organizations are considered special-purpose governments. A special-purpose government may also be considered a primary government if they meet **all** the following criteria:

- Members of the governing board are chosen in a general election.
- The government functions as a separate legal entity.
- The government is fiscally independent.

Knowledge check

1. Which statement is correct regarding the primary government?

    a. The primary government is at the core of the financial reporting entity.
    b. The reporting entity for a government is defined as the primary government and its employees.
    c. Few state and general-purpose local governments meet the definition of a primary government.
    d. A special-purpose government must only meet one of the criteria to be considered a primary government.

Component units: Special-purpose governments

If a special-purpose government does not meet all the criteria that defines a primary government, it becomes a *potential component unit* of a primary government. To be classified as a component unit of a primary government, a special-purpose government must first be a legally separate entity. Entities that are not legally separate would normally be included as part of the government that holds the related legal powers.

To be a component unit of a primary government, the legally separate special-purpose government must also be financially accountable to the elected officials of the primary government. How is this determined? If a legally separate special-purpose government meets **any** of the following three tests, then it is a component unit of the primary government.

Test 1
The primary government appoints the voting majority of the governing board of the entity.

Governments often appoint the majority of certain entities' boards. However, just appointing a majority is not enough to determine if the primary government is financially accountable for this entity. **One** of the following tests must also be met:

- The primary government must be able to impose its will (see the following examples).
- There is a financial benefit or burden relationship between the primary government and the separate legal entity (see the following examples).

Examples of a government being able to impose its will

- It can remove appointed members of the entity's board at will.
- It can modify or approve the entity's budget.
- It can modify or approve rate or fee changes that affect revenue.
- It can veto, overrule, or modify decisions of the entity's board.
- It can appoint, hire, reassign, or dismiss those persons responsible for day-to-day operations of the entity.

Examples of a financial benefit or burden relationship

- The government is legally entitled to the entity's resources.
- The government has access to the entity's resources.
- The government is legally obligated or has assumed the obligation to finance the entity's deficit or to provide support to the entity.
- The government is "obligated in some manner" for the debt of the entity.

For entities where the voting majority of the board is not appointed by the government, the following two tests apply.

Test 2

The entity is fiscally dependent on the primary government.

Separate legal entities sometimes are fiscally dependent on the primary government. The following are examples of fiscal dependency:

- The primary government's approval is needed for the entity's budget.
- The primary government's approval is needed for the entity to set taxes or charges.
- The primary government's approval is needed to issue bonded debt.

In addition, to meet the fiscally dependent test, there must also be an ongoing financial benefit or burden relationship between the primary government and the separate legal entity.

Test 3

The financial statements would be misleading if data from the entity were not included.

This test requires professional judgment. In most cases, special-purpose governments are reported as component units because they meet the first two tests. However, there may be special circumstances where it would be misleading to exclude a separate legal entity from the financial statements of a primary government. Such determination is based on the nature and significance of the potential component unit's relationship with the primary government. An example would be a special financing authority created to provide temporary financial assistance to a local government in financial distress; such an entity might not meet the first two tests but nevertheless should be included in the primary government's financial statements.

Component units: Certain tax-exempt organizations

Certain other organizations warrant inclusion in the primary government's financial statements because of their relationship and significance to the primary government, such as foundations and other organizations that support the programs of the primary government. A legally separate, tax-exempt organization[1] is considered a component unit of a primary government if it meets **all** the following three tests:

- The economic resources received or held by the organization are entirely or almost entirely for the direct benefit of the primary government, its component units, or its constituents.
- The primary government, or its component units, is entitled to, or has the ability to otherwise access, a majority of the economic resources of the organization.

---

[1] Guidance for tax-exempt organizations is contained in GASB Statement No. 39, *Determining Whether Certain Organizations Are Component Units.*

- The economic resources received or held by the individual organization that the specific primary government (or its component units) is entitled to, or has the ability to otherwise access, are significant to that primary government.

In addition, other organizations should be evaluated as potential component units if they are closely related to or financially integrated with the primary government. Professional judgment is used to determine whether the relationship and significance of the organization to the primary government warrant inclusion as a component unit.

Some component units issue separate financial statements. These financial statements should also include any component units of the entity producing the financial statement. If a component unit of the primary government has its own component units, these component units must also be included in the financial statements of the primary government. Separately issued financial statements of a component unit should acknowledge that it is a component unit of another government. The notes to the financial statements should identify the primary government in whose financial reporting entity it is included and describe its relationship to the primary government.

Finally, it is important to note that an entity can be included as a component unit by only one primary government. This is true even if the entity passes the tests to be reported as a component unit for more than one government. For example, a state government may appoint an entity's governing board, but the entity may be fiscally dependent on a local government. Usually, the fiscally dependent test takes precedence over the other tests. In this example, the entity is considered a component unit of the local government, not of the state government.

Reporting component units

Once an entity has been determined to be a component unit of the primary government, the next decision is how to report it in the financial statements. There are two different methods: blending and discrete presentation.

Blending combines the financial information of the component unit with the existing funds of the primary government in the financial statements. Essentially, a blended component unit appears as just another fund in the financial statements of the primary government. However, the general fund of a blended component unit should be reported as a special revenue fund; it should not be combined with the general fund of the primary government.

A government is required to blend the financial information of a component unit if **any** of the following circumstances applies:

1. The board of the component unit is "substantively" the same as that of the primary government and there is a financial benefit or burden relationship between the primary government and the component unit.
2. The board of the component unit is "substantively" the same as that of the primary government and management of the primary government has operational responsibility for the component unit.
3. The component unit serves the primary government exclusively, or almost exclusively (for example, a financing authority used to finance the government's construction projects).
4. The component unit's total debt is expected to be paid entirely or almost entirely with resources from the primary government.
5. The component unit is incorporated as a not-for-profit corporation in which the government is the sole corporate member (see GASB Statement No. 80, *Blending Requirements for Certain Component Units — An Amendment to GASB Statement No. 14*).[2]

If none of the listed circumstances are met, then the component unit will be discretely reported in the financial statements (discrete presentation). *Discrete presentation* reports the financial information of a component unit in a column separate from the primary government in the government-wide financial statements.

---

[2] This criterion does not apply to component units included in the reporting entity pursuant to the provisions of GASB Statement No. 39.

Knowledge check

2. Which is correct regarding the reporting of component units?

   a. There are five different methods.
   b. A blended component unit appears differently than individual funds in the financial statements of the primary government.
   c. Once an entity has been determined to be a component unit of the primary government, the next decision is how it should be reported in the financial statements.
   d. Component units are always reported separately from the primary government.

When there is more than one discretely presented component unit, generally accepted accounting principles requires that information about each major component unit be provided in the basic financial statements. There are three ways a government can meet this requirement, as follows:

1. Use a separate column for each component unit in the government-wide statements.
2. Include a combining statement of major component units after the fund financial statements.
3. Present condensed financial information in notes to the financial statements.

Component units that are fiduciary activities should not be reported in the government-wide statements. Government-wide statements exclude all fiduciary funds and fiduciary component units. Fiduciary component units are reported only in the fund financial statements along with the primary government's fiduciary funds.

Lastly, a component unit may have a different fiscal year than the primary government. Such a component unit is presented in the basic financial statements using the component unit's fiscal year. Generally, component units' information should not be more than nine months older than the primary government, unless including the newer information would unduly delay issuing the financial statements.

Joint ventures and other organizations

A local government may join with other area governments to provide certain services. These multigovernment arrangements often do not meet the criteria to be treated as a component unit by any individual government. How, then, should each government report their participation in such arrangements? That depends on the nature of the arrangement.

There are two general types of multigovernment arrangements: joint ventures and jointly governed organizations. The main difference between the two is that a joint venture creates an ongoing financial relationship with the participating governments; a jointly governed organization does not create such a relationship. Both types of organizations are included in note disclosures by the participating governments.

For joint ventures, the arrangement may create an explicit, measurable equity interest for the participating governments in some or all the resources of the joint venture. In this case, a government should report its interest in the joint venture in the government-wide statements as a single line item. For the fund financial statements, governmental funds should report an interest in joint ventures only to the extent that the interest represents financial assets. For proprietary funds, the "investment in joint venture" account reported in a proprietary fund should report the participating government's equity interest calculated in accordance with the joint venture agreement.

Summary

A government's reporting entity includes the primary government and its component units. Component units are separate legal entities that are financially accountable to the elected officials of the primary government. In addition, certain other tax-exempt organizations warrant inclusion in the primary government's financial statements as component units because of their relationship and significance to the primary government. A variety of tests is used to determine whether an entity is a component unit.

Component units are either blended or discretely presented in the financial statements of the primary government. Blending reports component units as funds of the primary government. Discrete presentation reports component units in separate columns of the government-wide statements. Other related organizations, such as joint ventures and jointly governed organizations, should be disclosed in the notes to the financial statements.

Key foundational points	
1	The reporting entity for a government is defined as the primary government and its component units.
2	GASB Statement No. 39 relies on a financially accountable criterion to determine which entities should be included in the financial statements of a government.
3	There are three tests used to determine if an entity should be reported as a component unit.
4	Once an entity has been determined to be a component unit of the primary government, the next decision is how it should be reported in the financial statements. There are two different methods: blending and discrete presentation.
5	Joint ventures and jointly governed organizations are disclosed in the notes to the financial statements.

Practice questions

Please note that the following practice questions are not required reading material.

1. For a special-purpose government to be considered a primary government, which criterion must be met?

   a. Be fiscally independent.
   b. Be a legally separate entity.
   c. Members of the governing board are chosen in a general election.
   d. All the above.

2. Which is **not** a test to determine if a special-purpose government is a component unit?

   a. A voting majority of its governing body is appointed by a primary government.
   b. It is fiscally dependent on a primary government.
   c. Its governing board is substantially the same as that of the primary government.
   d. The financial statements of the primary government would be misleading if data from the entity were not included.

3. In a case where the majority of the board is appointed by the primary government, which additional criterion must be met for an entity to be classified as a component unit?

   a. The primary government can impose its will.
   b. There is a financial benefit relationship with the primary government.
   c. There is a financial burden relationship with the primary government.
   d. Any of the above.

4. A tax-exempt organization would be considered a component unit if it meets which criterion?

   a. The primary government can impose its will.
   b. There is a financial benefit relationship with the primary government.
   c. There is a financial burden relationship with the primary government.
   d. None of the above.

5. How are component units presented in the financial statements of a primary government?

   a. Reported only in the notes to the financial statements.
   b. Blended in the financial statements.
   c. Discretely presented in the financial statements.
   d. Either (*b*) or (*c*).

6. Which criterion must be met for a component unit to be "blended" in the financial statements?

   a. The component unit's total debt is expected to be paid entirely or almost entirely with resources from the primary government.
   b. Have substantively the same governing board of the primary government and there is a financial benefit or burden relationship between the primary government and the component unit.
   c. Provide services exclusively, or almost exclusively, to the primary government.
   d. Either (*b*) or (*c*).

7. Financial information for blended component units would be reported in which financial statements?

    a. The fund financial statements.
    b. The government-wide financial statements.
    c. Both (*a*) and (*b*).
    d. None of the above.

8. Which is accurate regarding joint ventures?

    a. They should be reported as component units.
    b. They should not be discussed in the notes to the financial statements.
    c. They should be disclosed in the notes to the financial statements.
    d. Both (*a*) and (*c*).

9. Explain the difference between reporting component units as blended or discretely presented.

10. How should a government present information about each major discretely presented component unit?

11. The following are examples of related organizations to a county government. Determine if the entities should be included in the financial statements of the county. If so, how should they be reported?

A county transit authority. The authority is a separate legal entity; however, the governing board of the authority is made up of members of the county's board of supervisors. The authority receives no financial support from the county. The county does guarantee the debt of the authority.

A tax-exempt foundation. The foundation supports the county's public library by raising funds for the purchase of books. The foundation receives requests for the director of the county's library systems and routinely funds those requests based on the amount of donations raised that year. The amount of resources raised and held each year is not significant to the overall county.

Chapter 10

Government-Wide Financial Statements

Learning objectives

- Recognize the format and requirements of the government-wide financial statements.

- Identify steps in the process required to produce the government-wide financial statements.

Constructing government-wide financial statements

Government-wide statements were created with the advent of GASB Statement No. 34, *Basic Financial Statement — and Management's Discussion and Analysis — for State and Local Governments*. They are constructed from the information in the fund-based accounting system and other records maintained by a government. However, these statements are more than just a summary of the fund financial statements. They present a different view of the government's resources. Understanding how they are constructed is an important step in understanding and interpreting government-wide financial statements.

Purpose of the government-wide statements

The purpose of the government-wide financial statements is to demonstrate *operational accountability*, which is the provision of information about the results of operations and the financial condition of the overall government. The fund financial statements are used to address fiscal accountability.

Operational accountability provides information about the medium and long-term effects of current and past financial decisions. It should assist users in assessing

- the service levels that can be provided from existing revenues,
- the effects of current-period operations on future service needs, and
- the government's financial position and financial condition.

To meet the goal of providing operational accountability, the government-wide statements use the flow of economic resources measurement focus and the accrual basis of accounting to report activities. The statements provide information about the economic resources and activity available to the overall government, including the primary government and its component units (reporting entity). However, fiduciary funds and fiduciary component units are excluded from the government-wide statements because these resources are not available to support the government's programs.

Knowledge check

1. Choose the correct statement regarding the government-wide financial statements.

    a. The government-wide financial statements are used to address fiscal accountability.
    b. Government-wide statements were created with the advent of GASB Statement No. 68, *Accounting and Financial Reporting for Pensions — An Amendment of GASB Statement No. 27.*
    c. The purpose of the government-wide financial statements is to demonstrate operational accountability.
    d. The fund financial statements are used to address operational accountability.

2. Which fund type is excluded from the government-wide statements?

    a. Fiduciary funds.
    b. Proprietary funds.
    c. Governmental funds.
    d. Capital project funds.

The government-wide statements

The two government-wide financial statements follow:

- The statement of net position
- The statement of activities

In both statements, information is reported in separate columns to distinguish between resources and activities of the primary government and its component units[1]. In addition, separate columns and rows are used to distinguish between the primary government's governmental activities and business-type activities. Governmental activities are usually reported in governmental funds and internal service funds. Business-type activities are usually reported in enterprise funds. The government-wide statements must report the following columns:

- Primary government's governmental activities
- Primary government's business-type activities
- Total for the primary government
- Component units (if there is more than one component unit, each major component unit may be displayed in separate columns or this information may be displayed in other sections of the basic financial statements)

The government also has an option to report a total column for the reporting entity.

The statement of net position

The *statement of net position* is like a balance sheet in that it reports assets plus deferred outflows of resources, liabilities plus deferred inflows of resources, and net position for the government. Governments are encouraged to use a net position format (assets + deferred outflows of resources − liabilities − deferred inflows of resources = net position) for this statement, but a balance sheet format (assets + deferred outflows of resources) = (liabilities + deferred inflows of resources + net position) may also be used. Governments should present assets and liabilities in order of their relative liquidity (although a classified approach is also allowed). For liabilities that have average maturities of more than one year, separate amounts are reported for the amount due within one year and the amount due in more than one year.

The statement of net position should minimize the reporting of internal balances (the reporting of receivables and payables among the different parts of the government). Interfund receivables and payables among the funds that make up governmental activities are eliminated. The same is true for business-type activities. Payables and receivables between governmental activities and business-type activities are eliminated in the total primary government column. Receivables and payables between the primary government and its component units are treated as external transactions and are not eliminated.

The difference between assets plus deferred outflows of resources and liabilities plus deferred inflows of resources should be reported as net position. Net position is divided into the following three components:

1. *Net investment in capital assets* is the component of net position that represents the government's net equity in its capital assets. It consists of capital assets, net of accumulated depreciation less any outstanding debt related to the capital assets. If there are unspent debt proceeds related to capital assets, both the unspent proceeds and related debt should be reported as part of restricted net position.

---

[1] See appendix A for examples of government-wide financial statements.

---

2. *Restricted net position* is used when constraints are placed on net position. The constraints can be either externally imposed (for example, debt covenants or grantor restrictions) or imposed by constitutional provisions or enabling legislation. In cases where there are endowment-type funds, two components of restricted net position should be displayed: expendable and nonexpendable net position.
3. *Unrestricted net position* includes all other net position not included in the previous two categories. Unlike fund balance, designations of unrestricted net position should not be reported on the face of the financial statements.

The statement of activities

The *statement of activities* reports the results of operations for the government. In some regards, it is like an income statement but looks nothing like one that a business would produce. This is because the purpose of a business is to generate income in such a fashion that it also generates net income for its owners. The purpose of government is to provide certain services to the public and to generate sufficient revenues to pay for those services. Therefore, the statement of activities begins with expenses, which are followed by revenues.

In the statement of activities, expenses are reported in three categories: governmental activities, business-type activities, and component units. Governmental activity expenses should be reported in at least as much detail as they are reported in governmental fund statements. Business-type activities expenses should be reported by different identifiable activities.

The statement format is designed to report the net expense or revenues of the different functions of governments. The first column in the statement of activities reports the expenses of the different functions of government. The next three columns are used to report different types of program revenues. Program revenues reduce the net cost of the function. The net (expense) revenue of a function indicates the function's relative benefit to or burden on the taxpayers and other general revenues of the government.

Separate columns are used in the statement of activities to report the net (expense) revenues for governmental activities, business-type activities, total for the primary government, and component units.

For example, assume that the public safety function reports $100,000 of expenses for the year. Also assume that this function generated $25,000 in fees and charges for services and received $10,000 in grants (restricted for this purpose) from other governments. The net cost of this function would be $65,000 ($100,000 − $25,000 − $10,000), which must be paid from taxes and other general revenues. The reporting of net (expense) revenues of functions is unique to the government-wide statements. The fund financial statements do not show the relationship of program revenues to expenditures.

Program revenues relate to the different functions of governments and reduce the net costs of these functions. They are generally generated from fees, fines, and forfeitures and charges for services from the different functions; they also may come from parties other than the government's taxpayers or citizens (such as intergovernmental grants restricted to a particular function). All taxes, even if restricted in purpose, should be reported as general revenue.

Program revenues are normally reported in the statement of activities using the following three separate columns:

1. *Charges for services* — This category includes charges to customers or applicants for the purchase of goods and services or for privileges provided. Some examples are fees charged for services (water and garbage collection), licenses and permits (dog licenses and building permits), and for operating special assessments (street cleaning and street lights). Fines and forfeitures would also be reported under this category (parking tickets and court fines).
2. *Operating grants and contributions* — This category includes revenues generated from mandatory and voluntary nonexchange transactions (for example, grants and contributions) with other governments, organizations, and individuals; these revenues are restricted for use in a particular program. The grants and contributions reported in this category should be for operating purposes. Restricted operating grants and contributions reduce the net expenses of certain functions for the reporting government.
3. *Capital grants and contributions* — This category is very similar to operating grants and contributions; however, in this category, program revenue is for capital purposes. For example, grants for the purchase, construction, or renovation of a capital asset would fall into this category.

Revenues that do not fit the definition of program revenues are classified as general revenues. All taxes and interest, grants, and contributions that are not restricted to a particular program are reported as general revenues. General revenues of the government are reported in the bottom of the statement.

Any contributions to endowments and permanent funds, special and extraordinary items, and transfers are reported immediately after general revenues in the statement of activities.

The statement also reports the change in net position for the year. This is the bottom-line measure for the results of operations for the government.

Generally, the statement of activities should eliminate the double recording of expenses related to goods and services provided by internal service funds. Only the programs that consume the goods and services should report the expenses (this is discussed in more detail later in the chapter). However, the revenues and expenses of services provided and used between different functions of governments should not be eliminated. For example, the sale of water by an enterprise fund to the general government should be reported as revenue by the function providing the water and as an expense by the function consuming the water.

This completes the discussion of the requirements and general format of the two government-wide statements. The next section discusses how the statements are prepared.

The worksheet approach

This section will give a general overview of how government-wide financial statements are produced.

Governments generally maintain their accounting records on a fund basis. This facilitates budgetary reporting throughout the year and is helpful in producing the fund financial statements. Where this is the case, producing the government-wide statements will be a worksheet exercise. This section will discuss a worksheet approach to creating these statements.

First, it is important to remember that fund financial statements use two different measurement focuses and bases of accounting, as follows:

- Governmental funds follow the flow of financial resources measurement focus and the modified accrual basis of accounting.
- Proprietary funds follow the flow of economic resources management focus and the accrual basis of accounting.

Government-wide financial statements report all financial information using the flow of economic resources measurement focus and the accrual basis of accounting.

The challenge in producing the government-wide statements is with converting governmental funds to governmental activities. Information from proprietary funds should flow easily into the government-wide statements. Therefore, the discussion in this chapter is focused on converting governmental funds to governmental activities.

How is a worksheet set up to convert governmental funds to governmental activities? There are different ways to do a worksheet but they all follow the same basic approach. They begin with the totals from the fund financial statements. Next, one makes adjustments for capital assets and long-term liabilities and makes other adjustments to convert from the modified accrual basis to the accrual basis of accounting and to account for deferred inflows and outflows of resources. The chart that follows summarizes this approach.

Producing governmental activities statements

Funds	→	Adjustments	→	Government-wide
General fund		Capital assets		Governmental activities
Special revenue		Long-term liabilities		
Debt service		Adjustment to the accrual basis		
Capital projects				
Permanent fund		Deferred inflows and outflows		
		Internal service*		

* If predominantly used to serve governmental funds

Let's apply this approach first to the statement of net position. A worksheet would begin with the total column from the fund-based balance sheet (assets, liabilities, and fund balances). Adjustments are made to add capital assets, long-term liabilities, deferred inflows and outflows of resources, and other adjustments needed to convert from the modified accrual to the accrual basis of accounting. Eliminations are also needed to remove interfund receivables and payables among the governmental funds.

Some explanation is needed regarding internal service funds. When internal service funds primarily serve governmental funds, they should be reported as part of governmental activities. When they primarily serve enterprise funds, they should be reported as part of business-type activities. When internal service funds are reported as part of governmental activities, their assets, deferred outflows of resources, liabilities, deferred inflows of resources, and net position are added to the worksheet. Any receivables or payables with governmental funds are eliminated.

One more step is needed to complete the worksheet. The balance sheet for governmental funds reports fund balances where the statement of net position reports net position. Annually, fund balance needs to be reclassified into the three components of net position.

Another way to view this process is in reviewing the reconciliation that must be reported as part of the balance sheet in the fund financial statements. This schedule reconciles fund balance for governmental funds to net position for governmental activities. The reconciliation contains the adjustments needed to produce the government-wide statements. Eliminations are not reported in the reconciliation because they do not affect net position. The following is an example of a reconciliation schedule.

Any City

Reconciliation of the balance sheet of governmental funds to the statement of net position

June 30, 202X

Fund balances — total governmental funds	$ 2,240,000
Amounts reported for governmental activities in the statement of net position are different because:	
Capital assets used in governmental activities are not financial resources and therefore are not reported in the funds.	1,680,000
Other long-term assets are not available to pay for current-period expenditures and therefore are deferred in the funds.	920,000
Long-term liabilities, including bonds payable, are not due and payable in the current period and therefore are not reported in the funds.	(1,200,000)
Deferred outflows/(inflows) for governmental activities are not current financial resources and therefore are not reported in the governmental funds.	

Deferred inflows of resources	(300,000)
Deferred outflows of resources	200,000

Internal service funds are used by management to charge the cost of certain activities to individual funds. The assets and liabilities of certain internal service funds are included in governmental activities in the statement of net position:

Internal service funds	520,000
Net position of governmental activities	$ 4,060,000

The statement of activities is somewhat more difficult to set up on a worksheet because of the format of the statements. However, the process and adjustments needed to the fund financial information is similar to those for the statement of net position. A worksheet would begin with the totals from the statement of revenues, expenditures, and changes in fund balances. Adjustments are made to convert the year's activities related to capital assets and long-term liabilities from the flow of financial resources to the flow of economic resources measurement focus. For example, purchase of capital assets needs to be removed from the fund financial information and depreciation expenses recorded. These adjustments are discussed in more detail in the following paragraphs.

Adjustments to the worksheet are also needed to convert the fund financial information from the modified accrual basis to the accrual basis of accounting. For example, certain revenue sources need adjustments and interest on long-term liabilities needs to be accrued.

Adjustments for internal service funds — assuming they are reported as part of governmental activities — are somewhat more complicated. Eliminations are needed to remove the double recording of expenses related to goods and services provided by internal service funds. The goal of this process is to have only the programs that consume the goods and services report the expenses. This can be done on a worksheet in a number of ways.

Most nonoperating Items of an Internal service fund, such as interest expenses and income, would not be eliminated. These items represent revenues and expenses of the government.

Eliminations are also needed for any transfers among governmental funds (and internal service funds when they are reported as part of governmental activities).

Additional adjusting entries are needed to properly report program revenues. These are adjustments to reclassify certain revenues as program revenues; they do not affect the change in net position. Revenues that are program revenues must first be identified as to what function of government they support and then classified into one of the three types of program revenues discussed earlier.

Again, another way to view this process is in the reconciliation that must be reported in the statement of revenues, expenditures, and changes in fund balances in the fund financial statements. This schedule reconciles the change in fund balances for governmental funds to the change in net position for governmental activities. The reconciliation contains the adjustments needed to produce the government-wide statements. Eliminations and the reclassification of program revenues are not reported in the reconciliation because they do not affect the change in net position.

An example of a reconciliation schedule included in the statement of revenues, expenditures, and changes in fund balance follows:

Any City reconciliation of the statement of revenues, expenditures, and changes in fund balances of governmental funds to the statement of activities for the year ended June 30, 202X

Net change in fund balances — total governmental funds	$ 410,000
Amounts reported for governmental activities in the statement of activities are different because:	
Governmental funds report capital outlays as expenditures, whereas governmental activities report depreciation expense to allocate those expenditures over the life of the assets.	110,000
Add capital acquisitions 830,000 *Subtract depreciation (720,000)*	
In the statement of activities, only the gain (loss) on capital assets is reported, whereas in the governmental funds, the proceeds from the sale increase financial resources. Therefore, the change in net position differs from the change in fund balance by the cost of the capital asset.	(90,000)
Revenues in the statement of activities that do not provide current financial resources are not reported as revenues in the funds.	70,000
Bond proceeds provide current financial resources to governmental funds, but issuing debt increases long-term liabilities in the statement of net position. Repayment of bond principal is an expenditure in the governmental funds, but the repayment reduces long-term liabilities in the statement of net position.	130,000
Add debt repayment 680,000 *Subtract debt proceeds (550,000)*	
Some expenses reported in the statement of activities do not require the use of current financial resources and therefore are not reported as expenditures in governmental funds (such as changes in compensated absences and deferred inflows and outflows of resources).	(50,000)
Add amortization of deferred outflow resources 40,000 *Subtract amortization of deferred inflows resources (60,000)* *Subtract compensated absences (40,000)*	
Internal service funds are used by management to charge the costs of certain services to individual funds. The net revenue (expense) of the internal service funds is reported with governmental activities.	200,000
Change in net position of governmental activities	$ 780,000

Capital assets adjustments

Because capital assets are not reported by governmental funds, they play a major role in the conversion of governmental funds from the flow of financial resources to the flow of economic resources measurement focus. The government must maintain detailed capital assets records to support this conversion.

To convert the balance sheet of governmental funds to the statement of net position for governmental activities, capital assets — net of accumulated depreciation — need to be added to assets and an equal amount added to net position.

Several adjustments related to capital assets are needed to convert the statement of revenues, expenditures, and changes in fund balances for governmental funds to the statement of activities for governmental activities. Governmental funds report capital purchases as expenditures. No depreciation is recorded. Also, if a government sells a general capital asset, the proceeds from the sale are recorded in a governmental fund as other financing source.

The adjustments convert the information in the statement of revenues, expenditures, and changes in fund balances to the flow of economic resources measurement focus. The following list of adjustments indicates either an increase or decrease to the reconciliation schedule for the amount reported as changes in fund balances for governmental funds and the amount reported as change in net position for governmental activities:

- *Add capital assets purchased*. The purchase of a capital asset is not reported as an expense in the statement of activities but is recorded as an expenditure by governmental funds. Therefore, the amount of capital assets purchased is added back on the reconciliation. This amount would reduce reported expenses in the worksheet for the functional areas that reported the purchase.
- *Subtract depreciation*. Depreciation expense reduces net position but is not recorded in the fund financial statements. Therefore, the amount of depreciation expense is subtracted on the reconciliation. This amount would increase expenses in the worksheet for the function that used the capital assets.
- *Subtract the book value of capital assets disposed of during the year*. Gains and losses from disposal of assets should be reported in the statement of activities — not proceeds — from sale of capital assets reported by governmental funds. Proceeds can be converted to gains and losses by subtracting the book value of the assets sold. This adjustment on the worksheet will convert an other financing source to a gain or loss from the sale of capital assets, which generally is reported as general revenue.

A few additional comments are needed about infrastructure assets. *Infrastructure assets* are long-lived capital assets that are normally stationary in nature and can be preserved for a long time. Roads, bridges, tunnels, and dams are some examples. Governments were required for the first time to report general infrastructure assets under GASB Statement No. 34. GASB Statement No. 63, *Financial Reporting of Deferred Outflows of Resources, Deferred Inflows of Resources, and Net Position*, amends GASB Statement No. 34.

An important point about infrastructure assets is that governments are given the option to use a modified approach for these capital assets. Under the *modified approach*, infrastructure assets that are part of a network or subsystem of a network are not depreciated provided that two requirements are met. The requirements are (1) that the government maintains an asset management system and (2) that the assets are being preserved at or above a condition level established by the government. If this approach is used, all expenditures made to maintain the assets are expensed. In addition, certain information about these assets must be reported in the required supplementary information section of the financial statements.

GASB Statement No. 51, *Accounting and Financial Reporting for Intangible Assets*, addresses the accounting and reporting for intangible assets and requires that all intangible assets covered by its scope be classified as capital assets. Therefore, intangible assets may require adjustments. As an update to the information presented herein, it also should be noted that paragraph 6 (identifiable intangible assets) and footnote 4 of GASB Statement No. 51 are amended by paragraph 8 of GASB Statement No. 63.

The previously listed adjustments are needed to properly reflect capital-asset activities in the conversion of governmental funds from the flow of financial resources to the flow of economic resources measurement focus.

A final comment regarding capital assets is that GASB Statement No. 42, *Accounting and Financial Reporting for Impairment of Capital Assets and for Insurance Recoveries*, addresses the accounting and financial reporting for impairment of capital assets and for insurance recoveries.

Pensions, postemployment benefits other than pensions, long-term liabilities, and deferred inflows and outflows of resources adjustments

Because pension, postemployment benefits other than pensions (OPEB), and long-term liabilities are not reported by governmental funds, they also play a major role in the conversion of governmental funds from the flow of financial resources to the flow of economic resources measurement focus. The government must maintain detailed long-term liabilities records to support this conversion.

To convert the balance sheet for governmental funds to net position for governmental activities, pensions and long-term liabilities need to be added to liabilities and an equal amount needs to be subtracted from net position. The adjustment for long-term liabilities should include any unamortized premiums or discounts on debt.

Several adjustments related to long-term liabilities are needed to convert the statement of revenues, expenditures, and changes in fund balances for governmental funds to the statement of activities for governmental activities. Governmental funds report in the statement of revenues, expenditures, and changes in fund balances transactions that deal with capital-related long-term liabilities. Payment of long-term debt principal is reported as an expenditure. Proceeds from the issuance of debt are reported as an other financing source.

Activities related to noncapital long-term liabilities are not reported in the statement of revenues, expenditures, and changes in fund balances. This includes liabilities for compensated absences, claims and judgments, landfill closure costs, net pension obligations, OPEB, termination benefits, pollution remediation obligations, and asset retirement obligations.

GASB Statement No. 68 brought significant changes to how pension expense is measured and reported in government-wide statements. This statement uses an accounting approach instead of a funding approach to report pension costs.

GASB Statement No. 75, *Accounting and Financial Reporting for Postemployment Benefits Other Than Pensions,* requires that OPEB follow similar accounting and reporting requirements for pensions as those under GASB Statement No. 68. Some governments extend financial guarantees for the obligations of another organization without directly receiving equal or approximately equal value in exchange (a nonexchange transaction). GASB Statement No. 70, *Accounting and Financial Reporting for Nonexchange Financial Guarantees*, provides guidance for these types of costs.

GASB Statement No. 70 requires a government that extends a nonexchange financial guarantee to recognize a liability when qualitative factors and historical data, if any, indicate that it is more likely than not that the government will be required to make a payment on the guarantee. The amount of the liability to be recognized should be the discounted present value of the best estimate of the future outflows related to the guarantee expected to be incurred. When there is no best estimate but a range of the estimated future outflows can be established, the amount of the liability to be recognized should be the discounted present value of the minimum amount within the range.

The adjustments convert the information in the statement of revenues, expenditures, and changes in fund balances to the flow of economic resources measurement focus. The following list of adjustments indicates either an increase (add) or decrease (subtract) to the reconciliation schedule for the amount reported as changes in fund balances for governmental funds and the amount reported as change in net position for governmental activities:

- *Add principal payments*. The payment of principal is not reported as an expense in the statement of activities but is reported as an expenditure by governmental funds. Therefore, the amount of expenditures reported for principal payments is added back on the reconciliation. This amount would reduce reported expenses in the worksheet for principal payments.
- *Subtract debt proceeds*. Debt proceeds do not increase net position in the statement of activities but increase fund balance for governmental funds. Therefore, the amount reported as an other financing source for debt proceeds is subtracted on the reconciliation. This amount would eliminate the amount reported for debt proceeds in the worksheet.
- *Add or subtract changes in noncapital long-term liabilities*. The changes in these liabilities are not reported in the fund financial statements. Therefore, the amount of changes in these liabilities needs to be reported on the reconciliation. For example, if the liability for compensated absences increases for the year, an increase in expenses needs to be recorded and this amount subtracted in the reconciliation. The increase in expense would adjust the appropriate functional expenses on the worksheet (for example, the functional areas related to employees who earned the compensated absences).
- *Add or subtract changes in unamortized discounts and premiums*. Interest expense in the statement of activities should reflect the amortization of any premiums or discounts on debt issued. The

statement of revenues, expenditures, and changes in fund balances does not report such amortization. Therefore, the amount of amortization is reported on the reconciliation. The adjustment would either increase or decrease interest expense on the worksheet.

- *Add or subtract changes in deferred inflows and outflows of resources.* Deferred inflows and outflows of resources need to be amortized over their respective amortization periods.

The preceding adjustments are needed to properly reflect long-term liability activities in the conversion of governmental funds from the flow of financial resources to the flow of economic resources measurement focus.

Other adjustments

There are a few additional adjustments needed to convert the fund financial information from the modified accrual basis to the accrual basis of accounting.

The first adjustment is related to recognition of revenues. Governmental funds recognize revenues under the modified accrual basis when it is measurable and available. Under the accrual basis, revenues do not need to be available to be recognized. For example, property taxes must be collected during the year or no later than 60 days after the end of the year to be reported as revenues by the general fund. However, the full amount of the tax levied for that year (less the amount expected to be uncollectible) should be reported as revenue under the accrual basis of accounting.

The second adjustment is related to recognition of interest expense. Governmental funds recognize interest expenditures when they become due. Under accrual accounting, interest expense should be recognized when incurred. This would include accruing interest at year-end and amortizing any premiums or discounts on debt issued.

The last major adjustment is related to debt refunding. Debt refunding is reported differently for governmental funds than it is for proprietary funds. Adjustments are needed to report debt refunding consistent with the treatment used by proprietary funds.

Remember that, in most cases, the adjustments needed to produce the government-wide statements would be made only on worksheets. Governments will generally maintain accounting records on a fund basis using the flow of financial resources measurement focus and modified accrual basis of accounting for governmental funds. Worksheets will have to be prepared anew each year.

Government combinations

GASB Statement No. 69, *Government Combinations and Disposals of Government Operations*, addresses certain types of combinations. The statement defines these as mergers, acquisitions, and transfers of operations. *Government mergers* include combinations of legally separate entities without the exchange of significant consideration. This statement requires the use of carrying values to measure the assets and liabilities in a government merger and certain transfers of operations.

Government acquisitions are transactions in which a government acquires another entity, or its operations, in exchange for significant consideration. GASB Statement No. 69 requires measurements of assets acquired and liabilities assumed generally to be based on their acquisition values.

In some cases, the consideration paid in an acquisition will exceed the amount of net position acquired. The acquiring government should report the excess as a deferred outflow of resources. For other acquisitions where the consideration is less than the amount of net position acquired, the excess net position should be eliminated by reducing the noncurrent assets (other than financial assets) that are acquired. If the allocation reduces noncurrent assets to zero, the remaining amount should be recognized as a special item in the government-wide statement of activities.

Summary

Governments are required to produce two government-wide statements: the statement of net position and the statement of activities. These statements report the financial position and results of operations for the primary government and its component units. The format of the statement of activities also allows a government to report the net (expenses) revenues of the different functions of the government.

The government-wide statements for governmental activities are generally produced each year by using a worksheet approach. The worksheet takes the governmental fund financial statements and converts them to the flow of economic resources measurement focus and the accrual basis of accounting. Adjustments are needed for capital assets, long-term liabilities, and other accrual items. Worksheet entries are also needed to make certain eliminations for interfund items and to reclassify program revenues. Internal service funds are often included as part of governmental activities and must be added as part of the adjustment process.

Key foundational points	
1	The two government-wide financial statements are the statement of net position and the statement of activities.
2	The government-wide statements use the flow of economic resources measurement focus and the accrual basis of accounting to report all activities.
3	The statement of net position (the preferred reporting format) reports separate columns for governmental activities, business-type activities, and component units. However, a balance-sheet format also may be used.
4	Revenues in the statement of activities are reported as either program revenues or general revenues.
5	The government-wide financial statements for governmental activities are generally produced each year by using a worksheet approach.

Knowledge check

3. Which statement is correct regarding the government-wide financial statements?

   a. The format of the statement of activities keeps a government from reporting the net (expenses) revenues of the different functions of the government.
   b. The challenge in producing the government-wide statements is with converting proprietary activities to governmental activities.
   c. The government-wide statements for governmental activities are generally produced each year using a worksheet approach.
   d. The government-wide statements for governmental activities report five separate columns of program revenue.

Practice questions

Please note that the following practice questions are not required reading material.

1. Which is **not** required to be reported in the statement of net position?

   a. Governmental activities.
   b. Business-type activities.
   c. Component units.
   d. Total for reporting entity.

2. Which component of net position would **not** be reported in a statement of net position?

   a. Unrestricted net position.
   b. Designated net position.
   c. Net investment in capital assets.
   d. Restricted net position.

3. In the statement of activities, depreciation expense is reported for

   a. Governmental activities.
   b. Business-type activities.
   c. Component units.
   d. All the above.

4. Which item **cannot** be classified as program revenue?

   a. Contributions.
   b. Taxes restricted for a specific purpose.
   c. Operating grants.
   d. Capital grants.

5. Which item would appear on the reconciliation of the governmental fund balance sheet to net position?

   a. Capital assets.
   b. Internal service funds.
   c. Long-term liabilities.
   d. All the above.

6. Which item would **not** appear on the reconciliation of the governmental funds statement of revenues, expenditures, and changes in fund balances to the changes in net position?

   a. Depreciation.
   b. Amortization of bond premiums.
   c. Program revenues.
   d. Bond proceeds.

7. Which item would be subtracted on the reconciliation of governmental funds statement of revenues, expenditures, and changes in fund balances to the changes in net position?

    a. Depreciation.
    b. Capital outlay expenditures.
    c. Internal service fund increase in net position.
    d. Long-term debt principal payment.

8. Explain how internal service funds' (included as part of governmental activities) revenues and expenses should be reported in the statement of activities.

9. What are program revenues and how are they reported in the statement of activities?

10. Prepare a reconciliation of governmental funds statement of revenues, expenditures, and changes in fund balances to the change in net position in the statement of activities.

Net increase in all governmental funds' fund balances	$300,000
Increase in deferred inflows all related to property taxes	200,000
Expenditures — capital asset	1,500,000
Expenditures — principal on bonds	2,000,000
Depreciation expenses on capital assets	800,000
Proceeds from bonds	2,500,000
Increase in liability for compensated absences	50,000
Internal service increase in net position	100,000

Reconciliation of the statement of revenues, expenditures, and changes in fund balance to the statement of activities	
Net change in fund balances — total governmental funds	$
Amounts reported for governmental activities in the statement of activities are different because:	
Governmental funds report capital outlays as expenditures whereas governmental activities report depreciation expense to allocate those expenditures over the life of the assets.	

Reconciliation of the statement of revenues, expenditures, and changes in fund balance to the statement of activities (continued)

Add capital acquisitions		
Subtract depreciation		
Revenues in the statement of activities that do not provide current financial resources are not reported as revenues in the funds.		
Bond proceeds provide current financial resources to governmental funds but issuing debt increases long-term liabilities in the statement of net position. Repayment of bond principal is an expenditure in the governmental funds, but the repayment reduces long-term liabilities in the statement of net position.		
Add debt principal repayment		
Subtract debt proceeds		
Some expenses reported in the statement of activities do not require the use of current financial resources and therefore are not reported as expenditures in governmental funds (such as compensated absences).		
Internal service funds are used by management to charge the costs of certain services to individual funds. The net revenue (expense) of the internal service funds is reported with governmental activities.		
Change in net position of governmental activities		$

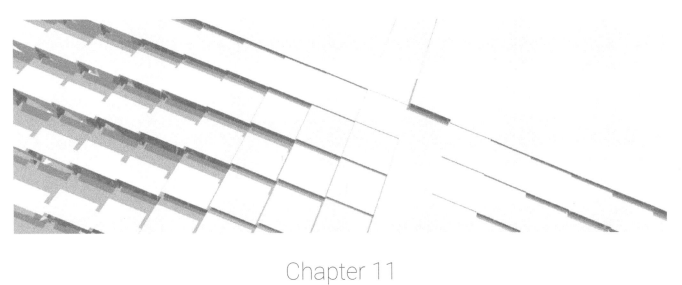

Chapter 11

Financial Reporting and the Comprehensive Annual Financial Report

---

Learning objectives

- Recall the minimum requirements for general-purpose external financial statements.

- Identify what must be included in management's discussion and analysis (MD&A).

- Identify what must be included in required supplementary information (RSI).

- Identify what must be included in a comprehensive annual financial report (CAFR).

Refer to appendix C for an example of MD&A and a statistical section.

Contents of a CAFR

Governments must include certain minimum financial statements, reports, and other information in their external financial reports. Governments are encouraged, however, to go beyond the minimum requirements and to issue a CAFR. What information must be included in the different reports and where does it go? This chapter will try to answer those questions.

The minimum requirements for general-purpose external financial statements

The key objective of financial reporting for governments is accountability. To meet this objective, certain minimum requirements have been established for external financial reports; these requirements are designed to meet the basic needs of a broad group of external users. A government's general-purpose external financial statements must contain, at minimum, the following items:

- MD&A
- Basic financial statements
  - Government-wide financial statements
  - Fund financial statements
  - Notes to the financial statements
- RSI (other than MD&A)

The relationship among the different elements required for general-purpose financial statements can be seen in the following chart.

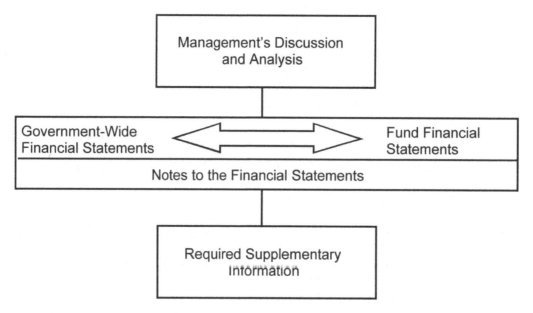

Some of these minimum requirements have been discussed in earlier chapters, such as government-wide financial statements and fund financial statements. To recap, the basic financial statements are as follows:

- Government-wide financial statements
  - Statement of net position
  - Statement of activities
- Fund financial statements
  - Governmental funds
    - Balance sheet
    - Statement of revenues, expenditures, and changes in fund balances

- Proprietary funds
  - Statement of net position or balance sheet
  - Statement of revenues, expenses, and changes in fund net position
  - Statement of cash flows
- Fiduciary funds
  - Statement of fiduciary net position
  - Statement of changes in fiduciary net position

Governments have unique requirements for notes to the financial statements. Items that must be included in the notes are contained in GASB Statement No. 38, *Certain Financial Statement Note Disclosures,* and in other statements. In addition to the information presented here, it should be noted that paragraph 13, "Disaggregation of Receivable and Payable Balances," of GASB Statement No. 38 is amended by GASB Statement No. 63, *Financial Reporting of Deferred Outflows of Resources, Deferred Inflows of Resources, and Net Position.* Additionally, paragraph 8 is amended by GASB Statement No. 68, *Accounting and Financial Reporting for Pensions — An Amendment of GASB Statement No. 27.*

MD&A and RSI are discussed in succeeding sections of this chapter.

MD&A

MD&A should be presented before the basic financial statements and is part of the RSI that must be presented in the financial statements. (The nature of RSI is discussed in the next section.) It provides an objective and easily readable analysis of the government's financial activity for the year.

MD&A is based on currently known facts, decisions, and conditions; it must discuss both positive and negative aspects of current-year activity.

Depending on the government, MD&A comprises eight separate elements, as follows:

A discussion of the basic financial statements. The MD&A should focus on the activities of the primary government. The decision to include comments about a government's component units is a matter of professional judgment and should be based on the significance and relationship of the component unit with the primary government. Any information presented for a component unit should be clearly distinguished from that of the primary government.

The MD&A includes a discussion on the basic financial statements and the relationship between government-wide statements and fund financial statements. This discussion enables readers to understand the differences between financial results reported in the two sets of financial statements.

Condensed comparative data. The MD&A should compare current-year results with those of the prior year. This is the only place in the general-purpose external financial reports where governments are required to present comparative information.

An analysis of the government's overall financial position and results of operations. The MD&A discusses the overall financial position and results of operations for the government. This analysis explains why the financial position of the government has either increased or decreased for the year. The analysis should also address the financial activities of both governmental and business-type activities as reported in the government-wide statements.

An analysis of the funds. The MD&A addresses any significant changes in the fund balances or fund net position for the year and comments on any significant restrictions or commitments affecting the availability of fund resources at year-end.

An analysis between the budget to the actual statement or schedule. The MD&A should also analyze any significant variation between the original budget and final budget and between the final budget and actual results for the general fund.

Capital asset and debt activities. A description of significant capital asset and long-term debt activities is also included in the MD&A. This discussion should include any significant commitments, changes in credit ratings, debt limitations that may affect the financing of planned facilities or services, and new debt issuances.

Infrastructure, if applicable. If a government is using the modified approach for certain infrastructure capital assets, the MD&A should discuss any significant changes in assessed condition of eligible infrastructure, how the current assessed condition compares with the level set by the government, and any significant differences in the amount spent to maintain infrastructure from the annual amount estimated to maintain those assets.

Economic conditions and outlook. The MD&A also includes a description of any currently known facts, decisions, or conditions that are expected to have a significant financial effect on the government. Currently known facts would include any items that occurred after year-end but before the date of the auditors' report. Governments are also encouraged to use charts, graphs, and tables in the MD&A to enhance the understandability of the information.

Items to describe could include the following:

- Changes in tax rates, tax base, or population
- Loss of significant employers
- Settlement of significant lawsuits
- New labor contracts
- Deficit reduction measures

Governments also must provide condensed financial information (from the government-wide statements) comparing the current year with the prior year. Governments are required to report the following condensed government-wide financial information:

- Total assets, distinguishing between capital and other assets
- Total liabilities, distinguishing between long-term liabilities and other liabilities
- Total net position, distinguishing between the three components of net position
- Program revenues by major source
- General revenues by major source
- Total revenues
- Program expenses, at a minimum by function
- Total expenses

- Excess (deficiency) of revenues over expenses
- Contributions
- Special and extraordinary items
- Transfers
- Change in net position
- Ending net position

Knowledge check

1. Which statement is correct regarding MD&A?

    a. It is based on currently known facts, decisions, and conditions and must discuss both positive and negative aspects of the current-year activity.
    b. Any information presented for a component unit should not be distinguished from that of the primary government.
    c. MD&A should be presented after the basic financial statements.
    d. Comparative financial information is not reported in the MD&A.

2. Which is **not** required to be included in a government's general-purpose external financial statements?

    a. Government-wide financial statements..
    b. Fund financial statements.
    c. Certificate of Achievement for Excellence in Financial Reporting.
    d. Notes to the financial statements.

RSI (Other than MD&A)

RSI (including MD&A) is unaudited information that a government must present as part of its financial presentation. Auditors are required to perform certain limited procedures on RSI; however, the absence of, or deficiencies in, RSI does not affect the auditor's opinion on the financial statements. In such cases, the auditor adds information to the audit report describing the situation.

As stated earlier, the MD&A is presented before the basic financial statements. Other RSI is presented after the basic financial statements. Governments may be required to report the following additional items as part of RSI:

Budgetary comparison schedule. Governments must present budgetary comparison schedules for the general fund and each major special revenue fund with a legally adopted annual budget. Governments have the option of including these schedules as part of the fund financial statements as opposed to reporting them as part of RSI.

These schedules must contain a minimum of three columns for each governmental fund reported: original budget, final budget, and actual amounts reported using the budgetary basis of accounting. A variance column may be included to facilitate the comparison of budget amounts and actual amounts; this is not required, however. The budget comparison schedule may be prepared using the same format and terminology of the budget document or using the same format as the statement of revenues, expenditures, and changes in fund balances.

Infrastructure assets. When a government uses the modified approach for certain networks or subsystems of infrastructure, certain information must be disclosed as part of RSI. A schedule must be provided that gives the assessed condition of the infrastructure assets over a period of time. Also, a schedule for the last five years must be provided with the estimated annual amount needed to maintain the assets at the condition level established by the government and the actual amount expensed.

Additional information must be provided about the basis for the condition measurement and the scale used to assess and report condition. The condition level at which the government intends to preserve the infrastructure assets must also be disclosed. Factors that significantly affect trends in the information reported in the required schedules must be disclosed.

Pensions and postemployment benefits other than pensions (OPEB). RSI requirements exist related to pensions and OPEB. These requirements are mainly found in the following GASB statements:

- GASB Statement No. 67, *Financial Reporting for Pension Plans — An Amendment of GASB Statement No. 25*
- GASB Statement No. 68, *Accounting and Financial Reporting for Pensions — An Amendment of GASB Statement No. 27*
- GASB Statement No. 73, *Accounting and Financial Reporting for Pensions and Related Assets That Are Not Within the Scope of GASB Statement 68, and Amendments to Certain Provisions of GASB Statements 67 and 68*
- GASB Statement No. 74, *Financial Reporting for Postemployment Benefit Plans Other than Pension Plans*
- GASB Statement No.75, *Accounting and Financial Reporting for Postemployment Benefits Other Than Pensions*
- GASB Statement No. 78, *Pensions Provided through Certain Multiple-Employer Defined Benefit Pension Plans*
- GASB Statement No. 82, *Pension Issues — An Amendment of GASB Statements No. 67, No. 68, and No. 73*

Knowledge check

3. Which statement is correct regarding RSI?

    a. When a government uses the modified approach for certain networks or subsystems of infrastructure, certain information must be disclosed as part of RSI.
    b. RSI requirements do not exist related to pensions and OPEB.
    c. All RSI is presented before the basic financial statements.
    d. Budgetary comparison schedules are reported for all governmental funds.

The CAFR

The preceding sections discussed the minimum requirements for general-purpose external financial statements for governments. However, to meet the key financial reporting objectives of accountability, governments are encouraged to go beyond the minimum requirements by preparing a CAFR. The CAFR provides a variety of additional information outside the audited financial statements that is useful in assessing a government's performance and financial condition.

The Government Finance Officers Association (GFOA) provides guidance on what information should be included in the CAFR. The GFOA also administers an award program (the Certificate of Achievement for Excellence in Financial Reporting) for governments that meet their requirements.

A CAFR consists of at least three sections: introductory, financial, and statistical.

Each section requires certain information and tables. Governments need to present only the information and tables applicable to them. The requirements of the three sections follow.

The introductory section

The introductory section provides an overview of the government's financial position and results of operations. The following items are included in the introductory section:

- Report cover
- Title page
- Table of contents
- Certificate of Achievement for Excellence in Financial Reporting, if applicable
- List of principal officials
- Organizational chart
- Audit committee letter
- Letter of transmittal

The financial section

The financial section provides the financial statements, RSI, and related notes. The following items are included in the financial section:

- Independent auditor's report
- MD&A
- Basic financial statements
- RSI (other than MD&A)
- Combining and individual fund presentation and supplementary information

One of the goals of the CAFR is to present information about each individual fund and component unit. Because the basic financial statements present information only on major funds and major component units, the combining statements are where information is reported for funds and component units not reported individually in the basic financial statements. Separate combining statements are needed for any nonmajor governmental funds, nonmajor enterprise funds, internal service funds, fiduciary funds, and nonmajor component units. The combining statements should include a total column that agrees with the related column in the fund financial statements.

The statistical section

The statistical section of the CAFR provides information that is useful in evaluating the economic condition of a government.

GASB Statement No. 44, *Economic Condition Reporting: The Statistical Section — An Amendment of NCGA Statement 1,* as amended, requires governments to report five categories of statistical information as follows:

- Financial trends
  - Net position
  - Change in net position
  - Fund balances for governmental funds
  - Changes in fund balances for governmental funds
- Revenue capacity (This is information about the most significant own-source revenue. If a government has other own-source revenues that are nearly as significant as its largest source, it should consider presenting revenue capacity information for those own-source revenues as well.)
  - Revenue base
  - Revenue rates
  - Principal revenue payers
  - Property tax levies and collections (If a government presents revenue capacity information about a property tax.)
- Debt capacity
  - Ratios of outstanding debt
  - Ratios of general bonded debt
    Direct and overlapping debt
  - Debt limits
  - Pledged-revenue coverage
- Demographic and economic
  - Demographic and economic indicators
  - Principal employers
- Operating
  - Government employees
  - Operating indicators (demand or level of service)
  - Capital asset indicators (volume, usage, or nature)
  - GASB Statement No. 44 also contains requirements related to operating information reported by pension and OPEB plans in separately issued reports.

Knowledge check

4. Which statement is correct regarding the CAFR?

    a. The IASB provides guidance on what information should be included in the CAFR.
    b. The statistical section of the CAFR provides information that is useful in evaluating the social condition of a government.
    c. The CAFR provides a variety of additional information outside the audited financial statements that is useful in assessing a government's performance and financial condition.
    d. GASB Statement No. 44 requires governments to report six categories of statistical information.

Other sections

In addition to the three sections included in the CAFR, governments are free to include additional sections. For example, a government might include a single audit section or investment section.

The relationship between the minimum requirements for external financial statements and the CAFR is summarized in the following table.

Minimum requirements for external financial statements versus the CAFR

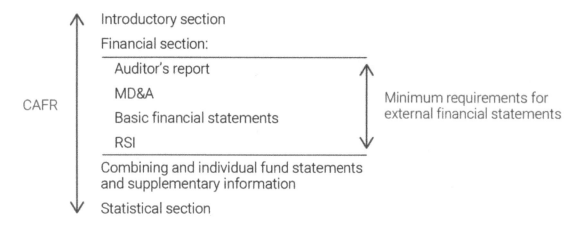

Summary

Governments are required to include certain minimum information in their external financial reports. The requirements are designed to meet the basic needs of a broad group of external users. At minimum, a government's general-purpose external financial statements contain MD&A, basic financial statements, and RSI.

Governments are encouraged to go beyond the minimum requirements by preparing a CAFR. The CAFR provides a variety of additional information outside the audited financial statements that is useful in assessing a government's performance and financial condition. The CAFR has three sections: introductory, financial, and statistical.

	Key foundational points
1	MD&A should be presented before the basic financial statements and is part of RSI that must be presented in the financial statements.
2	Other RSI is presented after the basic financial statements.
3	Governments are encouraged to go beyond the minimum requirements by preparing a CAFR.
4	The introductory section of the CAFR includes a letter of transmittal and other information about the government.
5	The statistical section of the CAFR provides information that is useful in evaluating the economic condition of a government.

Practice questions

Please note that the following practice questions are not required reading material.

1. Choose the correct statement concerning a government.

    a. A government can issue only a CAFR.
    b. A government can issue its basic financial statements, MD&A, and other RSI without its CAFR.
    c. Both (*a*) and (*b*) are permitted.
    d. Neither (*a*) nor (*b*) is permitted.

2. Which is **not** part of the introductory section of a CAFR?

    a. Transmittal letter.
    b. Organizational chart.
    c. RSI.
    d. Table of contents.

3. Which is part of the financial section of a CAFR?

    a. Transmittal letter.
    b. Auditor's report.
    c. Computation of overlapping debt.
    d. Demographic statistics.

4. Which is **not** part of the statistical section of a CAFR?

    a. List of principal officials.
    b. Debt capacity information.
    c. Demographic and economic information.
    d. Financial trends information.

5. Combining financial statements are required in the CAFR when there is more than one fund of which type or category of funds?

    a. Nonmajor governmental funds.
    b. Internal service funds.
    c. Private-purpose trust funds.
    d. All the above.

6. Explain the difference between the minimum requirements for general-purpose external financial reporting and the CAFR. Must a government issue both?

7. What should be the focus of the MD&A? Is comparative information required in the MD&A?

8. Explain how information about individual funds is presented in the financial reports of a government.

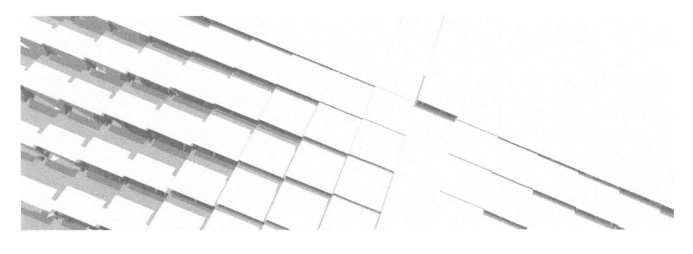

Chapter 12

Special-Purpose Governments

Learning objectives

- Recognize the reporting requirements for special-purpose governments engaged only in governmental activities.

- Recognize the reporting requirements for special-purpose governments engaged only in business-type activities.

- Recognize the reporting requirements for special-purpose governments engaged only in fiduciary activities.

Are these reports different?

How should financial statements for entities like public colleges, hospitals, housing authorities, or organizations engaged only in one program be reported? Do they have to produce both fund financial statements and government-wide statements? Do the statements have to look the same? The answers to these questions depend on different factors. This chapter will try to answer these questions.

Background

Most information in this course has focused on general-purpose governments, such as those for states, cities, counties, and towns. However, many governmental entities do not fit this category; these are referred to as *special-purpose governments*. These organizations are separate legal entities that may be component units of another government or stand-alone governments that do not meet the definition of a general-purpose government.

Special-purpose governments that are engaged in more than one program or that engage in both governmental and business-type activities should produce both fund financial statements and government-wide financial statements. For example, a school district may have programs for regular instruction, special education, vocational education, and adult education. Those entities should generally follow the guidance set out in previous chapters. However, for entities engaged only in a single program or only in a business-type or fiduciary activity, different financial statements are appropriate.

Special-purpose governments engaged only in governmental activities

Some governmental entities are engaged only in a single program. Some examples include cemetery districts, levee districts, assessment districts, and drainage districts.

For these entities engaged only in a single program, the fund financial statements and government-wide statements may be combined using a columnar format. This format would present the reconciling items in separate columns as opposed to presenting them at the bottom of the statement.

However, a special-purpose government engaged only in governmental activities may also present separate fund financial statements and government-wide statements. In this case, it may use a different format to report the statement of activities. This alternative format presents the statement in a single column by reporting expenses first, followed by program revenues and then general revenues. Other items, like special and extraordinary items and transfers, would then be reported.

Knowledge check

1. Choose the correct statement regarding special-purpose governments.

    a. Special-purpose governments engaged in more than one program or that engage in both governmental and business-type activities should produce both fund financial statements and government-wide financial statements.
    b. All special-purpose governments report government-wide statements.
    c. For special-purpose governments engaged only in a single program or only in a business-type or fiduciary activity, different financial statements are not appropriate.
    d. Special-purpose governments are not separate legal entities.

Special-purpose governments engaged only in business-type activities

Some special-purpose governments are engaged only in business-type activities; these include entities such as water and electric authorities, housing authorities, public colleges and universities, and hospitals.

These entities report as special-purpose governments engaged only in business-type activities.

Business-type activities are reported as enterprise funds. Because information in fund financial statements for enterprise funds is basically the same information presented in government-wide statements for business-type activities, there is no need to present both types of statements. For this type of governmental entity, the basic financial statements and required supplementary information (RSI) comprise the following items:

- Management's discussion and analysis (MD&A)
- Enterprise fund financial statements
  - Statement of net position or balance sheet
  - Statement of revenues, expenses, and changes in fund net position
  - Statement of cash flows
- Notes to the financial statements
- RSI (other than MD&A), if applicable

These entities follow the financial reporting requirements for enterprise funds.

Knowledge check

2. Which entity is an example of a special-purpose government engaged only in business-type activities?

    a. Cemetery district.
    b. Levee district.
    c. Electric authority.
    d. Drainage district.

Special-purpose governments engaged only in fiduciary activities

Some special-purpose governments are engaged only in fiduciary activities. Some examples include pension plans, other employee benefit trust funds, and investment trust funds.

These entities need report only the financial statements required for fiduciary funds. The basic financial statements and RSI for these entities comprise the following items:

- MD&A
- Statement of fiduciary net position
- Statement of changes in fiduciary net position
- Notes to the financial statements

The reporting format for pensions is defined by GASB Statement No. 67, *Financial Reporting for Pension Plans — An Amendment of GASB Statement No. 25,* as amended.

Note that a special-purpose government may be engaged in both business-type and fiduciary activities. In this case, the government should present the financial statements for both enterprise funds and fiduciary funds.

Public colleges and universities

GASB Statement No. 35, *Basic Financial Statements — and Management's Discussion and Analysis — for Public Colleges and Universities — an Amendment of GASB Statement No. 34*, extends the reporting requirements for special-purpose governments of GASB Statement No. 34 to public colleges and universities.

This statement allows colleges and universities issuing separate financial statements to select the reporting requirements for special-purpose governments engaged only in business-type activities, engaged only in governmental activities, or engaged in both governmental and business-type activities.

Most public colleges and universities report as special-purpose governments engaged only in business-type activities. In such cases, the reporting requirements are as follows:

- MD&A)
- Enterprise fund financial statements
  - Statement of net position or balance sheet
  - Statement of revenues, expenses, and changes in fund net position
  - Statement of cash flows
- Notes to the financial statements
- RSI (other than MD&A), if applicable

An example of the fund financial statements for a university is in appendix D.

Summary

Not all governmental entities are required to produce both fund financial statements and government-wide financial statements. Special-purpose governments are separate legal entities that do not meet the definition of a general-purpose government. Special-purpose governments engaged in more than one program or that engage in both governmental and business-type activities are required to produce both types of statements. Special-purpose governments engaged only in a single governmental program may combine the fund financial statements and government-wide statements using a columnar format.

However, some special-purpose governments do not report government-wide statements. Special-purpose governments engaged only in business-type activities report the fund financial statements required for enterprise funds. Special-purpose governments engaged only in fiduciary activities report the fund financial statements required for fiduciary funds.

	Key foundational points
1	Special-purpose governments are separate legal entities that may be component units of another government or they may be stand-alone governments that do not meet the definition of a general-purpose government.
2	Not all governmental entities are required to produce both fund financial statements and government-wide financial statements.
3	Special-purpose governments engaged in more than one program or that engage in both governmental and business-type activities should produce both fund financial statements and government-wide financial statements.
4	Governmental entities engaged only in governmental activities and only in a single program may combine the fund financial statements and government-wide statements using a columnar format.
5	For entities engaged only in a single program or only in a business-type or fiduciary activity, different financial statements are appropriate.

Practice questions

Please note that the following practice questions are not required reading material.

1. Which special-purpose governments' financial reports must include MD&A?

    a. Governments engaged only in governmental activities.
    b. Governments engaged only in business-type activities.
    c. Governments engaged only in fiduciary activities.
    d. All the above.

2. Which special-purpose governments' financial reports must include a statement of cash flows?

    a. Governments engaged only in governmental activities.
    b. Governments engaged only in business-type activities.
    c. Governments engaged only in fiduciary activities.
    d. All the above.

3. What are the reporting requirements for a special-purpose government engaged only in governmental activities?

4. Explain the reporting requirements of a governmental authority engaged only in business-type activities.

Appendix A

CITY OF CHARLOTTESVILLE — BASIC FINANCIAL STATEMENTS

CITY OF CHARLOTTESVILLE, VIRGINIA

Comprehensive Annual Financial Report
Fiscal Year Ended June 30, 2019

Prepared by
Department of Finance

STATEMENT OF NET POSITION
JUNE 30, 2019

	Primary Government			Component Units	
	Governmental Activities	Business-type Activities	Total	Economic Development Authority	School Board
ASSETS					
Cash, cash equivalents and investments (note 3)	$ 89,368,860	$ 19,685,974	$ 109,054,834	$ 2,532,933	$ 8,713,223
Interest receivable	207,536	-	207,536	-	-
Accounts receivable, net	2,576,664	4,336,171	6,912,835	-	344,161
Taxes receivable, net	42,595,895	-	42,595,895	-	-
Loans receivable (note 5)	4,274,840	-	4,274,840	1,193,974	-
Due from other governments (note 6)	10,965,858	-	10,965,858	-	2,635,929
Inventories	127,968	586,518	714,486	-	-
Prepaid expenses	112,856	1,568,654	1,681,510	17	-
Restricted cash and investments (note 3)	4,504,678	3,409,644	7,914,322	-	-
Capital assets (note 8):					
Capital assets not being depreciated	57,128,446	2,064,048	59,192,494	-	982,889
Capital assets being depreciated	183,812,333	89,834,955	273,647,288	-	22,477,259
Total assets	395,675,934	121,485,964	517,161,898	3,726,924	35,153,461
DEFERRED OUTFLOWS OF RESOURCES					
Deferred charges on refunding resulting in loss transactions	1,326	38,935	40,261	-	-
Deferred charges - pension (notes 11 and 15)	19,393,499	2,376,045	21,769,544	-	7,595,816
Deferred charges - OPEB (notes 13 and 16)	4,849,042	519,753	5,368,795	-	1,018,159
Total deferred outflows of resources	24,243,867	2,934,733	27,178,600	-	8,613,975
LIABILITIES					
Accounts payable	3,227,698	2,196,325	5,424,023	4,108	1,230,414
Accrued liabilities	10,230,457	2,327,468	12,557,925	67,430	5,841,645
Customer deposits	15,291	991,437	1,006,728	-	-
Due to other governments	1,799,744	-	1,799,744	-	-
Unearned revenue	75,234	-	75,234	20,000	302,347
Accrued interest payable	1,143,409	557,057	1,700,466	49,687	-
Long-term liabilities (note 9):					
Due within one year	10,410,800	3,425,734	13,836,534	130,000	413,187
Due in more than one year	89,070,194	48,785,214	137,855,408	-	3,415,268
Net pension liability (notes 9,11 and 15)	72,925,795	8,681,297	81,607,092	-	55,942,044
Net OPEB liability (notes 9, 13 and 15)	38,001,806	4,612,838	42,614,644	-	12,917,000
Total liabilities	226,900,428	71,577,370	298,477,798	271,225	80,061,905
DEFERRED INFLOWS OF RESOURCES					
Deferred tax revenue	40,565,408	-	40,565,408	-	-
Deferred charges on refunding resulting in gain transactions	883,682	233,886	1,117,568	-	-
Deferred charges - pension (notes 11 and 15)	5,150,677	591,728	5,742,405	-	6,597,336
Deferred charges - OPEB (notes 13 and 16)	2,204,550	231,357	2,435,907	-	570,000
Total deferred inflows of resources	48,804,317	1,056,971	49,861,288	-	7,167,336
NET POSITION					
Net investment in capital assets	150,327,831	43,208,912	193,536,743	-	23,460,148
Restricted for (note 2a):					
Public safety	470,480	-	470,480	-	-
Community services	17,071	-	17,071	-	-
Parks, recreation and culture	6,560	-	6,560	-	-
Education	-	-	-	-	2,008,369
Conservation and development	10,000	-	10,000	-	-
Permanent fund, nonexpendable	164,422	-	164,422	-	-
Unrestricted	(6,781,306)	8,577,443	1,796,137	3,455,699	(68,930,324)
Total net position	$ 144,215,058	$ 51,786,355	$ 196,001,413	$ 3,455,699	$ (43,461,807)

The accompanying notes are an integral part of the basic financial statements.

Functions/Programs	Expenses	Program Revenues		
		Charges for Services	Operating Grants and Contributions	Capital Grants and Contributions
PRIMARY GOVERNMENT				
Governmental activities:				
General government	$ 28,445,537	$ 2,171,318	$ 3,065,503	$ -
Public safety	39,513,247	56,035	4,686,110	154,845
Community services	22,110,867	1,305,654	7,623,041	661,930
Health and welfare	35,670,836	5,235,853	1,838,249	-
Parks, recreation and culture	14,061,131	1,588,889	621,157	-
Education	55,709,768	210,003	-	-
Conservation and development	15,426,140	4,803,067	3,502,830	60,800
Interest on long term debt	860,768	-	-	-
Total governmental activities	211,798,294	15,370,819	21,336,890	877,575
Business-type activities:				
Water	10,037,485	11,815,767	-	-
Sewer	13,623,419	15,201,858	-	-
Gas	22,276,461	27,104,835	9,173	-
Stormwater	684,091	1,936,374	-	-
Golf	932,038	784,088	15,114	-
Total business-type activities	47,553,494	56,842,922	24,287	-
Total Primary Government	$ 259,351,788	$ 72,213,741	$ 21,361,177	$ 877,575
COMPONENT UNITS				
Economic Development Authority	$ 608,192	$ 23,250	$ -	$ -
School Board	74,459,716	2,906,219	8,750,937	-
Total Component Units	$ 75,067,908	$ 2,929,469	$ 8,750,937	$ -

Continued

CITY OF CHARLOTTESVILLE, VIRGINIA
STATEMENT OF ACTIVITIES
FOR THE YEAR ENDED JUNE 30, 2019

| Functions/Programs | Net (Expense) Revenue and Changes in Net Position | | | Component Units | |
	Governmental Activities	Business Type Activities	Total Primary Government	Economic Development Authority	School Board
PRIMARY GOVERNMENT					
Governmental activities:					
General government	$ (23,208,716)	$ -	$ (23,208,716)		
Public safety	(34,616,257)	-	(34,616,257)		
Community services	(12,520,242)	-	(12,520,242)		
Health and welfare	(28,596,734)	-	(28,596,734)		
Parks, recreation and culture	(11,851,085)	-	(11,851,085)		
Education	(55,499,765)	-	(55,499,765)		
Conservation and development	(7,059,443)	-	(7,059,443)		
Interest on long term debt	(860,768)	-	(860,768)		
Total governmental activities	(174,213,010)	-	(174,213,010)		
Business-type activities:					
Water	-	1,778,282	1,778,282		
Sewer	-	1,578,439	1,578,439		
Gas	-	4,837,547	4,837,547		
Stormwater	-	1,252,283	1,252,283		
Golf	-	(132,836)	(132,836)		
Total business-type activities	-	9,313,715	9,313,715		
Total Primary Government	(174,213,010)	9,313,715	(164,899,295)		
COMPONENT UNITS					
Economic Development Authority				$ (584,942)	$ -
School Board				-	(62,802,560)
Total Component Units				(584,942)	(62,802,560)
GENERAL REVENUES					
General property taxes	80,460,113	-	80,460,113	-	-
Sales tax	11,876,599	-	11,876,599	-	-
Utility tax	4,764,420	-	4,764,420	-	-
Communications tax	2,716,128	-	2,716,128	-	-
Meals tax	12,212,802	-	12,212,802	-	-
Lodging tax	5,659,226	-	5,659,226	-	-
Public service corporation tax	1,447,032	-	1,447,032	-	-
Franchise tax	3,500	-	3,500	-	-
Wills and deeds tax	751,569	-	751,569	-	-
Rolling stock tax	36,940	-	36,940	-	-
Short-term rental tax	56,557	-	56,557	-	-
Cigarette tax	671,562	-	671,562	-	-
State recordation tax	236,226	-	236,226	-	-
Bank stock tax	1,369,883	-	1,369,883	-	-
Business license tax	9,134,801	-	9,134,801	-	-
Grants & contributions not restricted to specific programs	39,975,597	-	39,975,597	-	15,697,356
Payment from City	-	-	-	343,422	47,229,709
Unrestricted revenue from use of money and property	1,893,575	16,855	1,910,430	240,100	-
Interest on investment earnings	1,033,337	206,128	1,239,465	67,587	-
Miscellaneous	896,195	297,137	1,193,332	-	-
Transfers, net	5,567,298	(5,567,298)	-	-	-
Total general revenues and transfers	180,763,360	(5,047,178)	175,716,182	651,109	62,927,065
Change in net position	6,550,350	4,266,537	10,816,887	66,167	124,505
Net Position - July 1, 2018 as restated	137,664,708	47,519,818	185,184,526	3,389,532	(43,586,312)
Net Position - June 30, 2019	$ 144,215,058	$ 51,786,355	$ 196,001,413	$ 3,455,699	$ (43,461,807)

The accompanying notes are an integral part of the basic financial statements.

CITY OF CHARLOTTESVILLE, VIRGINIA

EXHIBIT C

BALANCE SHEET
GOVERNMENTAL FUNDS
JUNE 30, 2019

	General Fund	Capital Projects Fund	Debt Service Fund	Social Services Fund	Other Governmental Funds	Total
ASSETS						
Cash, cash equivalents and investments	$ 46,159,103	$ 12,590,697	$ 12,842,718	$ 59,106	$ 2,046,548	$ 73,698,172
Interest receivable	207,536	-	-	-	-	207,536
Accounts receivable, net	545,315	3,997	-	9,486	7,461	566,259
Taxes receivable, net	42,595,895	-	-	-	-	42,595,895
Due from other governments (note 6)	3,110,601	2,439,808	-	785,173	4,630,275	10,965,857
Due from other funds (note 7)	2,010,405	-	-	-	-	2,010,405
Loans receivable (note 5)	-	2,530,000	-	-	1,744,840	4,274,840
Prepaid items	1,920	-	-	-	-	1,920
Total assets	$ 94,630,775	$ 17,564,502	$ 12,842,718	$ 853,765	$ 8,429,124	$ 134,320,884
LIABILITIES, DEFERRED INFLOWS OF RESOURCES AND FUND BALANCES						
LIABILITIES						
Accounts payable	$ 1,219,893	$ 1,470,445	$ 7,394	$ 13,425	$ 458,891	$ 3,170,048
Accrued liabilities	3,836,202	639,772	5,250	347,900	1,676,757	6,505,881
Due to other governments	-	-	-	-	1,799,744	1,799,744
Due to other funds (note 7)	-	-	-	372,742	1,637,663	2,010,405
Unearned revenue-other	42,224	-	-	-	33,010	75,234
Total liabilities	5,098,319	2,110,217	12,644	734,067	5,606,065	13,561,312
DEFERRED INFLOWS OF RESOURCES						
Unavailable tax revenue	41,710,372	1,435,766	-	-	-	43,146,138
FUND BALANCES (Note 2b):						
Nonspendable	1,920	-	-	-	162,502	164,422
Restricted	327,770	-	-	-	176,341	504,111
Committed	7,990,059	-	12,830,074	-	-	20,820,133
Assigned	6,229,997	14,018,519	-	119,698	2,484,216	22,852,430
Unassigned	33,272,338	-	-	-	-	33,272,338
Total fund balances	47,822,084	14,018,519	12,830,074	119,698	2,823,059	77,613,434
Total liabilities, deferred inflows of resources and fund balances	$ 94,630,775	$ 17,564,502	$ 12,842,718	$ 853,765	$ 8,429,124	$ 134,320,884

(continued)

BALANCE SHEET
GOVERNMENTAL FUNDS
JUNE 30, 2019

Total fund balances per the Balance Sheet for Governmental Funds	$	77,613,434
Amounts reported in the Statement of Net Position (Exhibit A) are different because:		
Capital assets are not financial resources and therefore are not reported in the funds statements. The Statement of Net Position, however, includes these assets, net of accumulated depreciation:		240,940,779
Other long-term assets are not available to pay current period expenditures and therefore are deferred in the governmental funds and are not included in fund balance:		
Net deferred inflows and outflows of resources for pension charges		14,242,822
Net deferred amount on OPEB		2,644,492
Internal service funds area used by management to charge the cost of certain activities such as insurances and telecommunication to individual funds. The assets and liabilities of certain internal service funds are included in governmental activities in the Statement of Net Position:		
Internal service funds net position, less amounts reflected in capital assets, deferred inflows/outflows, and net pension liabilities		17,425,721
Some of the city's property taxes will be collected after year-end, but are not available soon enough to pay for the current year's expenditures, and therefore are unavailable in the funds:		1,144,964
Some liabilities, including general bonds payable, are not due as payable in the current period and therefore are not reported as fund liabilities. All liabilities are included in the Statement of Net Position:		
Accrued interest payable		(1,143,409)
Unamortized premiums on bonds		(6,419,819)
Bonds payable		(87,670,733)
Net deferred amount on refunding		(882,356)
Net pension liability		(72,925,795)
Net OPEB liability		(38,001,806)
Compensated absenses		(2,753,236)
Net position per the Statement of Net Position (Exhibit A)	$	144,215,058

The accompanying notes are an integral part of the basic financial statements.

STATEMENT OF REVENUES, EXPENDITURES AND CHANGES IN FUND BALANCES
FOR THE YEAR ENDED JUNE 30, 2019

	General Fund	Capital Projects Fund	Debt Service Fund	Social Service Fund	Other Governmental Funds	Total
REVENUES						
Taxes	$ 130,457,652	$ -	$ -	$ -	$ -	$ 130,457,652
Fees and permits	2,801,483	50,575	-	-	-	2,852,058
Intergovernmental	29,230,238	3,938,162	148,845	10,152,679	16,570,360	60,040,284
Charges for services	9,587,144	-	-	7,925	5,718,814	15,313,883
Fines	362,381	-	-	-	-	362,381
Investment earnings	882,355	-	147,680	-	3,303	1,033,338
Miscellaneous	2,006,747	250,012	-	9,638	94,567	2,360,964
Total revenues	175,328,000	4,238,749	296,525	10,170,242	22,387,044	212,420,560
EXPENDITURES						
Current:						
General government	23,177,528	2,826,493	193,281	-	783,562	26,980,864
Public safety	37,803,772	69,520	-	-	367,156	38,240,448
Community services	7,928,717	1,808,532	-	-	9,269,226	19,006,475
Health and welfare	5,017,088	-	-	13,382,868	17,336,351	35,736,307
Parks, recreation and culture	12,877,191	359,784	-	-	89,045	13,326,020
Education	53,168,613	1,629,867	-	-	-	54,798,480
Conservation and development	7,664,413	5,192,994	-	-	387,446	13,244,853
Debt service:						
Retirement of principal	-	-	7,140,323	-	-	7,140,323
Interest	-	-	3,041,563	-	-	3,041,563
Capital outlay	2,069,092	10,209,265	-	23,624	1,009,771	13,331,752
Total expenditures	149,726,414	22,096,455	10,375,167	13,406,492	29,242,557	224,847,085
Revenues over (under) expenditures	25,601,586	(17,857,706)	(10,078,642)	(3,236,250)	(6,855,513)	(12,426,525)
OTHER FINANCING SOURCES (USES)						
Transfers in (note 7)	6,344,655	9,265,627	11,003,348	3,236,250	6,870,258	36,720,138
Transfers out (note 7)	(30,292,594)	(1,144,534)	-	-	(113,938)	(31,551,066)
Issuance of debt (note 9)	-	9,520,000	-	-	-	9,520,000
Premium on issuance of debt (note 9)	-	1,126,606	-	-	-	1,126,606
Total other financial sources (uses)	(23,947,939)	18,767,699	11,003,348	3,236,250	6,756,320	15,815,678
Net change in fund balance	1,653,647	909,993	924,706	-	(99,193)	3,389,153
Fund Balance July 1, 2018 as restated	46,168,437	13,108,526	11,905,368	119,696	2,922,252	74,224,281
Fund Balance June 30, 2019	$ 47,822,084	$ 14,018,519	$ 12,830,074	$ 119,696	$ 2,823,059	$ 77,613,434

(continued)

CITY OF CHARLOTTESVILLE, VIRGINIA
STATEMENT OF REVENUES, EXPENDITURES AND CHANGES IN FUND BALANCES
FOR THE YEAR ENDED JUNE 30, 2019

EXHIBIT D, Continued

Net change in fund balances - total governmental funds (Exhibit D) $ 3,389,153

Amounts reported for governmental activities in the Statement of Activities (Exhibit B) are different because:

Governmental funds report the cost of equipment and facilities required as current expenditures while the Statement of Activities reports depreciation expense to allocate those expenses over the life of the assets:

Capital outlay	13,346,753
Depreciation expense	(10,522,854)
Net gain (loss) on disposal of assets	(4,255)

Revenues in the statement of activities that do not provide current financial resources are not reported as revenues in the funds. Details of this item consist of the following:

Change in deferred property taxes	345,786

Debt proceeds provide current financing resources to governmental funds but debt issues increase long-term liabilities in the Statement of Net Position. Principal payments are expenditures in governmental funds but reduce long-term liabilities in the Statement of Net Position:

New debt issued	(9,520,000)
Principal payments	7,140,323

Governmental funds report interest on long-term debt as expenditures when payments are due, while the Statement of Activities reports interest expense on the accrual basis:

Change in accrued interest	(26,883)
Change in amortization of bond premium	871,938
Interest earned on bond refunding	209,134

Some expenses reported in the Statement of Activities do not require the use of current financial resources and therefore are not reported as expenditures in governmental funds:

Change in compensated absences	(168,122)
Change in net pension liability	743,686
Net change in deferred outflows and deferred inflows of resources related to net pension liability	(3,033,849)
Change in net OPEB liability	1,667,380
Net change in deferred outflows and deferred inflows of resources related to net OPEB liability	(646,469)

The change in net position of internal service funds, less amounts reflected in long term assets and liabilities, and deferred outflows of resources, and deferred inflows of resources, is combined with governmental activities on the Statement of Activities.   2,758,629

Change in net position per the Statement of Activities (Exhibit B) $ 6,550,350

The accompanying notes are an integral part of the basic financial statements.

STATEMENT OF NET POSITION
PROPRIETARY FUNDS
JUNE 30, 2019

| | Business - Type Activities - Enterprise Funds | | | | | | Internal Service Funds |
	Water	Sewer	Gas	Stormwater	Golf	Total	
ASSETS							
Current assets:							
Cash and cash equivalents	$ 1,187,459	$ 3,496,389	$ 8,879,686	$ 6,042,005	$ 41,114	$ 19,646,653	$ 20,214,688
Accounts receivable, net	764,797	687,487	333,432	46,440	987	1,833,143	27,844
Unbilled accounts receivable	818,950	1,051,683	604,550	-	-	2,475,183	
Inventories	-	-	-	-	26,905	26,905	687,580
Prepaid expenses	-	-	1,568,654	-	-	1,568,654	110,936
Restricted cash and investments	3,100	2,081,904	-	1,324,640	-	3,409,644	-
Total current assets	2,774,306	7,317,463	11,386,322	7,413,085	69,006	28,960,182	21,041,048
Noncurrent assets:							
Land	-	-	584,291	-	1,337,432	1,921,723	-
Easements	12,625	95,600	34,100	-	-	142,325	
Buildings and Improvements	18,919	39,014	-	-	1,819,260	1,877,193	48,364
Vehicles	478,139	765,934	2,075,089	82,350	13,732	3,415,244	66,848
Transmission lines and mains	44,507,045	46,480,786	43,188,795	1,016,825	-	135,193,452	
Storm drainage	-	-	-	5,046,966	-	5,046,966	-
Equipment	552,415	338,063	1,793,602	19,374	241,498	2,944,952	9,394,956
Accumulated depreciation	(14,516,656)	(10,742,910)	(31,282,162)	(444,903)	(1,660,571)	(58,647,202)	(9,361,103)
Total noncurrent assets	31,052,487	36,976,487	16,393,715	5,720,613	1,751,351	91,894,653	149,065
Total assets	33,826,793	44,293,950	27,780,037	13,133,696	1,820,357	120,854,835	21,190,113
DEFERRED OUTFLOWS OF RESOURCES							
Deferred charges on refunding losses	1,419	35,493	2,023	-	-	38,935	-
Deferred charges-pension	359,387	368,012	1,464,306	74,653	66,427	2,332,785	621,339
Deferred charges-OPEB	85,664	91,657	313,536	10,778	7,009	508,644	89,779
Total deferred outflows of resources	446,470	495,162	1,779,865	85,431	73,436	2,880,364	711,118
LIABILITIES							
Current liabilities:							
Accounts payable	1,113,155	863,054	138,498	60,235	2,338	2,177,280	104,076
Accrued liabilities	439,972	432,600	1,141,611	257,566	49,637	2,321,386	2,909,600
Accrued interest payable	200,768	314,260	2,309	39,719	-	557,056	-
Customer deposits	257,437	-	734,001	-	-	991,438	
Liabilities due in less than one year	1,506,037	1,638,157	23,224	255,998	1,855	3,425,271	8,230
Total current liabilities	3,517,369	3,248,071	2,039,643	613,518	53,830	9,472,431	3,021,906
Noncurrent liabilities:							
Liabilities due in more than one year	17,858,373	25,950,458	344,408	4,614,970	13,601	48,781,810	60,355
Net pension liability	1,348,827	1,221,268	5,432,854	108,071	433,119	8,544,139	2,731,559
Net OPEB liability	722,967	677,702	2,824,557	133,987	177,267	4,536,480	1,563,526
Total noncurrent liabilities	19,930,167	27,849,428	8,601,819	4,857,028	623,987	61,862,429	4,355,440
Total liabilities	23,447,536	31,097,499	10,641,462	5,470,546	677,817	71,334,860	7,377,346
DEFERRED INFLOWS OF RESOURCES							
Deferred charges on refunding gains	119,601	113,850	435	-	-	233,886	-
Deferred charges-pension	101,747	83,044	371,715	1,071	23,912	581,489	205,008
Deferred charges-OPEB	39,837	35,577	136,802	6,447	8,780	227,443	82,673
Total deferred inflows of resources	261,185	232,471	508,952	7,518	32,692	1,042,818	287,681
NET POSITION							
Net investment in capital assets	11,618,629	11,434,280	16,217,705	2,182,599	1,751,351	43,204,564	149,067
Unrestricted	(1,054,086)	2,024,862	2,191,785	5,558,466	(568,066)	8,152,961	14,087,139
Total net position	$ 10,564,543	$ 13,459,142	$ 18,409,490	$ 7,741,065	$ 1,183,285	$ 51,357,525	$ 14,236,206

Total net position $ 51,357,525

Allocated internal services:		
Warehouse assets		631,125
Warehouse deferred outflows		54,369
Warehouse liabilities		(242,511)
Warehouse deferred inflows		(14,153)
Total allocation of warehouse net position		428,830
Net position of business-type activities		$ 51,786,355

The accompanying notes are an intregal part of the basic financial statements.

STATEMENT OF REVENUES, EXPENSES AND CHANGES IN FUND NET POSITION
PROPRIETARY FUNDS
FOR THE YEAR ENDED JUNE 30, 2019

	Business - Type Activities - Enterprise Funds						Internal Service Funds
	Water	Sewer	Gas	Stormwater	Golf	Total	
OPERATING REVENUES							
Utility charges	$ 11,382,693	$ 16,317,525	$ 26,962,660	$ 1,922,072	$ -	$ 56,584,950	$ -
Charges for services	314,905	73,126	212,183	14,303	804,604	1,419,121	24,653,980
Total operating revenues	11,697,598	16,390,651	27,174,843	1,936,375	804,604	58,004,071	24,653,980
OPERATING EXPENSES							
Purchases for resale	5,638,812	9,765,889	12,077,595	-	37,384	27,519,680	1,990,032
Personnel costs	1,247,526	1,220,864	5,134,263	355,976	382,680	8,341,309	1,817,250
Materials and supplies	460,015	80,152	775,242	(1,566)	65,031	1,378,874	792,366
Contractual services and charges	1,105,509	2,384,703	2,925,315	59,188	419,101	6,893,816	1,345,613
Depreciation	1,127,558	1,060,052	1,316,693	152,833	28,040	3,685,176	34,980
Claims incurred	-	-	-	-	-	-	13,281,774
Insurance premiums	-	-	-	-	-	-	3,011,602
Total operating expenses	9,579,420	14,511,660	22,229,108	566,431	932,236	47,818,855	22,273,617
Operating income (loss)	2,118,178	1,878,991	4,945,735	1,369,944	(127,632)	10,185,216	2,380,363
NONOPERATING REVENUES (EXPENSES)							
Gain/Loss on capital asset disposition	3,938	-	-	-	-	3,938	3,654
Interest expense	(451,264)	(718,644)	(14,282)	(94,282)	-	(1,278,472)	-
Interest income	23,930	46,974	55,204	80,020	-	206,128	109,342
Bond issuance expense	(30,549)	(40,432)	-	(23,511)	-	(94,492)	-
Capacity fees	307,450	500,485	-	-	-	807,935	-
Insurance recovery	-	-	-	-	-	-	48,204
Total nonoperating revenues (expenses), net	(146,495)	(211,617)	40,922	(37,773)	-	(354,963)	161,200
Income (loss) before contributions and transfers	1,971,683	1,667,374	4,986,657	1,332,171	(127,632)	9,830,253	2,541,563
Transfers in	-	-	59,700	-	149,204	208,904	-
Transfers out	(866,528)	(928,278)	(3,981,395)	-	-	(5,776,201)	(101,774)
Total transfers, net	(866,528)	(928,278)	(3,921,695)	-	149,204	(5,567,297)	(101,774)
Change in net position	1,105,155	739,096	1,064,962	1,332,171	21,572	4,262,956	2,439,789
Total net position - July 1, 2018	9,459,388	12,720,046	17,344,528	6,408,894	1,161,713	47,094,569	11,796,416
Total net position - June 30, 2019	$ 10,564,543	$ 13,459,142	$ 18,409,490	$ 7,741,065	$ 1,183,285	$ 51,357,525	$ 14,236,205

Total business-type change in net position	$	4,262,956
Warehouse sales operating revenues		986,772
Expenses associated with warehouse sales		(983,191)
Net internal service fund allocation		3,581
Change in net position of business-type activities	$	4,266,537

The accompanying notes are an integral part of the basic financial statements.

STATEMENT OF CASH FLOWS
PROPRIETARY FUNDS
FOR THE YEAR ENDING JUNE 30, 2019

	Business - Type Activities - Enterprise Funds						Internal Service Funds
	Water	Sewer	Gas	Stormwater	Golf	Total	
OPERATING ACTIVITIES							
Receipts from customers	$ 11,488,821	$ 14,509,475	$ 27,264,705	$ 1,907,535	$ 808,276	$ 55,978,812	$ 24,645,321
Payments to suppliers	(6,697,143)	(10,668,943)	(16,018,853)	(207,459)	(560,829)	(34,153,227)	(20,522,051)
Payments to employees	(1,199,491)	(1,224,708)	(5,112,771)	(317,486)	(355,537)	(8,209,993)	(1,514,204)
Net cash provided by (used for) operating activities	3,592,187	2,615,824	6,133,081	1,382,590	(108,090)	13,615,592	2,609,066
NONCAPITAL FINANCING ACTIVITIES							
Insurance recovery	-	-	-	-	-	-	48,204
Transfers in	-	-	59,700	-	149,204	208,904	-
Transfers out	(866,528)	(928,278)	(3,981,395)	-	-	(5,776,201)	(101,774)
Net cash provided by (used for) noncapital financing activities	(866,528)	(928,278)	(3,921,695)	-	149,204	(5,567,297)	(53,570)
CAPITAL AND RELATED FINANCING ACTIVITIES							
Acquisition of capital assets	(6,051,584)	(1,384,521)	(907,490)	(1,233,508)	-	(9,577,103)	-
Proceeds from sale of capital assets	3,936	-	-	-	-	3,936	3,654
Capacity fees	307,450	500,485	-	-	-	807,935	-
Bond proceeds	2,040,000	2,700,000	-	1,570,000	-	6,310,000	-
Bond principal paid	(1,388,994)	(1,963,721)	(122,633)	(156,159)	-	(3,631,507)	-
Interest paid	(602,690)	(842,745)	(18,647)	(102,172)	-	(1,566,254)	-
Bond issuance expenses	(30,549)	(40,432)	-	(23,511)	-	(94,492)	-
Premium on bonds issued	243,649	342,193	-	204,967	-	790,809	-
Net cash provided by (used for) capital and related financing	(5,478,782)	(688,741)	(1,048,770)	259,617	-	(6,956,676)	3,654
INVESTING ACTIVITIES							
Interest on investments	23,930	46,974	55,203	80,020	-	206,127	109,342
Net cash provided by investment activities	23,930	46,974	55,203	80,020	-	206,127	109,342
Net increase (decrease) in cash and cash equivalents	(2,729,193)	1,045,779	1,217,819	1,722,227	41,114	1,297,746	2,668,492
Balance - July 1, 2018	3,919,752	4,532,516	7,661,867	5,644,418	$ -	21,758,553	17,546,197
Balance - June 30, 2019	$ 1,190,559	$ 5,578,293	$ 8,879,686	$ 7,366,645	$ 41,114	$ 23,056,297	$ 20,214,688
Reconciliation of operating income (loss) to net cash used in operating activities							
Operating income (loss)	$ 2,118,178	$ 1,878,991	$ 4,945,735	$ 1,369,944	$ (127,632)	$ 10,185,216	$ 2,380,363
Adjustments to reconcile operating income (loss) to net cash provided by (used in) operating activities:							
Depreciation expense	1,127,558	1,060,052	1,316,693	152,833	28,040	3,685,176	34,981
(Increase) decrease in accounts receivable	(170,473)	(234,358)	36,819	(28,840)	(986)	(397,838)	(8,659)
(Increase) decrease in inventories	-	-	-	-	1,267	1,267	(71,921)
(Increase) decrease in prepaid expenses	-	-	(19,060)	-	-	(19,060)	-
Increase (decrease) in accounts payable	484,011	(85,017)	(186,385)	(117,837)	(40,581)	54,191	104,464
Increase (decrease) in accrued liabilities	7,984	(3,034)	4,997	2,934	(10,529)	2,352	(93,984)
Increase (decrease) in customer deposits	(15,122)	-	17,786	-	-	2,664	-
Increase (decrease) in unredeemed gift certificates	-	-	-	-	4,659	4,659	-
Increase (decrease) in compensated absenses	5,165	(792)	(276)	4,562	1,662	10,321	(28,500)
Increase (decrease) in insurance claims payable	-	-	-	-	-	-	(19,376)
Net pension liability change for measurement year	49,802	25,406	99,156	2,173	28,848	205,385	257,896
Net OPEB liability change for measurement year	(14,916)	(25,424)	(82,384)	(3,179)	7,162	(118,741)	53,802
Net cash provided by (used for) operating activities	$ 3,592,187	$ 2,615,824	$ 6,133,081	$ 1,382,590	$ (108,090)	$ 13,615,592	$ 2,609,066

The accompanying notes are an integral part of the basic financial statements.

CITY OF CHARLOTTESVILLE, VIRGINIA

STATEMENT OF FIDUCIARY NET POSITION
FIDUCIARY FUNDS
JUNE 30, 2019

	Pension Trust Funds
ASSETS	
Cash and cash equivalents (note 3b)	$ 2,708,237
Interest receivable	288,331
Investments (note 3b):	
Common stocks	48,862,848
Corporate fixed income securities	12,808,646
Government and agency fixed income securities	19,370,040
Mutual Funds:	
Domestic	32,966,763
International	21,899,671
Alternative Investments:	
Agriculture	7,060,872
Real Estate	16,551,164
Total Investments	159,520,004
Total assets	162,516,572
LIABILITIES	
Accounts payable	48,441
Total liabilities	48,441
NET POSITION	
Net position - restricted	$ 162,468,131

The accompanying notes are an integral part of the basic financial statements.

CITY OF CHARLOTTESVILLE, VIRGINIA

STATEMENT OF CHANGES IN FIDUCIARY NET POSITION
FIDUCIARY FUNDS
JUNE 30, 2019

	Pension Trust Funds
ADDITIONS	
Contributions:	
Employer	$ 15,632,242
Plan members	2,437,111
Total contributions	18,069,353
Investment earnings:	
Net increase in fair value of investments	10,500,429
Interest	1,132,785
Dividends	1,416,845
Total investment earnings	13,050,059
Less investment expenses	750,275
Net investment earnings	12,299,784
Total additions	30,369,137
DEDUCTIONS	
Pension benefits	12,666,079
Refund of plan member contributions	114,365
Other post-retirement benefits	5,537,826
Administrative expenses	330,998
Total deductions	18,649,268
Increase in net position	11,719,869
Net Position - July 1, 2018	150,748,262
Net position - June 30, 2019	$ 162,468,131

The accompanying notes are an integral part of the basic financial statements.

Appendix B

CITY OF CHARLOTTESVILLE – REQUIRED SUPPLEMENTARY INFORMATION

REQUIRED SUPPLEMENTARY INFORMATION

102

CITY OF CHARLOTTESVILLE, VIRGINIA

NOTE TO REQUIRED SUPPLEMENTARY INFORMATION
FOR THE YEAR ENDED JUNE 30, 2019

1. BUDGETARY ACCOUNTING

Demonstrating compliance with the adopted budget is an important component of a government's accountability to the public. Many citizens participate in the process of establishing the annual operating budgets of state and local governments, and have a keen interest in following the actual financial progress of their governments over the course of the year. The City and many other governments revise their original budgets over the course of the year for a variety of reasons. Accordingly, GAAP requires that governments include the original budget with the comparison of final budget and actual results.

The City's budget process begins in December with the preparation of estimated revenue forecasts. Departmental budget requests are submitted to the City Manager in early January. By early March the Manager's proposed budget is presented to City Council. A series of City Council work sessions and public hearings are held. The budget is formally adopted by April 15.

An annual operating budget is adopted for the General Fund and the Social Services Fund. Within the General Fund, budgets are legally adopted at the departmental level. The City Manager is authorized to transfer the budget for personnel cost (salaries and fringe benefits) between departments if necessary; however, any other revisions that alter the total expenditures of any department or agency must be approved by City Council. Unexpended appropriations lapse at the end of the fiscal year unless carried over by Council action.

The budgets are integrated into the accounting system and the budgetary data, as presented in the Required Supplementary Information for all major funds with annual budgets, compares the expenditures with the amended budgets. All budgets are presented on the modified accrual basis of accounting. Accordingly, the Budgetary Comparison Schedules for the General and Social Services Funds present actual expenditures in accordance with GAAP on a basis consistent with legally adopted budgets as amended. Original, final budget and actual revenues and expenditures, including encumbrances, for the General Fund and Social Services Fund are presented on Exhibits G-1 and G-2, respectively. Original budget amounts are the budgets originally adopted by City Council, plus any approved amounts carried over from the previous fiscal year. Final budgets are these amounts plus any adjustments, through additional appropriations or reductions.

CITY OF CHARLOTTESVILLE, VIRGINIA

SCHEDULE OF REVENUES, EXPENDITURES AND
CHANGES IN FUND BALANCE - BUDGET AND ACTUAL - BUDGET BASIS
GENERAL FUND
FOR THE YEAR ENDED JUNE 30, 2019

| | Budgeted Amounts | | Actual-Budget | Variance Positive |
	Original	Final	Basis (see Note 1)	(Negative)
REVENUES				
Taxes:				
Real estate	$ 68,267,343	$ 68,267,343	$ 70,263,898	$ 1,996,555
Personal property	8,629,200	8,629,200	9,310,203	681,003
Public service corporation	1,350,000	1,350,000	1,447,032	97,032
Penalties and interest on delinquent taxes	350,000	350,000	540,225	190,225
Sales and use	11,663,391	11,663,391	11,876,599	213,208
Business license	7,400,000	7,400,000	8,540,881	1,140,881
Utilities	4,699,842	4,699,842	4,764,420	64,578
Communications	3,000,000	3,000,000	2,716,128	(283,872)
Meals	11,817,375	11,817,375	12,212,802	395,427
Lodging	5,100,000	5,100,000	5,659,226	559,226
Franchise	-	-	3,500	3,500
Tax on bank stock	1,200,000	1,200,000	1,369,883	169,883
Tax on wills and deeds	550,000	550,000	751,569	201,569
Rolling stock	21,000	21,000	36,940	15,940
Short-term rental	60,000	60,000	56,557	(3,443)
Cigarette	725,000	725,000	671,562	(53,438)
Recordation	203,191	203,191	236,226	33,035
Total Taxes:	125,036,342	125,036,342	130,457,652	5,421,310
Licenses and permits:				
Vehicle license fees	915,000	915,000	902,902	(12,098)
Dog licenses	15,000	15,000	9,024	(5,976)
Electrical, heating and mechanical permits	250,000	250,000	265,251	15,251
Building and plumbing permits	400,000	400,000	726,066	326,066
Erosion control fees	27,000	27,000	37,125	10,125
Sign permits	8,000	8,000	8,750	750
Other permits	570,500	570,500	852,365	281,865
Total Licenses and permits:	2,185,500	2,185,500	2,801,483	615,983
Intergovernmental:				
Revenue from Federal government	-	6,937	13,171	6,234
Revenue from State agencies:				
State highway assistance	4,103,696	4,103,696	4,206,501	102,805
Reimbursement for constitutional officers	1,634,635	1,634,635	1,680,881	46,246
Police assistance	2,012,664	2,012,664	2,154,332	141,668
Trailer titling tax	1,200	1,200	3,750	2,550
PPTRA revenue	3,498,256	3,498,256	3,498,256	-
Other State assistance	150,000	150,000	226,866	76,866
Revenue from other local governments:				
Revenue sharing - Albemarle County	15,696,360	15,696,360	15,696,360	-
Fire Department operations	191,850	191,850	194,465	2,615
Juvenile and Domestic Relations Court	124,668	124,668	124,668	-
Court revenue	490,000	490,000	438,947	(51,053)
Circuit Court reimbursement	10,000	10,000	10,178	178
University of Virginia service charge	46,000	46,000	76,538	30,538
Payment in lieu of taxes - CRHA	33,828	33,828	24,726	(9,102)
Other local governments	3,350,657	3,354,177	880,599	(2,473,578)
Total Intergovernmental:	31,343,814	31,354,271	29,230,238	(2,124,033)

(continued)

CITY OF CHARLOTTESVILLE, VIRGINIA

SCHEDULE OF REVENUES, EXPENDITURES AND
CHANGES IN FUND BALANCE - BUDGET AND ACTUAL - BUDGET BASIS
GENERAL FUND
FOR THE YEAR ENDED JUNE 30, 2019

| | Budgeted Amounts | | Actual-Budget | Variance Positive |
	Original	Final	Basis (see Note 1)	(Negative)
Charges for services:				
Recreation income	1,426,129	1,428,249	1,313,825	(114,424)
Parking meter receipts	1,500	1,500	50,571	49,071
Parking garage revenue	774,828	1,751,983	1,354,591	(397,392)
Solid waste collection fees	1,050,000	1,050,000	1,117,434	67,434
Emergency Medical Services	1,440,000	1,440,000	1,427,530	(12,470)
Tax abatement application fees	-	-	1,750	1,750
DMV Select Commissions	-	-	4,392	4,392
Other charges for services	3,422,463	3,479,399	4,317,050	837,651
Total Charges for services:	8,114,920	9,151,131	9,587,144	436,013
Fines:				
Parking fines	450,000	450,000	362,381	(87,619)
Investment earnings:				
	515,000	515,000	882,355	367,355
Miscellaneous revenues:				
Rent	495,832	500,080	566,941	66,861
Proceeds from drug seizures	-	6,781	20,778	13,997
Contributions	-	34,218	40,671	6,453
Refund of prior year expenditures	30,000	30,000	273,202	243,202
Indirect cost recovery	125,000	125,000	109,258	(15,742)
Other miscellaneous revenues	921,500	997,172	995,898	(1,274)
Total Miscellaneous revenues:	1,572,332	1,693,251	2,006,747	313,496
Total Revenues	169,217,908	170,385,495	175,328,001	4,942,506
EXPENDITURES-CURRENT				
General government:				
Legislative:				
Mayor and Council	574,520	584,520	514,767	69,753
Reserve for Council	606,400	1,751,050	1,077,437	673,613
First Cities	18,000	18,000	17,870	130
Sister Cities	15,000	72,191	18,179	54,012
Judicial:				
City Circuit Court	928,628	933,465	877,866	55,599
General District Court	21,208	24,273	24,273	-
Court Services Unit	9,820	9,820	9,726	94
Juvenile and Domestic Relations Court	340,227	346,252	346,251	1
Commonwealth's Attorney	1,166,741	1,115,866	1,076,319	39,547
City Sheriff	1,395,065	1,766,581	1,374,844	391,737
Executive:				
City Manager	2,043,785	2,199,954	1,889,141	310,813
Human Rights Commission	250,301	250,301	222,779	27,522
Citywide Reserve	945,281	2,101,799	564,127	1,537,672
Legal:				
City Attorney	1,040,151	1,040,151	923,864	116,287
Financial administration:				
Commissioner of Revenue	1,344,682	1,377,595	1,377,595	-
Real Estate Assessor	823,069	823,069	822,135	934
Treasurer	1,331,312	1,331,312	1,311,265	20,047
Finance - Administration	1,380,986	1,389,656	1,389,656	-
Purchasing	345,052	336,382	308,706	27,675
Personnel administration:				
Human Resources Department	1,226,916	1,226,916	1,147,157	79,759
Elections:				
Office of the Registrar	560,232	598,691	598,691	-

(continued)

CITY OF CHARLOTTESVILLE, VIRGINIA

SCHEDULE OF REVENUES, EXPENDITURES AND
CHANGES IN FUND BALANCE - BUDGET AND ACTUAL - BUDGET BASIS
GENERAL FUND
FOR THE YEAR ENDED JUNE 30, 2019

EXHIBIT G-1
Page 3 of 5

	Budgeted Amounts		Actual-Budget Basis (see Note 1)	Variance Positive (Negative)
	Original	Final		
General government buildings and plant:				
Public Works - Administration	1,058,663	1,062,183	901,048	161,135
Custodial	457,252	500,452	500,435	17
Maintenance	2,939,658	2,727,013	2,209,758	517,255
Information technology:				
IT Operations	2,881,027	2,934,801	2,851,882	82,919
Total General government	23,703,975	26,522,292	22,355,772	4,166,521
Public safety:				
Police protection:				
Police Department	17,020,666	17,347,788	17,121,822	225,967
Drug investigation	-	32,067	28,875	3,191
Fire protection:				
Fire Department	11,669,751	11,851,039	11,747,018	104,021
Volunteer Fire Company	22,342	22,342	9,912	12,430
Other protection:				
Contribution - Charlottesville-Albemarle Regional Jail	5,030,787	5,030,787	4,952,622	78,165
Blue Ridge Juvenile Detention Center	892,045	892,045	871,266	20,779
Office of the Magistrate	8,300	8,343	8,343	-
Traffic Engineering	855,075	873,805	902,946	(29,142)
Contribution - Emergency Communications Center	1,585,328	1,585,328	1,573,094	12,234
Four for Life	-	19,747	4,050	15,697
Emergency medical services	777,080	886,972	886,972	-
Crisis Intervention Training	106,449	106,449	82,913	23,536
Total Public safety	37,967,823	38,656,712	38,189,833	466,879
Community services				
Highways and streets:				
Public Service - Administration	405,792	482,381	482,378	3
Streets and sidewalks	4,537,130	4,442,780	3,602,254	840,526
Public Works - Stormwater	338,681	338,681	320,456	18,225
Street lighting	705,358	713,358	713,092	266
Sanitation:				
Refuse collection and disposal	1,907,571	1,964,821	1,946,009	18,812
Contribution to Ivy Landfill	-	271,189	271,189	-
Transportation:				
Contribution to JAUNT	1,377,047	1,377,047	1,377,047	-
Total Community services	9,271,579	9,590,257	8,712,424	877,833
Health and welfare:				
Health:				
Thomas Jefferson Health Department	561,344	626,344	626,344	-
Region Ten Community Services Board	1,001,865	1,021,865	1,021,865	-
Society for the Prevention of Cruelty to Animals	264,039	264,039	264,039	-
Offender Aid and Restoration	242,403	242,403	242,403	-
Welfare:				
Tax relief for the elderly	400,000	431,179	431,178	1
Rent relief for the elderly	18,000	18,000	16,111	1,889
Tax relief for the disabled	120,000	120,000	105,756	14,244
Rent relief for the disabled	195,000	195,000	188,429	6,571
CHAR homeowners tax relief prog	569,500	569,500	506,800	62,700
Stormwater fee assistance program	20,000	20,000	-	20,000
Education Extension program	49,961	49,961	48,636	1,325
Contributions to community organizations	2,219,333	2,220,713	2,173,023	47,690
Total Health and welfare	5,661,445	5,779,004	5,624,584	154,420

(continued)

CITY OF CHARLOTTESVILLE, VIRGINIA

SCHEDULE OF REVENUES, EXPENDITURES AND
CHANGES IN FUND BALANCE - BUDGET AND ACTUAL - BUDGET BASIS
GENERAL FUND
FOR THE YEAR ENDED JUNE 30, 2019

	Budgeted Amounts		Actual-Budget Basis (see Note 1)	Variance Positive (Negative)
	Original	Final		
Parks, recreation and culture:				
Culture:				
Contribution to Jefferson - Madison Regional Library	-	1,941,399	1,941,399	-
Contributions to community organizations	178,198	178,198	128,198	50,000
Contributions to festivals	73,000	68,500	43,513	24,987
Recreation:				
Administration	1,003,521	1,009,775	993,763	16,012
Athletics	264,487	270,782	250,687	20,095
Aquatics	2,195,260	2,273,401	2,168,281	105,119
Recreation centers	2,088,565	2,027,685	1,930,235	97,450
Special activities	826,589	937,893	870,794	67,100
Therapeutic programs	370,327	429,983	401,886	28,098
Parks:				
Park maintenance	4,469,616	4,499,356	4,336,065	163,291
Contribution to Towe Park operations	87,553	108,153	108,153	-
Total Parks, recreation and culture:	11,557,115	13,745,126	13,172,973	572,153
Education:				
Contribution to School Board component unit	50,321,149	50,321,149	47,229,709	3,091,440
School pupil transportation	3,346,234	3,185,595	2,558,207	627,388
School maintenance and energy management	3,664,358	3,824,996	3,703,579	121,417
Piedmont Virginia Community College	11,126	11,126	11,126	-
Lighthouse Studio	38,321	38,321	38,321	-
Schoolyard Garden	19,200	19,200	19,200	-
Contributions to community organizations	73,180	73,180	73,180	-
Total Education:	57,473,568	57,473,567	53,633,322	3,840,245
Conservation and development:				
Economic development:				
Office of Economic Development	952,435	1,009,524	862,828	146,696
Chamber of Commerce	1,605	1,605	1,605	-
Contribution to Convention and Visitors Bureau	-	1,038,546	1,038,546	-
Urban redevelopment and housing:				
Parking enterprise	826,621	1,803,776	1,958,573	(154,797)
Neighborhood Development Services Department	4,157,426	4,091,106	3,878,528	212,577
Historic Preservation Task Force	5,000	42,093	-	42,093
Thomas Jefferson Planning District	68,590	68,590	68,590	-
Albemarle Housing Improvement Program	99,050	99,050	99,050	-
Small Business Development Center	12,000	12,000	12,000	-
Contributions to community organizations	145,763	145,763	145,763	-
Total Conservation and development:	6,268,490	8,312,053	8,065,483	246,570
Other activities:				
Virginia Municipal League	16,820	17,342	17,342	-
Employee benefits	1,258,024	1,038,534	1,020,097	18,437
Corporate training program	-	257,029	166,019	91,010
Thomas Jefferson Soil & Water	12,669	12,669	12,669	-
Virginia Institute for Government	2,500	2,500	2,500	-
Alliance for Innovation	2,550	2,550	2,550	-
Rivanna Conservation Alliance	11,000	11,000	11,000	-
National League of Cities	5,000	7,740	7,740	-
Center for Nonprofit Excellence	600	600	600	-
Total Other activities:	1,309,163	1,349,964	1,240,517	109,447
Total Expenditures - Budgetary Basis	153,213,158	161,428,976	150,994,909	10,434,069

(continued)

CITY OF CHARLOTTESVILLE, VIRGINIA

SCHEDULE OF REVENUES, EXPENDITURES AND
CHANGES IN FUND BALANCE - BUDGET AND ACTUAL - BUDGET BASIS
GENERAL FUND
FOR THE YEAR ENDED JUNE 30, 2019

| | Budgeted Amounts | | Actual-Budget | Variance |
	Original	Final	Basis (see Note 1)	Positive (Negative)
ENCUMBRANCES				
Less open encumbrances - June 30, 2019	-	-	(1,268,494)	1,268,494
Total Expenditures	153,213,158	161,428,976	149,726,415	11,702,563
Revenues Over Expenditures	16,004,750	8,956,520	25,601,586	16,645,069
OTHER FINANCING SOURCES (USES)				
Transfers in:				
Transfer from Information Technology Fund	-	101,774	101,774	-
Transfer from Capital Projects Fund	-	66,680	66,680	-
Transfer from Water Fund	-	866,528	866,528	-
Transfer from Sewer Fund	-	928,278	928,278	-
Transfer from Gas Fund	-	3,981,395	3,981,395	-
Total Transfers in:	-	5,944,655	5,944,655	-
Transfers out:				
Transfer to State Grants Fund	(33,000)	(46,306)	(20,359)	25,947
Transfer to Social Services Fund	(3,302,777)	(3,302,777)	(3,236,250)	66,527
Transfer to Human Services Fund	(662,030)	(1,074,537)	(1,074,537)	-
Transfer to Children's Services Act Fund	(1,804,722)	(2,064,092)	(2,064,092)	-
Transfer to Virginia Juvenile Comm Crime Control Act Fund	(108,415)	(108,415)	(108,415)	-
Transfer to Transit Fund	(2,437,365)	(2,942,409)	(2,942,409)	-
Transfer to Debt Service Fund	(10,924,263)	(11,003,348)	(11,003,348)	-
Transfer to Capital Projects Fund	(5,458,198)	(8,817,712)	(8,734,280)	83,432
Transfer to Golf Fund	(149,204)	(149,204)	(149,204)	-
Transfer to Gas Fund	-	(59,700)	(59,700)	-
Transfer to Retirement Fund	-	(500,000)	(500,000)	-
Total Transfers out:	(24,879,974)	(30,066,499)	(29,892,594)	175,905
Total Other Financing Sources (Uses), Net	(24,879,974)	(24,123,844)	(23,947,939)	175,905
Net Change in Fund Balance	$ (8,875,224)	$ (15,167,325)	1,653,647	$ 16,820,975
Fund Balance - July 1, 2018 as restated			46,168,437	
Fund Balance - June 30, 2019			$ 47,822,084	

See Accompanying Note to Required Supplementary Information

Appendix C

CITY OF CHARLOTTESVILLE — MD&A AND STATISTICAL SECTION

CITY OF CHARLOTTESVILLE, VIRGINIA

Management's Discussion and Analysis
Year Ended June 30, 2019

As management of the City of Charlottesville, Virginia, we offer readers this narrative overview and analysis of the financial activities of the City of Charlottesville, Virginia for the fiscal year ended June 30, 2019. Please read it in conjunction with the transmittal letter at the front of this report and the City's financial statements, which follow this section. The intent of this discussion and analysis is to evaluate the City's financial performance as a whole.

FINANCIAL HIGHLIGHTS

Government-wide

- The City's total net position, on a government-wide basis excluding component units, totaled $196.0 million at June 30, 2019. Of this amount, $1.8 million is unrestricted.
- The City's total net position increased by $10.8 million over the prior year. This increase is the sum of a $6.6 million increase, as restated, for the governmental net position and a $4.3 million increase in business-type net position.

Government Funds

- At June 30, 2019, the City's governmental funds reported combined ending fund balances of $77.6 million, an increase of $3.4 million over the prior year. Approximately 38.0 percent, or $33.5 million, of this amount is unassigned.
- The General Fund, on a current financial resource measurement focus and the modified accrual basis of accounting, reported revenues over budget of $1,653,647, primarily due to several of the tax revenues (real estate, personal property, business license, and lodging) performing better than expected. The expenditures and other financing sources (net) finished out the year under budget primarily due City departments continued budget monitoring, which resulted in expenditures less than budget. Savings resulted from vacancies, efficiencies and staff's constant due diligence with city tax dollars.
- At the end of the fiscal year, unassigned fund balance for the General Fund was $33.5 million, or 17.1 percent of total General Fund expenditures and net transfers.

Long-term Liabilities

- The City's total long-term liabilities, consisting of general obligation bonds, compensated absences, pension, and OPEB obligations decreased by $268,039 during the current fiscal year.

OVERVIEW OF THE FINANCIAL STATEMENTS

This discussion and analysis is intended to serve as an introduction to the City of Charlottesville's basic financial statements. The City's basic financial statements comprise the following three components:
- *Government-wide financial statements, Exhibits A and B*
- *Fund financial statements, Exhibits C, D, E, and F*
- *Notes to the financial statements*

This report contains other supplementary information in addition to the basic financial statements themselves.

The basic financial statements include two kinds of statements presenting different views of the City:
- The first two statements are *government-wide financial statements* that provide both *long-term* and *short-term* information about the City's *overall financial status.*
- The remaining statements are *fund financial statements* that focus on *individual parts* of the City's government, reporting the City's operations in *more detail* than the government-wide statements.
  - *Governmental fund* statements tell how *general government* services such as public safety were financed in the *short term* as well as what amounts remain for future spending.
  - *Proprietary fund* statements offer *short-* and *long-term* financial information about the activities the government operates *like businesses,* such as the public utility systems (water, sewer, and gas) and the golf course.
  - *Fiduciary fund* statements provide information about the financial relationship in which the City acts solely as a *trustee or agent* for the benefit of others, to whom the resources in question belong, such as the City's retirement and post-employment benefit plans.

The financial statements also include *notes* that explain some of the information in the financial statements and provide more detailed data. The statements are followed by a section of *required supplementary information* that further explains and supports the information in the financial statements. Figure A shows how the required parts of this *Management's Discussion and Analysis* and the City's *basic financial statements* are arranged and relate to one another.

Figure A
Required Components of City's Financial Statements

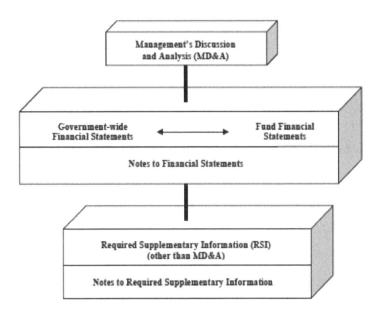

The government-wide financial statements provide both long-term and short-term information about the City's overall financial status. The fund financial statements focus on the individual parts of the City government, reporting the City's operations in more detail than the government-wide statements. Both perspectives (government-wide and fund) allow the user to address relevant questions, broaden the basis of comparison (year-to-year or government-to-government) and enhance the City's accountability.

GOVERNMENT-WIDE FINANCIAL STATEMENTS

The *government-wide financial statements* are designed to provide readers with a broad overview of the City's finances, in a manner similar to a private-sector business.

The *Statement of Net Position* presents financial information on all of the City's assets and liabilities, with the difference reported as net position. Over time, increases or decreases in net position may serve as a useful indicator of whether the financial position of the City is improving or deteriorating.

The *Statement of Activities* presents information showing how the City's net position changed during the most recent fiscal year. All changes in net position are reported as soon as the underlying event giving rise to the change occurs, *regardless of the timing of related cash flows*. Thus, revenues and expenses are reported for some items that will only result in cash flows in future fiscal periods (e.g., uncollected taxes and earned but unused accrued vacation leave.)

The government-wide financial statements distinguish functions of the City that are principally supported by taxes and intergovernmental revenues *(governmental activities)* from other functions that are intended to recover all or a significant portion of their costs through user fees and charges *(business-type activities)*.

In the Statement of Net Position and the Statement of Activities, the City is divided into three categories:

- *Governmental activities* – Most of the City's basic services are included here, such as the activities of the police, fire, public works, social services, parks and recreation departments, and general administration. Property taxes and state and federal grants finance most of these activities.
- *Business-type activities* – The City charges fees to customers to cover the cost of certain services it provides. The City's water, sewer, and gas systems as well as the golf course are included here.
- *Component units* – The City includes two separate legal entities in its report – the City of Charlottesville Economic Development Authority and the Charlottesville Public Schools. Although legally separate, these "component units" are important because the City is financially accountable for them and provides operating funding.

FUND FINANCIAL STATEMENTS

A fund is a grouping of related accounts that is used to maintain control over resources that have been segregated for specific activities or objectives. The City, like other state and local governments, uses fund accounting to ensure and demonstrate compliance with finance-related legal requirements. All the funds of the City of Charlottesville, Virginia can be divided into three categories: governmental funds, proprietary funds, and fiduciary funds.

* *Governmental Funds*. Most of the City's basic services are included in governmental funds, which focus on (1) how cash and other financial assets that can readily be converted to cash flow in and out and (2) the balances remaining at year-end that are available for spending. Consequently, the governmental fund statements provide a detailed *short-term* view that helps the reader determine whether there are more or fewer financial resources that can be spent in the near future to finance the City's programs. Because this information does not encompass the long-term focus of the government-wide financial statements, additional information is provided on a subsequent page that explains the relationship (or differences) between the government-wide and fund financial statements.

* *Proprietary Funds*. Services for which the City charges customers a fee are generally reported in proprietary funds. Proprietary fund statements, like the government-wide financial statements, provide

both short-term and long-term financial information. The City's enterprise funds (one type of proprietary fund) are the same as its business-type activities, with the exception of the Internal Service Funds' allocation, but they provide more detail and additional information, such as a *statement of cash flows*. The City also uses internal service funds (another kind of proprietary fund) to report activities that provide supplies and services for the City's other programs and activities – such as the Risk Management Fund and the Information Technology Fund.

* *Fiduciary Funds*. Fiduciary funds are used to report assets held in a trustee or agency capacity for others outside the government. The City maintains two pension trust funds for retirement and post-employment benefits. These activities are reported in a separate statement of fiduciary net assets. The City excludes this activity from its government-wide financial statements because the City cannot use these assets to finance its operations.

The Total Governmental Funds column requires reconciliation because of the different measurement focus from the government-wide statements (current financial resources versus total economic resources) which is reflected at the bottom of or following each statement. The flow of current financial resources will reflect bond proceeds and inter-fund transfers as other financing sources as well as capital expenditures and bond principal payments as expenditures. The reconciliation will eliminate these transactions and incorporate the capital assets and long-term obligations (bond and others) into the Governmental Activities column (in the government-wide statements).

NOTES TO THE FINANCIAL STATEMENTS

The notes provide additional information that is necessary to acquire a full understanding of the data provided in the government-wide and fund financial statements. The notes to the financial statements can be found following Exhibit F-2 at the end of the basic financial section of this report.

OTHER INFORMATION

In addition to the basic financial statements and accompanying notes, this report also presents *required supplementary information and notes*. General and Social Service major fund budget and actual reports are presented on a budgetary reporting basis as Exhibits G-1 and G-2. Progress in funding its obligations to provide pension and other post-employment benefits (OPEB) plans to its employees is provided as Exhibits H-1, H-2, H-3, H-4, and H-5.

The supplementary section has other major fund budget and actual reports presented on a budgetary reporting basis as Exhibits I-1 and I-2, as well as individual fiduciary statements in Exhibits I-3, and I-4. Non-major governmental funds are presented in Exhibits J, K, K-1, K2, K-3, K-4, K-5, and K-6. Proprietary fund statements are presented as Exhibits E-1, E-2, and E-3. Internal Service funds are presented as Exhibits L-1, L-2, and L-3.

Financial Statements for the Charlottesville School Board – Component unit are presented in Exhibits M-1, M-2, M-3, M-4, M-5, M-6 and M-7. Progress in funding School Board obligation to provide pension and other postemployment benefits (OPEB) plans to its employees is provided as Exhibits N-1, N-2, N-3, N-4, N-5, N-6, and N-7.

FINANCIAL ANALYSIS OF THE CITY AS A WHOLE

Statement of Net Position

The following table reflects the condensed Statement of Net Position:

City of Charlottesville, Virginia
Condensed Statement of Net Position
June 30, 2019 and 2018   **Table I**

	Governmental Activities		Business-Type Activities		Total		Total Percentage Change
	2019	2018*	2019	2018*	2019	2018*	2018-2019
Assets:							
Current and other assets	$ 154,735,155	$ 142,769,674	$ 29,586,961	$ 27,837,914	$ 184,322,116	$ 170,607,588	8.0 %
Capital assets	240,940,779	238,121,136	91,899,003	86,006,083	332,839,782	324,127,219	2.7
Total assets	395,675,934	380,890,810	121,485,964	113,843,597	517,161,898	494,734,807	4.5
Deferred Outflow of							
Resources	24,243,867	27,722,665	2,934,733	3,255,204	27,178,600	30,977,869	(12.3)
Liabilities:							
Long-term liabilities outstanding	199,997,795	208,506,596	62,079,349	62,569,770	262,077,144	271,076,366	(3.3)
Other liabilities	26,902,631	16,551,531	9,498,021	5,927,403	36,400,652	22,478,934	61.9
Total liabilities	226,900,426	225,058,127	71,577,370	68,497,173	298,477,796	293,555,300	1.7
Deferred Inflow of							
Resources	48,804,317	46,298,441	1,056,971	1,085,210	49,861,288	47,383,651	5.2
Net position:							
Net investment in capital assets	150,327,831	147,349,262	43,208,912	41,719,356	193,536,743	189,068,618	2.4
Restricted							
Public safety	470,480	142,581	-	-	470,480	142,581	230.0
Parks, recreation, and culture	6,560	197,518	-	-	6,560	197,518	-
Health and welfare	17,071	-	-	-	17,071	-	
Conservation and development	10,000	-	-	-	10,000	-	100.0
Nonexpendable permanent fund	164,422	184,504	-	-	164,422	184,504	(10.9)
Unrestricted	(6,781,306)	(10,209,157)	8,577,443	5,800,462	1,796,137	(4,408,695)	(140.7)
Total net position *	$ 144,215,058	$ 137,664,708	$ 51,786,355	$ 47,519,818	$ 196,001,413	$ 185,184,526	5.8

*As restated.

Net position (the difference between assets and liabilities plus deferred outflows of resources less deferred inflows of resources) may serve over time as a useful indicator of a government's financial position. In the case of the City of Charlottesville, the net position was $196.0 million at the close of fiscal year 2019. The largest portion of the City's net position reflects its net investment in capital assets (e.g., land, buildings, equipment, and infrastructure) less accumulated depreciation, less any related outstanding debt and adding unspent proceeds from debt used to acquire those assets. The City uses these assets to provide services to its citizens and consequently, these assets are not available for future spending. The resources needed to repay the debt related to these capital assets must be provided from other sources.

Governmental Activities

The net position of the City's governmental activities increased from $137.7 million to $144.2 million.

Business-type Activities

The City's business-type activities net position increased by $4.3 million primarily due to a consistent increase in net position of all utility activities. Business-type activity resources are not to be used to make up for a net position deficit in the governmental activities. In general, the City can only use the unrestricted net position of business-type activities to finance the continued operations of its enterprise operations, which include the Water, Sewer, Stormwater, Gas and Meadowcreek Golf Course funds.

Statement of Activities

The following table shows the revenues and expenses of the governmental and business-type activities:

City of Charlottesville, Virginia
Changes in Net Position
For the Years Ended June 30, 2019 and 2018   Table II

	Governmental Activities		Business-Type Activities		Total		Total Percentage Change
	2019	2018	2019	2018	2019	2018	2018-2019
Revenues:							
Program Revenues:							
Charges for services	$ 15,370,819	$ 12,111,145	$ 56,842,922	$ 50,811,369	$ 72,213,741	$ 62,922,514	14.8 %
Operating grants and contributions	21,336,890	11,797,231	24,287	-	21,361,177	11,797,231	81.1
Capital grants and contributions	877,575	3,490,466	-	-	877,575	3,490,466	(74.9)
General Revenues:							
Property taxes	80,460,113	75,042,232	-	-	80,460,113	75,042,232	7.2
Other taxes	50,937,245	44,503,888	-	-	50,937,245	44,503,888	14.5
Grants and contributions*	39,975,597	54,414,478	-	158,054	39,975,597	54,572,532	-
Miscellaneous	896,195	980,353	297,137	15,116	1,193,332	995,469	-
Use of money and property	2,926,912	1,297,431	222,983	125,665	3,149,895	1,423,096	121.3
Total revenues	212,781,346	203,637,224	57,387,329	51,110,204	270,168,675	254,747,428	6.1
Expenses:							
General government	28,445,537	21,921,172	-	-	28,445,537	21,921,172	29.8
Public safety	39,513,247	39,334,221	-	-	39,513,247	39,334,221	0.5
Community services	22,110,867	19,938,224	-	-	22,110,867	19,938,224	10.9
Health and welfare	35,670,836	34,893,670	-	-	35,670,836	34,893,670	2.2
Parks, recreation and culture	14,061,131	13,476,760	-	-	14,061,131	13,476,760	4.3
Education	55,709,768	52,237,967	-	-	55,709,768	52,237,967	6.6
Conservation and development	15,426,140	15,142,115	-	-	15,426,140	15,142,115	1.9
Interest on long term debt	860,768	3,705,543	-	-	860,768	3,705,543	(76.8)
Water	-	-	10,037,485	9,056,356	10,037,485	9,056,356	10.8
Sewer	-	-	13,623,419	10,762,194	13,623,419	10,762,194	26.6
Gas	-	-	22,276,461	23,467,175	22,276,461	23,467,175	(5.1)
Stormwater	-	-	684,091	570,454	684,091	570,454	-
Golf	-	-	932,038	889,392	932,038	889,392	4.8
Total expenses	211,798,294	200,649,672	47,553,494	44,745,571	259,351,788	245,395,243	5.7
Change in net position before transfers	983,052	2,987,552	9,833,835	6,364,633	10,816,887	9,352,185	15.7
Transfers	5,567,298	5,264,759	(5,567,298)	(5,264,759)	-	-	*
Change in net position	6,550,350	8,252,311	4,266,537	1,099,874	10,816,887	9,352,185	15.7
Net position - beginning of year, restated **	137,664,708	129,004,596	47,519,818	46,419,944	185,184,526	175,424,540	5.6
Net position - end of year	$ 144,215,058	$ 137,256,907	$ 51,786,355	$ 47,519,818	$ 196,001,413	$ 184,776,725	6.1

* Not restricted to specific programs.
** FY19 Net position beginning balance was restated due to restatement in the General Fund.

Governmental Activities

The City's total revenues from governmental activities were $212.8 million for the fiscal year ended June 30, 2019.

Approximately 61.3% of the City's revenue from governmental activities comes from property and other taxes (58.8% in 2018).

Revenues by Source – Governmental Activities

City of Charlottesville
Sources of Revenue for Fiscal Year 2019
Governmental Activities

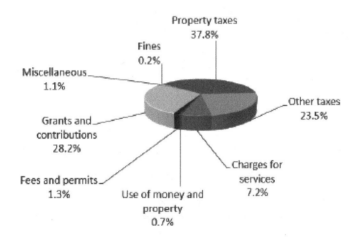

The City's governmental activity expenses increased by $7.5 million in 2019. Expenses for fiscal year 2019 cover a wide range of services, with 16.8% or $35.7 million related to health and welfare, 26.3% or $54.8 million for education (primarily payments to the City's Public Schools, a component unit), and 18.7% or $38.1 million related to public safety.

Expenses by Function – Governmental Activities

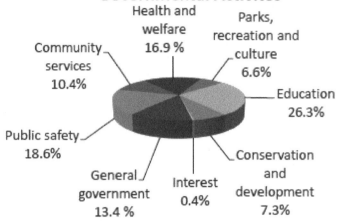

City of Charlottesville
Functional Expenses for Fiscal Year 2019
Governmental Activites

Health and welfare 16.9 %

Parks, recreation and culture 6.6%

Community services 10.4%

Education 26.3%

Public safety 18.6%

General government 13.4 %

Interest 0.4%

Conservation and development 7.3%

Business-Type Activities

Net position for the City's business-type increased by $4.3 million.

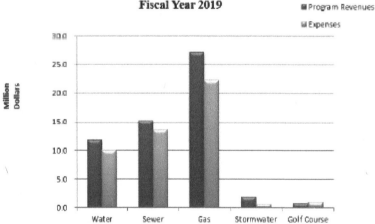

City of Charlottesville
Expenses and Program Revenues
Business-type Activities
Fiscal Year 2019

■ Program Revenues
■ Expenses

FINANCIAL ANALYSIS OF THE CITY'S FUNDS

The City of Charlottesville uses fund accounting to ensure and demonstrate compliance with finance-related legal requirements.

Governmental Funds

The focus of Charlottesville's governmental funds is to provide information on near-term inflows, outflows and balances of spendable resources. In particular, restricted, committed, assigned, and unassigned fund balances may serve as a useful measure of a city's net resources available at the end of a fiscal year. For the fiscal year ended June 30, 2019, the governmental funds reported combined ending fund balances of $77.6 million, an increase of $3.4 million, with restatement, in comparison with the prior year. Included in this are the following major transactions:

- $10.2 million spent in the Capital Projects Fund for capital outlay to fund McIntire Park trail, Circuit Court renovation, CHS track, Skateboard Park, replacement Fire apparatus, road and sidewalk construction and other projects.
- $54.8 million net, contributed by the City's governmental funds to finance the Public Schools' operations.

Approximately $43.5 million of the combined total fund balances constitutes committed and assigned fund balance, which generally is available for spending at the government's discretion. This balance includes $12.8 million committed for debt service.

Nonspendable fund balance is $164.4 thousand from the Permanent Fund. This amount represents assets that are not readily available to the City for current expenditures. The City also has $504.1 thousand in restricted fund balance. Restricted fund balance represents resources that have restrictions placed on them by an outside party. In this case, the City has received grant funds that must be used for a specific purpose but have not yet been spent.

The remaining fund balance at June 30, 2019, indicated as unassigned, is $33.5 million in the General Fund. This amount represents 17.9% of General Fund expenditures and transfers (net) and is a measure of the General Fund's liquidity. Total fund balance of the General Fund increased by $1.7 million in fiscal year 2019.

Proprietary Funds

The City of Charlottesville's proprietary fund statements provide the same type of information found in the government-wide financial statements, but in more detail.

The Water Fund had an increase in net position of $1,105,155. The Sewer Fund had an increase in net position of $739,096. The Gas Fund had an increase in net position of $1,064,962. The Stormwater Fund had an increase in net position of $1,332,171. The Golf Fund had an increase in net position of $21,572.

GENERAL FUND BUDGETARY HIGHLIGHTS

General Fund
For the Year Ended June 30, 2019   Table III

	Original Budget	Amended Budget	Actual	Variance Positive/(Negative)
Revenues				
Real Estate taxes	$ 68,267,693	$ 68,267,693	$ 70,804,123	$ 2,536,430
Other taxes	56,768,649	56,768,649	59,653,529	2,884,880
Intergovernmental	31,354,271	31,354,271	29,230,239	(2,124,032)
Other	13,994,882	5,893,842	15,640,113	9,746,271
Total	170,385,495	162,284,455	175,328,004	13,043,549
Expenditures and transfers (net)				
Expenditures	153,213,158	161,428,977	149,726,418	11,702,559
Transfers (net)	19,114,230	24,123,844	23,947,939	175,905
Total	172,327,388	185,552,821	173,674,357	11,878,464
Change in Fund Balance	$ (1,941,893)	$ (23,268,366)	$ 1,653,647	$ 24,922,013

The City's budget ordinance includes, as part of the original budget for expenditures, the amount of $1,107,752 for encumbrances re-appropriated from June 30, 2018, as well as continuing appropriations from the prior year totaling $2,839,995 for equipment and facilities as well as $2,390,433 for the Landfill Remediation Reserve.

Differences between the original and the final amended budget for the City's General Fund for expenditures, totaled $13,225,433. This difference is primarily due to the continuing appropriations from the prior year and supplemental appropriations during the year.

Actual total revenues were greater than the amended budget by $1,653,648, primarily due to higher than estimated tax revenues. Several of the significant differences between budgeted and actual revenue were in meals tax, lodging tax, real estate tax and personal property tax. Expenditures and transfers were below budget by $11,878,467.

CAPITAL ASSETS AND DEBT ADMINISTRATION

Capital Assets

The City of Charlottesville's investment in capital assets for its governmental and business-type activities as of June 30, 2019, amounts to $332.7 million (net of depreciation). This investment includes land, municipal and school buildings and improvements, water, sewer and gas distribution systems, machinery and equipment, roads, and bridges.

City of Charlottesville's Capital Assets
(net of accumulated depreciation)
June 30, 2019 and 2018

Table IV

| | Governmental Activities | | Business-Type Activities | | Total | | Percentage Change |
	2019	2018	2019	2018	2019	2018	2018-2019
Land	$ 21,786,374	$ 21,725,574	$ 2,064,048	$ 2,064,048	$ 23,850,422	$ 23,789,622	0.3 %
Assets under construction	35,342,072	31,068,020	-	-	35,342,072	31,068,020	-
Buildings and improvements	99,517,726	99,887,488	449,553	485,544	99,967,279	100,373,032	(0.4)
Vehicles	10,125,601	8,396,885	1,285,903	1,018,550	11,411,504	9,415,435	21.2
Equipment	3,937,585	3,809,991	360,947	464,100	4,298,532	4,274,091	0.6
Streets	40,382,215	42,235,196	-	-	40,382,215	42,235,196	(4.4)
Bridges	2,408,370	2,540,270			2,408,370	2,540,270	(5.2)
Infrastructure	27,440,836	28,457,712	87,738,552	81,976,840	115,179,388	110,434,552	4.3
Total	$ 240,940,779	$ 238,121,136	$ 91,899,003	$ 86,009,082	$ 332,839,782	$ 324,130,218	2.7

Major capital asset additions during the fiscal year included the following:

- Utility Infrastructure Improvements (Water, Sewer, and Stormwater)
- McIntire Park Trail Bridge
- Circuit Court Renovations
- CHS Track Improvements

The City's fiscal year 2019 capital budget provided approximately $24.9 million for various capital projects. Some of the major categories include $2.1 million in school related projects, $1.2 million for street projects, $7.7 million for parks and recreation facility improvements, $2.5 million for public safety, and $10.5 million for urban redevelopment and housing, General obligation bonds have been issued for a portion of the funding, in accordance with the City's on-going, five year capital plan.

Additional information about the City of Charlottesville's capital assets can be found in note 8 of the notes to the financial statements.

Long-term Liabilities

At the end of the current fiscal year, the City of Charlottesville had total bonded debt (including unamortized premiums, and notes payable) outstanding of $144.1 million. This entire amount is backed by the full faith and credit of the City and $48.7 million is being repaid by the City's utilities.

City of Charlottesville's Outstanding Debt
General Obligation Bonds
June 30, 2019 and 2018

Table V

| | Governmental Activities | | Business-Type Activities | | Total | | Total Percentage Change |
	2019	2018	2019	2018	2019	2018	2018-2019
General obligation bonds	$ 87,670,733	$ 92,582,812	$ 49,234,305	$ 48,728,590	$ 136,905,038	$ 141,311,402	(3.1) %
Total	$ 87,670,733	$ 92,582,812	$ 49,234,305	$ 48,728,590	$ 136,905,038	$ 141,311,402	(3.1) %

Charlottesville's total debt increased by $2.8 million during the fiscal year. On its most recent bond issue in May 2019, the City's bond rating was reaffirmed by Standard & Poor's Corporation and Moody's Investors Service, as AAA and Aaa, respectively.

State statutes limit the amount of general obligation debt a government entity may issue to 10 percent of its total assessed valuation of real property. The current debt limitation for the City of Charlottesville is $766 million. This is significantly more than the City's current total outstanding debt.

Additional information on the City of Charlottesville's long-term liabilities can be found in note 9 of the notes to the financial statements.

ECONOMIC FACTORS AND NEXT YEAR'S BUDGET AND RATES

- The City's unemployment rate has stabilized from its high in 2010 and as of July 2019 is at 2.6%. This compares favorably to the national unemployment rate of 3.7%, and the state's rate of 2.9%.
- City labor force increased 0.99% from 25,758 in July 2018 to 26,014 in July 2019 based on current Virginia Employment Commission statistics.
- The City has an estimated population of 49,281 according to the Weldon Cooper Center for Public Service.

These indicators were taken into account when adopting the General Fund budget for 2020. Amounts available for appropriation in the General Fund budget for 2020 are $192.8 million, an increase of 13.1% over the 2019 budget of $179.7 million.

CONTACTING THE CITY'S FINANCIAL MANAGEMENT

This financial report is designed to provide citizens, taxpayers, customers, investors, and creditors with a general overview of the City's finances and to demonstrate the City's accountability for the funds it receives. If you have questions about this report or need additional financial information, contact the Director of Finance, City of Charlottesville, 605 East Main Street, Charlottesville, Virginia 22902.

STATISTICAL SECTION

39

STATISTICAL SECTION

This section of the City of Charlottesville's comprehensive annual financial report presents detailed information as a context for understanding what the information in the financial statements, note disclosures, and required supplementary information says about the City of Charlottesville's overall financial health.

Contents

Financial Trends **Tables 1 - 4**

These schedules show comparative information about how the City's financial performance has changed over time.

Revenue Capacity **Tables 5 - 10**

These schedules show the City's significant local revenue sources and how they have changed over time.

Debt Capacity **Tables 11 - 14**

These schedules demonstrate the affordability of the City's outstanding debt along with the City's ability to issue additional debt in the future.

Economic and Demographic Information **Tables 15 - 17**

These schedules show the some of the economic and demographic trends that affect the financial health of the City.

Operating Information **Tables 18 - 20**

These schedules contain service and infrastructure data to show some of the services the City provides and the activities it performs.

Sources: Unless otherwise noted, the information in this section is derived from the City's Comprehensive Annual Financial Reports for the relevant year.

NET POSITION BY COMPONENT
LAST TEN FISCAL YEARS

		2019	2018	2017	2016	2015	2014	2013	2012	2011	2010
Governmental activities:											
Net investment in capital assets	$	150,327,831	$ 147,349,262	$ 129,422,307	$ 138,310,542	$ 132,554,513	$ 139,313,423	$ 105,462,444	$ 122,164,890	$ 116,844,116	$ 133,087,240
Restricted For:											
Expendable		-	340,099	378,342	1,097,425	2,200,311	2,441,436	2,191,647	6,402,164	10,000	10,000
Nonexpendable		668,533	184,504	5,663,251	4,891,126	162,501	162,501	162,501	162,501	162,501	162,501
Unrestricted		(6,781,306)	(10,616,958)	34,145,789	11,167,288	23,465,667	67,085,400	85,110,590	60,401,741	72,528,272	66,615,278
Total governmental activities net position	$	144,215,058	$ 137,256,907	$ 169,609,689	$ 155,466,381	$ 158,382,992	$ 209,002,760	$ 192,927,182	$ 189,131,296	$ 189,544,889	$ 199,875,019
Business-type activities:											
Net investment in capital assets	$	43,208,912	$ 41,719,356	$ 33,246,970	$ 28,416,350	$ 26,407,757	$ 25,036,215	$ 37,760,064	$ 21,862,917	$ 21,900,131	$ 21,576,238
Restricted-expendable		-	-	-	-	-	-	-	-	27,817	-
Unrestricted		8,577,443	5,800,462	19,663,499	24,816,588	21,070,253	25,377,815	11,374,395	24,882,257	24,327,004	22,368,111
Total business-type activities net position	$	51,786,355	$ 47,519,818	$ 52,910,469	$ 53,232,938	$ 47,478,010	$ 50,414,030	$ 49,134,459	$ 46,745,174	$ 46,254,952	$ 43,944,349
Primary Government:											
Net investment in capital assets	$	193,536,743	$ 189,068,618	$ 162,669,277	$ 166,726,892	$ 158,962,270	$ 164,349,638	$ 143,222,508	$ 144,027,807	$ 138,744,247	$ 154,663,478
Restricted For:											
Expendable		-	340,099	378,342	1,097,425	2,200,311	2,441,436	2,191,647	6,402,164	37,817	10,000
Nonexpendable		668,533	184,504	5,663,251	4,891,126	162,501	162,501	162,501	162,501	162,501	162,501
Unrestricted		1,796,137	(4,816,496)	53,809,288	35,983,876	44,535,920	92,463,215	96,484,985	85,283,998	96,855,276	88,983,389
Total primary government net position	$	196,001,413	$ 184,776,725	$ 222,520,158	$ 208,699,319	$ 205,861,002	$ 259,416,790	$ 242,061,641	$ 235,876,470	$ 235,799,841	$ 243,819,368

Source: City of Charlottesville Comprehensive Annual Financial Report - Exhibit A

Schedule prepared using the accrual basis of accounting

CHANGES IN NET POSITION
LAST TEN FISCAL YEARS

	2019	2018	2017	2016	2015	2014	2013	2012	2011	2010
Expenses										
Governmental activities:										
General government	$ 28,445,537	$ 21,921,172	$ 25,116,791	$ 27,127,028	$ 26,798,174	$ 24,270,356	$ 23,535,445	$ 22,483,808	$ 23,834,491	$ 20,411,785
Public safety	39,513,247	39,334,221	45,118,838	38,827,913	33,615,106	33,358,670	32,597,684	32,258,520	30,545,881	30,547,357
Community services	22,110,867	19,938,224	25,259,071	23,003,605	22,323,559	20,704,251	20,052,677	23,670,432	22,348,563	21,293,487
Health and welfare	35,670,836	34,893,670	37,155,165	31,493,208	31,115,213	29,785,068	30,274,066	30,034,547	30,820,530	31,358,502
Parks, recreation and culture	14,061,131	13,476,760	17,120,453	13,868,610	12,782,459	12,666,217	12,368,616	11,256,003	10,053,398	9,546,796
Education	55,709,769	52,237,967	52,714,685	50,053,416	52,968,559	45,368,328	51,677,155	42,460,291	57,974,958	41,990,709
Conservation and development	15,426,140	15,142,115	12,626,012	10,244,823	9,501,823	8,870,158	10,373,102	14,171,433	7,743,918	6,985,191
Interest on long-term debt	860,768	3,705,543	1,746,162	2,465,754	3,604,179	2,241,591	2,359,080	5,100,955	2,733,885	2,454,390
Total governmental activities	211,798,294	200,649,672	216,857,177	197,084,153	192,707,182	177,265,830	183,239,625	181,495,789	185,855,204	164,588,197
Business-type activities:										
Water	10,037,485	9,058,356	8,671,472	8,332,731	8,988,566	8,834,334	8,162,082	8,417,556	8,321,515	8,009,139
Sewer	13,623,419	10,782,194	10,301,902	10,583,241	10,770,341	11,503,795	9,858,802	9,829,843	8,416,888	8,640,500
Gas	22,278,461	23,467,175	23,898,603	18,420,330	26,493,000	28,239,126	23,788,374	22,288,691	24,889,854	25,111,699
Other enterprise funds	1,616,129	1,450,846	1,534,483	1,393,942	1,341,548	1,038,023	871,628	912,344	617,357	1,198,157
Total business-type activities	47,563,494	44,745,571	44,506,460	38,730,244	47,593,455	49,615,278	42,680,886	41,448,134	42,225,614	43,159,495
Total Primary Government Expenses	$ 259,351,788	$ 245,395,243	$ 261,383,637	$ 235,814,397	$ 240,300,617	$ 226,881,117	$ 225,920,511	$ 222,883,923	$ 228,080,818	$ 207,747,692
Program Revenues										
Governmental activities:										
Charges for Services										
General government	$ 2,171,318	$ 900,906	$ 7,808,336	$ 13,289,075	$ 13,365,582	$ 14,156,093	$ 14,000,028	$ 12,718,913	$ 11,509,211	$ 10,624,798
Public safety	56,035	165,172	7,130,597	12,349	16,206	10,969	29,778	29,919	31,416	42,850
Community services	1,305,654	1,336,122	5,112,907	1,968,282	1,808,948	1,820,062	1,843,984	1,840,737	1,786,899	1,945,796
Health and welfare	5,235,853	5,594,608	8,753,432	4,653,306	4,588,956	4,203,244	3,923,086	3,950,389	4,305,042	2,719,628
Parks, recreation and culture	1,588,889	1,117,006	5,350,770	1,630,679	1,744,910	1,785,912	1,610,587	1,372,958	1,214,220	943,705
Education	210,003	209,591	1,288,687	214,120	243,413	273,815	208,088	229,949	203,713	228,853
Conservation and development	4,803,087	2,787,740	3,922,782	40,047	34,406	27,506	21,321	28,322	23,487	27,885
Operating Grants and Contributions										
General government	3,065,503	2,503,684	29,242,564	151,621	2,212,016	2,275,879	1,782,119	1,643,234	2,022,309	2,099,757
Public safety	4,686,110	997,866	1,696,764	718,675	869,252	2,647,082	1,675,385	1,908,155	1,632,513	1,554,804
Community services	7,623,041	8,204,371	5,441,190	5,028,690	11,009,042	6,184,560	8,107,968	9,074,860	8,839,499	7,947,633
Health and welfare	1,838,249	18,423,390	17,076,168	18,790,098	17,046,748	15,864,102	16,278,179	16,481,539	17,810,096	18,163,800
Parks, recreation and culture	621,157	844,671	467,158	218,771	142,942	285,800	904,083	76,725	45,382	51,953
Education	-	228,081	347,685	217,188	269,716	232,043	562,087	566,776	566,586	224,203
Conservation and development	3,502,830	3,292,285	4,506,454	185,529	133,588	63,905	238,338	344,349	459,922	
Capital Grants and Contributions										
General government	-	-	-	-	-	-	-	350,876	11,728	630,275
Public safety	154,845	154,845	154,845	-	-	-	12,825	383,584	-	-
Community services	661,930	411,471	592,408	3,039,031	6,948,100	13,486,069	6,776,158	5,070,874	1,990,553	13,285,028
Education	-	-	-	119,915	144,700	-	-	458,441	113,912	22,432
Conservation and development	60,800	3,323,240	5,977,748	-	33,162	16,839	59,500	115,398	-	
Total governmental activities	37,585,284	50,294,829	104,810,495	48,217,374	60,631,775	65,113,570	58,014,392	58,641,972	52,566,462	60,512,800
Business-type activities:										
Charges for Services										
Water	11,815,767	11,049,045	11,189,238	10,311,760	9,868,917	9,183,447	9,064,161	8,923,040	9,244,578	9,134,985
Sewer	15,201,858	14,562,317	14,704,642	13,254,116	11,970,322	11,338,480	10,554,384	9,121,471	9,086,402	8,952,616
Gas	27,104,835	22,419,210	20,544,734	22,813,188	30,826,233	33,856,411	29,779,891	27,619,960	30,380,501	29,860,371
Other enterprise funds	2,720,462	2,780,797	2,810,284	2,719,146	2,818,345	1,780,508	842,787	939,797	949,264	1,084,929
Operating Grants and Contributions										
Other enterprise funds	-	-	-	-	-	-	-	-	17,105	54,667
Capital Grants and Contributions										
Other enterprise funds	-	-	-	-	68,552	-	-	18,800	-	-
Total business-type activities	56,842,922	50,811,369	49,248,898	49,098,210	55,552,369	56,138,826	50,241,223	46,623,068	49,637,850	49,087,568
Total Primary Government Revenues	$ 94,428,206	$ 101,106,198	$ 154,059,391	$ 97,315,584	$ 116,184,144	$ 121,252,396	$ 108,255,615	$ 103,265,040	$ 102,204,312	$ 109,580,368

CHANGES IN NET POSITION

LAST TEN FISCAL YEARS

	2019	2018	2017	2016	2015	2014	2013	2012	2011	2010
Net (Expense) Revenue										
Governmental activities:										
General government	$ (23,208,716)	$ (18,516,582)	$ 11,934,109	$ (13,686,330)	$ (11,218,576)	$ (7,838,584)	$ (7,773,298)	$ (7,770,585)	$ (10,091,249)	$ (7,056,935)
Public safety	(34,616,257)	(38,016,538)	(38,196,632)	(38,096,689)	(32,709,738)	(30,700,919)	(30,879,696)	(29,938,862)	(28,861,752)	(28,949,903)
Community services	(12,520,242)	(9,986,260)	(14,112,566)	(12,987,602)	(2,557,469)	2,786,440	(3,324,589)	(7,883,961)	(9,731,812)	1,884,970
Health and welfare	(28,596,734)	(10,875,672)	(11,325,585)	(10,109,804)	(9,479,511)	(9,916,622)	(10,073,701)	(9,602,645)	(8,705,392)	(10,475,274)
Parks, recreation and culture	(11,851,085)	(11,715,083)	(11,302,525)	(12,019,160)	(10,894,607)	(10,614,415)	(9,853,948)	(9,806,320)	(8,793,796)	(8,551,138)
Education	(55,499,765)	(51,800,295)	(51,078,313)	(49,502,193)	(52,310,730)	(44,862,670)	(50,908,080)	(41,207,125)	(57,060,767)	(41,515,221)
Conservation and development	(7,059,443)	(5,738,870)	1,780,972	(10,019,047)	(9,300,577)	(8,761,908)	(10,053,943)	(13,883,364)	(7,280,500)	(6,957,506)
Interest on long-term debt	(980,768)	(3,705,543)	(1,746,162)	(2,465,754)	(3,804,179)	(2,241,591)	(2,359,980)	(5,100,955)	(2,733,885)	(2,454,390)
Total governmental activities	(174,213,010)	(150,354,843)	(112,046,682)	(148,866,779)	(132,075,387)	(112,152,289)	(125,225,253)	(124,793,817)	(153,288,742)	(104,075,397)
Business-type activities:										
Water	1,778,282	1,992,689	2,217,764	1,979,029	880,351	329,113	902,079	505,484	923,063	1,125,846
Sewer	1,578,439	3,800,123	4,402,740	2,670,875	1,199,981	(185,395)	695,582	(708,172)	849,514	112,116
Gas	4,828,374	(1,047,965)	(3,153,869)	4,392,858	4,333,233	5,617,285	5,991,517	5,331,269	5,490,847	4,748,672
Other enterprise funds	1,104,333	1,320,951	1,275,801	1,325,204	1,545,349	742,485	(28,841)	46,353	349,012	(78,561)
Total business-type activities	9,289,428	6,065,798	4,742,436	10,367,966	7,958,914	6,523,548	7,560,337	5,174,934	7,412,236	5,908,073
Total Primary Government Net Expense	$ (164,923,582)	$ (144,289,045)	$ (107,304,246)	$ (138,498,813)	$ (124,116,473)	$ (105,628,721)	$ (117,664,896)	$ (119,618,883)	$ (125,876,506)	$ (98,167,324)
General Revenues and Other Changes in Net Position										
Governmental activities:										
General Revenues:										
General property taxes	$ 80,460,113	$ 75,042,292	$ 68,384,143	$ 62,940,310	$ 59,586,818	$ 58,158,711	$ 56,060,959	$ 55,819,958	$ 55,401,204	$ 55,625,137
Sales tax	11,876,599	11,819,460	11,870,485	11,466,250	10,767,283	10,747,757	9,901,299	9,995,523	8,956,683	9,312,884
Utility tax	4,764,420	4,616,495	4,540,179	4,478,748	4,614,299	4,539,149	4,422,168	4,252,785	4,491,381	4,419,303
Communications tax	2,716,128	2,927,794	3,022,277	3,098,436	3,192,060	3,221,105	3,276,861	3,288,192	3,335,988	3,352,581
Meals tax	12,212,802	11,761,447	11,746,648	11,320,042	8,703,398	8,156,709	8,103,257	7,378,230	6,861,086	6,454,883
Lodging tax	5,859,226	5,151,629	4,846,549	3,664,156	3,166,309	2,933,227	2,932,367	2,807,326	2,460,055	2,475,914
Other taxes	12,261,038	4,256,433	4,593,226	4,511,753	4,319,279	4,139,312	4,022,679	4,059,205	4,317,180	3,762,710
Business license tax	1,447,032	8,767,125	7,918,003	6,925,402	6,788,971	6,442,388	6,680,942	6,491,428	6,061,192	6,502,949
Grants and contributions not restricted	39,075,507	27,056,841	-	30,117,894	23,502,728	24,353,298	27,910,750	24,887,083	25,229,097	25,160,421
Unrestricted revenue from use of money and property	1,893,575	1,297,431	-	-	-	-	-	-	-	-
Interest and investment earnings	1,033,337	-	406,825	341,347	385,070	259,548	276,657	373,961	538,029	918,853
Miscellaneous	898,195	980,353	-	-	-	-	-	-	-	-
Transfers, net	5,567,298	5,284,759	-	-	-	-	-	-	-	-
Gain from sale of assets	-	-	-	-	-	-	-	252,742	-	-
Total governmental activities	180,783,380	158,761,999	117,128,225	138,864,338	124,987,095	122,951,202	123,787,939	119,586,433	117,652,755	117,985,195
Business-type activities:										
Interest and investment earnings	206,128	-	101,036	141,362	113,151	32,668	62,128	109,079	204,224	240,142
Total business-type activities	206,128	-	101,036	141,362	113,151	32,668	62,128	109,079	204,224	240,142
Total Primary Government Revenues	$ 180,989,488	$ 158,761,999	$ 117,229,261	$ 139,005,700	$ 125,100,246	$ 122,983,870	$ 123,850,067	$ 119,695,512	$ 117,856,979	$ 118,225,337
Change in net position										
Governmental Activities	$ 6,550,350	$ 8,252,311	$ 10,372,952	$ (4,803,942)	$ (1,773,911)	$ 16,075,578	$ 3,795,886	$ (413,593)	$ (10,330,130)	$ 16,452,891
Business-type Activities	4,266,537	1,099,874	(322,469)	5,310,729	2,757,684	1,279,571	2,389,285	490,222	2,310,803	1,132,261
Total change in net position	$ 10,816,887	$ 9,352,185	$ 10,050,483	$ 506,787	$ 983,773	$ 17,355,149	$ 6,185,171	$ 76,629	$ (8,019,527)	$ 19,584,952

Source: City of Charlottesville Comprehensive Annual Financial Report - Exhibit B

Schedule prepared using the accrual basis of accounting

FUND BALANCES OF GOVERNMENTAL FUNDS
LAST TEN FISCAL YEARS

							Fiscal Year												
	2019		2018		2017		2016		2015		2014		2013		2012		2011		2010
General Fund																			
Reserved	$ -	$	-	$	-	$	-	$	-	$	-	$	-	$	-	$	-	$	1,180,647
Unreserved:																			
Designated	-		-		-		-		-		-		-		-		-		10,363,172
Undesignated	-		-		-		-		-		-		-		-		-		24,271,261
Total General Fund	$ -	$	-	$	-	$	-	$	-	$	-	$	-	$	-	$	-	$	35,815,080
All Other Governmental Funds																			
Reserved	$ -	$	-	$	-	$	-	$	-	$	-	$	-	$	-	$	-	$	14,555,925
Unreserved:																			
Capital Projects Funds	-		-		-		-		-		-		-		-		-		6,866,651
Social Service Funds	-		-		-		-		-		-		-		-		-		483,543
Special Revenue Funds	-		-		-		-		-		-		-		-		-		1,328,208
Debt Service Funds	-		-		-		-		-		-		-		-		-		9,547,048
Permanent Fund	-		-		-		-		-		-		-		-		-		162,501
Total All Other Governmental Funds	$ -	$	-	$	-	$	-	$	-	$	-	$	-	$	-	$	-	$	32,943,876
General Fund																			
Nonspendable	$ 1,920	$	22,002	$	-	$	-	$	-	$	-	$	-	$	-	$	-	$	-
Restricted	327,770		637,910		-		656,777		728,278		725,441		545,723		472,096		462,244		-
Committed	7,990,059		8,779,538		4,931,956		6,732,612		6,363,639		7,004,685		6,737,955		8,206,185		7,880,346		-
Assigned	6,229,997		5,818,834		1,102,935		7,804,945		5,130,563		3,786,220		3,633,160		4,542,491		5,945,930		-
Unassigned	33,272,338		30,902,351		41,933,825		29,054,913		28,251,814		27,291,468		26,989,410		26,861,656		25,855,782		-
Total General Fund	$ 47,822,084	$	45,760,635	$	47,968,716	$	44,249,247	$	40,474,294	$	38,807,814	$	37,906,248	$	40,082,388	$	40,144,301	$	-
All Other Governmental Funds																			
Nonspendable	$ 162,502	$	162,502	$	5,663,250	$	4,891,126	$	1,260,860	$	1,542,501	$	1,272,501	$	3,316,211	$	3,380,174	$	-
Restricted	176,341		2,951,459		8,300,066		440,648		6,159,927		4,216,750		9,486,035		15,949,126		20,687,703		-
Committed	12,830,074		11,905,368		15,541,112		12,082,178		11,745,744		15,202,070		14,768,068		11,252,983		9,508,177		-
Assigned	16,622,433		18,153,704		1,977,246		7,770,919		5,928,263		1,364,421		1,303,256		1,906,602		1,681,261		-
Unassigned	-		(5,117,190)		-		-		-		-		-		-		-		-
Total All Other Governmental Funds	$ 29,791,350	$	28,055,843	$	31,481,674	$	25,184,871	$	25,094,794	$	22,325,742	$	26,829,860	$	32,424,922	$	35,257,315	$	-

Source: City of Charlottesville Comprehensive Annual Financial Report - Exhibit C

Note: Fiscal years 2009 through 2010 have not been restated per GASB 54. Fiscal years prior to 2018 have not been restated for GASB 75.

Schedule prepared using the modified accrual basis of accounting

CITY OF CHARLOTTESVILLE, VIRGINIA

TABLE 4

CHANGES IN FUND BALANCES OF GOVERNMENTAL FUNDS
LAST TEN FISCAL YEARS

	2019	2018	2017	2016	2015	2014	2013	2012	2011	2010
Revenues										
General property taxes	$ 130,457,652	$ 122,040,706	$ 116,721,600	$ 108,365,439	$ 101,869,696	$ 98,699,930	$ 95,714,241	$ 94,311,894	$ 92,111,297	$ 92,251,458
Fee and permits	2,852,058	2,719,933	2,575,469	2,169,777	2,283,548	1,986,695	2,464,889	2,042,063	1,825,729	1,640,727
Intergovernmental	60,040,284	61,456,198	61,924,408	55,288,548	60,955,984	66,426,300	60,215,042	61,026,601	58,295,118	67,888,839
Charges for services	15,313,883	11,917,913	12,117,670	11,701,232	11,685,158	10,920,381	10,607,302	10,065,910	10,291,768	8,088,430
Fines and forfeitures	362,381	419,344	481,032	481,630	476,632	393,396	392,763	552,075	567,027	392,515
Miscellaneous	3,394,302	3,381,950	2,789,931	2,386,349	2,296,159	2,226,308	5,056,883	2,036,426	2,011,104	2,734,433
Total governmental revenues	212,420,560	202,836,046	196,610,110	180,372,975	179,567,155	180,633,212	174,451,120	170,034,969	164,952,043	172,966,402
Expenditures										
General government	26,980,864	20,817,229	18,107,974	17,206,445	18,446,310	14,625,220	15,352,223	15,117,332	14,653,299	13,844,581
Public safety	38,240,448	39,397,475	35,081,163	36,357,223	33,290,687	32,609,199	31,987,432	32,231,433	30,480,298	30,780,038
Community services	19,006,475	16,980,656	17,257,531	18,470,598	20,824,429	21,796,529	18,524,126	23,573,132	21,264,573	21,000,353
Health and welfare	35,736,307	35,175,725	32,346,026	30,975,824	31,318,573	29,948,939	31,196,387	30,211,972	30,929,233	31,483,066
Parks, recreation and culture	13,326,020	12,709,049	11,912,756	13,023,170	12,152,256	11,739,822	12,229,739	10,586,859	9,870,613	9,129,591
Education	54,796,480	51,757,047	50,385,279	49,397,353	46,999,266	44,279,012	45,526,167	41,983,543	41,088,749	41,104,359
Conservation and development	13,244,853	13,070,791	9,620,535	10,710,688	8,928,692	7,469,535	8,764,632	13,711,905	7,109,914	6,395,913
Debt service										
Principal	7,140,323	7,417,376	7,146,682	6,379,799	6,064,318	6,685,521	6,430,175	6,611,249	6,236,895	5,926,398
Interest	3,041,563	3,099,780	2,832,293	2,591,814	2,680,459	2,725,366	2,452,754	2,855,961	2,550,831	2,407,670
Miscellaneous	-	-	123,892	172,063	384,966	100,571	87,599	198,062	94,848	107,867
Other activities	-	-	289,665	1,055,402	1,052,619	975,456	266,562	255,994	298,737	276,671
Capital outlay	13,391,752	16,960,272	19,795,285	5,613,733	11,713,606	23,165,369	21,380,655	11,213,317	9,882,212	28,702,858
Total governmental expenditures	224,847,085	217,385,401	204,900,181	191,954,112	193,856,381	196,320,539	194,198,451	188,548,759	174,420,140	191,133,353
Revenues over (under) expenditures	(12,426,525)	(14,547,355)	(8,290,071)	(11,581,137)	(14,289,226)	(15,687,327)	(19,747,331)	(18,513,790)	(9,468,097)	(18,166,951)
Other financing sources (uses)										
Transfers in	36,720,138	38,479,757	32,386,616	30,657,532	29,059,645	29,291,985	31,047,043	31,879,012	27,888,963	30,642,078
Transfers out	(31,551,066)	(31,547,212)	(27,186,718)	(25,140,392)	(22,880,748)	(23,356,855)	(25,108,773)	(26,698,163)	(22,054,595)	(24,733,114)
Issuance of debt	9,520,000	4,610,000	11,140,000	7,250,000	11,405,000	5,740,000	5,610,000	9,133,200	9,650,400	10,211,600
Refunding bonds issued	-	-	-	3,875,466	11,663,366	1,390,695	-	17,737,100	-	-
Premium on issuance of debt	1,126,806	420,561	1,076,892	1,282,326	2,261,124	417,486	427,859	3,411,666	616,989	93,887
Payment to refunded bond escrow agent	-	-	-	(4,385,996)	(13,098,411)	(1,506,186)	-	(20,195,331)	-	-
Sale of capital assets	-	-	-	-	312,782	107,650	-	352,000	9,000	-
Total other financing sources (uses)	15,815,878	11,963,106	17,436,790	13,558,936	18,724,758	12,084,775	11,976,129	15,619,484	16,110,757	16,214,449
Net change in fund balances	$ 3,389,153	$ (2,584,249)	$ 9,146,719	$ 1,977,799	$ 4,435,532	$ (3,602,552)	$ (7,771,202)	$ (2,894,306)	$ 6,642,660	$ (1,952,502)
Debt service as a percentage of noncapital expenditures										
Total debt service expenditures	$ 10,181,886	$ 10,517,156	$ 10,103,067	$ 8,971,613	$ 8,744,777	$ 9,410,887	$ 8,882,929	$ 9,467,210	$ 8,787,726	$ 8,334,066
Total governmental expenditures	224,847,085	217,385,401	204,900,181	191,954,112	193,856,381	196,320,539	194,198,451	188,548,759	174,420,140	191,133,353
Change in capital assets	(13,346,753)	(16,960,272)	(21,634,978)	(9,215,151)	(16,487,414)	(27,697,576)	(22,573,753)	(15,554,651)	(14,212,438)	(32,444,266)
Noncapital expenditures	$ 211,500,332	$ 200,425,129	$ 183,265,203	$ 182,738,961	$ 177,368,967	$ 168,622,963	$ 171,624,698	$ 172,994,108	$ 160,207,702	$ 158,689,087
Debt service as a percentage of noncapital expenditures	4.81%	5.25%	5.45%	4.91%	4.93%	5.58%	5.18%	5.47%	5.49%	5.25%

Source: City of Charlottesville Comprehensive Annual Financial Report - Exhibit D

Schedule prepared using the modified accrual basis of accounting

TAX REVENUES BY SOURCE
LAST TEN FISCAL YEARS

Fiscal Year	Total Taxes	Property Taxes (1)	Sales and Use Taxes	Utility and Communications Taxes (2)	Meals Tax	Lodging Tax	Business License Tax	Franchise Taxes (2)	Tax on Bank Stock	Tax on Wills and Deeds	Other Taxes
2019	$ 130,457,651	$ 81,561,358	$ 11,876,599	$ 7,480,548	$ 12,212,802	$ 5,659,226	$ 8,540,881	$ 3,500	$ 1,369,883	$ 751,569	$ 1,001,285
2018	122,940,708	75,616,895	11,619,460	7,658,576	11,781,447	5,151,629	8,230,107	3,500	1,348,260	581,600	949,234
2017	116,724,600	69,739,801	11,670,485	7,562,456	11,746,648	4,846,549	7,918,093	3,500	1,226,609	904,353	1,106,106
2016	108,365,439	64,620,157	11,466,250	7,577,184	11,320,042	3,664,156	6,925,402	3,500	1,138,188	585,246	1,065,314
2015	101,869,696	62,020,045	10,767,263	7,807,259	8,703,398	3,166,309	6,788,971	3,500	982,185	554,805	1,075,961
2014	98,699,930	60,203,592	10,747,757	7,760,254	8,156,709	2,933,227	6,442,386	7,000	923,869	565,320	959,816
2013	95,714,241	57,894,427	9,901,299	7,699,029	8,103,257	2,932,367	6,880,942	13,880	851,638	604,597	832,805
2012	94,311,894	57,774,887	9,995,523	7,520,977	7,378,230	2,807,326	6,491,428	10,440	1,051,723	493,248	788,112
2011	92,111,297	57,336,116	8,956,683	7,827,349	6,861,066	2,460,055	6,061,192	26,402	1,358,812	436,709	786,913
2010	92,251,458	57,520,194	9,312,664	7,771,884	6,454,663	2,475,914	6,502,949	3,500	975,779	403,918	829,993

Source: City of Charlottesville Comprehensive Annual Financial Report - Exhibit G

(1) Beginning in 1998, the Commonwealth of Virginia pays a portion of the personal property tax formerly paid by the property owner; the Commonwealth's share is reported as intergovernmental revenue.

(2) Beginning in January 1, 2007, the Commonwealth of Virginia enacted the Virginia Communication Tax. This new tax replaces most of the current Virginia state and local communications taxes and fees with a central administered Communications Sales and Use Tax, a uniform statewide E-911 tax on landline telephone service and a cable television provider's public right-of-way use fee.

CITY OF CHARLOTTESVILLE, VIRGINIA

TABLE 6

ASSESSED AND ESTIMATED MARKET VALUE OF REAL PROPERTY (1)
LAST TEN CALENDAR YEARS

Taxable Year	Real Estate	Public Service Real Estate	Total Taxable Real Property Assessed Value	Real Property Direct Tax Rate	Tax-Exempt Real Property	Total Value Real Property
2019	$ 7,647,893,000	$ 152,574,032	$ 7,800,467,032	0.95	$ 2,046,675,800	$ 9,847,142,832
2018	7,060,139,700	151,135,069	7,211,274,769	0.95	1,917,683,250	9,128,958,019
2017	6,740,234,600	143,303,198	6,883,537,798	0.95	1,746,952,600	8,630,490,398
2016	5,953,910,000	140,924,014	6,094,834,014	0.95	1,135,055,400	7,229,889,414
2015	5,704,217,700	142,650,296	5,846,867,996	0.95	1,027,382,800	6,874,250,796
2014	5,503,669,500	137,745,380	5,641,414,880	0.95	1,017,616,600	6,659,031,480
2013	5,281,021,000	138,256,036	5,419,277,036	0.95	1,012,716,900	6,431,993,936
2012	5,222,661,300	138,241,036	5,360,902,336	0.95	1,016,573,300	6,377,475,636
2011	5,282,859,100	135,463,526	5,418,322,626	0.95	1,016,346,400	6,434,669,026
2010	5,257,182,700	135,809,935	5,392,992,635	0.95	1,053,205,500	6,446,198,135

Source: Records of the City Assessor and State Corporation Commission

Note: The City has no overlapping property taxes.
(1) Assessed values of all classes of property are the approximate market value.

CITY OF CHARLOTTESVILLE, VIRGINIA

TABLE 7

DIRECT PROPERTY TAX RATES
(PER $100 OF ASSESSED VALUE)
LAST TEN CALENDAR YEARS

Year	Real Property (1)	Personal Property (2)	Machinery & Tools (2)	Total Direct Tax Rate of City Assessed Property	Public Service Real Property (3)	Public Service Personal Property (3)	Total Direct Tax Rate of State Assessed Property
2019	0.95	4.20	4.20	9.35	0.95	4.20	5.15
2018	0.95	4.20	4.20	9.35	0.95	4.20	5.15
2017	0.95	4.20	4.20	9.35	0.95	4.20	5.15
2016	0.95	4.20	4.20	9.35	0.95	4.20	5.15
2015	0.95	4.20	4.20	9.35	0.95	4.20	5.15
2014	0.95	4.20	4.20	9.35	0.95	4.20	5.15
2013	0.95	4.20	4.20	9.35	0.95	4.20	5.15
2012	0.95	4.20	4.20	9.35	0.95	4.20	5.15
2011	0.95	4.20	4.20	9.35	0.95	4.20	5.15
2010	0.95	4.20	4.20	9.35	0.95	4.20	5.15

Source: City of Charlottesville Director of Finance

    (1) Assessed by the City of Charlottesville Real Estate Assessor
    (2) Assessed by the City of Charlottesville Commissioner of Revenue
    (3) Assessed by the State Corporation Commission

Note: The City has no overlapping property taxes.

PRINCIPAL PROPERTY TAXPAYERS
CURRENT YEAR AND NINE YEARS AGO
JUNE 30, 2019

Taxpayer	Type of Business	2019 Assessed Valuation (1)	Tax Amount (2)	Rank	Percentage of Total Assessed Valuation (1)	2010 Assessed Valuation (1)	Tax Amount (2)	Rank	Percentage of Total Assessed Valuation (1)
Federal Realty Investment Trust	Shopping Center	$ 178,884,200	$ 1,699,400	1	2.65 %	$ 81,498,600	$ 774,237	1	1.55 %
Woodard United, LLC	Apartments	120,324,500	1,143,083	2	1.79	-	-		-
Pavilion UVA, LLC & Pavilion II, LLC	Apartments	80,636,900	766,051	3	1.20	-	-		-
Neighborhood Development, Inc.	Apartments	79,580,600	756,016	4	1.18	-	-		-
Madison Loft, LLC	Apartments	68,668,300	652,349	5	1.02	-	-		-
750 Harris Street, LLC	Apartments	68,423,000	650,019	6	1.02	-	-		-
Baron, LLC	Apartments	68,221,700	648,106	7	1.01	-	-		-
Pavilion, LLC	Apartments	67,260,000	638,970	8	1.00	34,605,700	328,754	6	0.66
Court Square, LLC	Real Estate	61,687,200	586,028	9	0.92	-	-		-
Cabell Limited Partnership	Apartments	59,259,400	562,964	10	0.88	-	-		-
Caton, Douglas E.	Real Estate	-	-		-	60,972,500	579,239	2	1.16
Dominion Virginia Power Company	Public Utility	-	-		-	43,700,147	415,151	3	0.83
Wade Apartments	Apartments	-	-		-	42,719,600	405,836	4	0.81
CenturyLink	Public Utility	-	-		-	37,559,490	356,815	5	0.71
Towers Limited Partnership, ETAL	Real Estate	-	-		-	34,285,000	325,708	7	0.65
Peyton Associates Partnership	Real Estate	-	-		-	33,392,400	317,228	8	0.64
University of Virginia Foundation	Real Estate	-	-		-	30,580,200	290,512	9	0.58
JA-Zan Limited Partnership	Retail, Office	-	-		-	25,493,400	242,187	10	0.48
		$ 852,945,800	$ 8,102,985		12.65 %	$ 424,807,037	$ 4,035,667		7.01 %

Source: City Assessor and Commissioner of Revenue, City of Charlottesville, Virginia
(1) Represents percentage of total City valuation of taxable property, real estate only.
(2) Tax rate of $0.95 in 2019; Tax rate of $0.95 in 2010

CITY OF CHARLOTTESVILLE, VIRGINIA

TABLE 9

PROPERTY TAX LEVIES AND COLLECTIONS
LAST TEN FISCAL YEARS

Fiscal Year	Total Tax Levy for Fiscal Year	Collected within the Fiscal Year of the Levy		Collections in Subsequent Years [1]	Total Collections to Date	
		Amount Collected	Percentage of Levy		Amount Collected	Percentage of Levy
2019	$ 83,339,710	$ 82,035,675	98.44 %	$ -	$ 82,035,675	98.44 %
2018	77,696,498	76,521,606	98.49	914,805	76,521,606	98.49
2017	71,965,946	71,139,950	98.85	586,244	71,726,194	99.67
2016	65,952,891	65,027,636	98.60	811,921	65,839,557	99.83
2015	63,892,891	62,863,991	98.39	945,634	63,809,626	99.87
2014	62,251,968	61,010,246	98.01	1,167,668	62,177,914	99.88
2013	60,538,454	59,304,770	97.96	1,178,139	60,482,909	99.91
2012	60,132,379	58,573,010	97.41	1,517,424	60,090,434	99.93
2011	60,231,991	58,308,249	96.81	1,306,712	60,186,665	99.92
2010	60,201,656	58,243,180	96.75 %	1,329,491	60,179,770	99.96 %

Source: Treasurer of the City of Charlottesville

(1) Beginning with Fiscal year 2015, supplements are reported in the year in which they were billed and due. Fiscal years 2009-2014 report supplemental tax levies back to the year they for which they are assessed, instead of reporting them in the fiscal year they were billed, causing the current year collection rate to decline in subsequent years.

ESTIMATED VALUE OF TAX-EXEMPT REAL PROPERTY
LAST TEN FISCAL YEARS

	2019	2018	2017	2016	2015	2014	2013	2012	2011	2010
Federal	$ 36,863,200	$ 32,717,600	$ 31,919,100	$ 23,817,800	$ 21,652,500	$ 21,652,500	$ 21,652,500	$ 21,652,500	$ 21,652,500	$ 21,652,500
State and regional	463,218,100	455,398,000	450,963,700	306,883,300	279,103,600	278,984,600	288,908,100	278,983,600	324,752,400	323,065,400
Local	446,420,700	417,963,500	362,990,800	214,399,600	194,685,500	192,076,800	191,927,100	181,085,000	192,885,400	190,835,500
Religious, charitable, educational and other	1,088,276,900	1,011,604,150	901,079,000	589,954,700	531,941,200	524,902,700	510,229,200	534,852,200	477,056,100	517,652,100
Total	2,034,778,900	1,917,683,250	$ 1,746,952,600	$ 1,135,055,400	$ 1,027,382,800	$ 1,017,616,600	$ 1,012,716,900	$ 1,016,573,300	$ 1,016,346,400	$ 1,053,205,500

Source: Office of the Real Estate Assessor, City of Charlottesville, Virginia. Reported to the State in April annually by the Assessor's Office.

CITY OF CHARLOTTESVILLE, VIRGINIA

TABLE 11

RATIO OF NET BONDED GOVERNMENTAL DEBT TO ASSESSED VALUE AND NET BONDED GOVERNMENTAL DEBT PER CAPITA
LAST TEN FISCAL YEARS

Fiscal Year	Population (1)	Real Estate Assessed Value	Total Bonded Debt	Total Bonded Business Type Debt	Governmental Bonded Debt Service Due (2)	General Fund Expenditures and Net Other Financing Sources	Ratio of Net Bonded Debt to Assessed Value	Total Bonded Debt per Capita	Ratio of Debt Service to Total General Fund Expenditures and Transfers
2019	49,281	$ 7,647,893,000	$ 136,905,038	$ 49,234,305	$ 7,443,208	$ 173,674,353	1.79 %	$ 2,778	4.29 %
2018	49,132	7,060,139,700	131,846,865	46,555,810	7,137,004	165,389,458	1.87	2,684	4.32
2017	49,071	6,740,234,600	132,121,039	44,022,607	7,417,376	152,655,215	1.96	2,692	4.86
2016	48,210	5,953,910,000	128,929,869	44,824,556	9,489,053	139,577,852	2.17	2,674	6.80
2015	47,783	5,704,217,700	130,376,506	48,052,860	9,121,289	139,577,852	2.29	2,729	6.53
2014	46,623	5,503,669,500	126,266,932	48,149,184	8,682,449	138,100,498	2.29	2,708	6.29
2013	45,073	5,281,021,000	122,474,814	43,325,574	6,938,939	137,559,888	2.32	2,717	5.04
2012	44,471	5,222,661,300	117,731,642	37,762,227	6,681,506	134,117,472	2.25	2,647	4.98
2011	43,475	5,282,859,100	114,532,934	36,693,311	6,847,707	127,413,032	2.17	2,634	5.37
2010	40,745	5,257,182,700	99,713,452	25,212,952	6,397,748	127,775,530	1.90	2,447	5.01

Note: The City has no overlapping debt.
(1) Weldon Cooper Center for Public Service, Demographics & Workforce Group
    http://www.coopercenter.org/demographics/virginia-population-estimates
(2) Governmental debt due within next fiscal year.

CITY OF CHARLOTTESVILLE, VIRGINIA

TABLE 12

RATIO OF ANNUAL DEBT SERVICE EXPENDITURES FOR
GENERAL BONDED DEBT TO GENERAL GOVERNMENTAL
EXPENDITURES AND TRANSFERS
LAST TEN FISCAL YEARS

Fiscal Year	Principal	Interest	Total Debt Service	General Governmental Expenditures and Transfers	Ratio of Debt Service to General Governmental Expenditures
2019	$ 7,140,323	$ 3,041,563	$ 10,181,885	$ 173,673,353	5.86 %
2018	7,417,377	3,099,780	10,517,157	224,199,432	4.69
2017	7,146,882	2,832,293	9,979,175	205,739,944	4.85
2016	6,379,799	2,591,814	8,971,613	195,491,554	4.59
2015	6,084,318	2,660,459	8,744,777	191,875,061	4.56
2014	6,685,521	2,725,366	9,410,887	190,189,617	4.95
2013	6,430,175	2,452,754	8,882,929	188,150,305	4.72
2012	6,611,249	2,855,961	9,467,210	188,952,877	5.01
2011	6,236,895	2,550,831	8,787,726	178,268,372	4.93
2010	5,926,396	2,407,670	8,334,066	178,323,894	4.67

Note: Excludes Capital Projects Fund expenditures and transfers.
The City has no overlapping debt.

CITY OF CHARLOTTESVILLE, VIRGINIA

TABLE 13

RATIOS OF OUTSTANDING DEBT BY TYPE
LAST TEN FISCAL YEARS

| | Governmental Activities | | | | Business-Type Activities | | | | |
Fiscal Year	General Obligation Bonds (1)	Literary Loans	Notes Payable	Total Governmental Debt	General Obligation Notes	Notes Payable	Total Primary Government	Percent of Personal Income	Per Capita Debt
2019	$87,670,733	$ -	$ -	$ 87,670,733	$49,234,305	$ -	$136,905,038	* %	2,778
2018	85,291,055	-	-	85,291,055	46,555,810	-	131,846,865	*	2,684
2017	88,098,432	-	-	88,098,432	44,022,607	-	132,121,039	*	2,692
2016	84,094,947	10,366		84,105,313	44,824,556	-	128,929,869	4.48	2,674
2015	82,293,261	30,385	-	82,323,646	48,052,860	-	130,376,506	4.53	2,729
2014	78,067,345	50,403	-	78,117,748	48,149,184	-	126,266,932	4.55	2,708
2013	78,676,333	70,421	402,486	79,149,240	43,325,574	-	122,474,814	5.00	2,717
2012	78,918,183	90,439	960,793	79,969,415	37,762,227	-	117,731,642	5.11	2,647
2011	76,002,100	118,343	1,641,771	77,762,214	36,693,311	77,409	114,532,934	5.50	2,630
2010	72,117,050	144,861	2,086,798	74,348,709	25,212,952	151,791	99,713,452	5.02	2,447

* Information not available at this time.

(1) Presented net of original issuance discounts and premiums, revised

Note: The City has no overlapping debt.

CITY OF CHARLOTTESVILLE, VIRGINIA

TABLE 14

COMPUTATION OF LEGAL DEBT MARGIN
LAST TEN FISCAL YEARS

	2019	2018	2017	2016	2015	2014	2013	2012	2011	2010
Assessed value of real property	$ 7,647,893,000	$ 7,060,139,700	$ 6,740,234,600	$ 5,953,910,000	$ 5,704,217,700	$ 5,503,669,500	$ 5,281,021,000	$ 5,222,661,300	$ 5,282,869,100	$ 5,257,182,700
Debt limit - 10% of assessed value	$ 764,789,300	$ 706,013,970	$ 674,023,460	$ 595,391,000	$ 570,421,770	$ 550,366,950	$ 528,102,100	$ 522,266,130	$ 528,286,910	$ 525,718,270
Amount of debt applicable to debt limit	136,905,038	131,846,865	132,121,039	128,929,869	119,460,105	114,398,907	110,304,028	106,478,659	104,947,348	90,014,613
Legal debt margin	$ 627,884,262	$ 574,167,105	$ 541,902,421	$ 466,461,131	$ 450,961,665	$ 435,968,043	$ 417,798,072	$ 415,787,471	$ 423,338,562	$ 435,703,657
Total net debt applicable to the limit as a percentage of debt limit	17.90%	18.67%	19.60%	21.65%	20.94%	20.79%	20.89%	20.39%	19.87%	17.12%

Note: The City has no overlapping debt.

PROPERTY VALUES, CONSTRUCTION AND BANK DEPOSITS
LAST TEN FISCAL YEARS

Fiscal Year	Institutional and other Construction (1)		Commercial Construction (1)		Residential Construction (1)		Bank deposits (2) (in thousands)	Calendar Year	Property Values (3)	
	Number of Permits	Value	Number of Permits	Value	Number of Permits	Value			Taxable	Nontaxable
2019	30	$ 1,015,033	468	$150,662,370	1,546	$ 218,624,551	$ 2,458,191	2019	$ 7,647,893,000	$ 1,088,276,900
2018	44	3,404,801	566	45,291,407	1,556	107,599,017	2,499,593	2018	7,060,139,700	1,917,683,250
2017	17	1,204,091	467	128,400,704	1,653	63,999,554	2,476,231	2017	6,740,234,600	1,746,952,600
2016	19	2,300,978	582	88,939,069	1,383	48,684,124	2,366,694 (4)	2016	5,953,910,000	1,135,055,400
2015	22	8,635,285	469	63,025,855	1,420	51,009,735	2,328,209 (4)	2015	5,704,217,700	1,027,382,800
2014	49	5,519,838	514	49,726,636	1,261	50,124,989	2,158,543	2014	5,503,669,500	1,017,616,600
2013	41	17,037,847	545	73,204,061	1,510	117,781,757	2,042,744	2013	5,281,021,000	1,012,716,900
2012	39	53,543,285	494	42,252,061	1,171	53,442,553	2,038,433	2012	5,222,661,300	1,016,573,300
2011	26	14,429,867	428	27,563,274	1,025	34,580,411	2,070,183	2011	5,282,859,100	1,016,346,400
2010	14	1,865,091	396	39,852,193	977	28,812,651	2,171,455	2010	5,257,182,700	1,053,205,500

(1) Department of Neighborhood Planning, City of Charlottesville
(2) FDIC Summary of deposits
(3) Real property values only
(4) FDIC Summary of deposits was corrected to reflect the actual value

CITY OF CHARLOTTESVILLE, VIRGINIA

TABLE 16

DEMOGRAPHIC STATISTICS
LAST TEN CALENDAR YEARS

Year	Population (1)	School Membership (2)	Unemployment Rate (3)	Total Personal Income (4) (thousands)	Per Capita Income (4)	Taxable Sales (5) (thousands)	Sales per Capita
2019	49,281	4,337	2.5	*	*	*	*
2018	49,132	4,313	3.1	*	*	$ 972,265	$ 19,789
2017	49,071	4,210	3.6	$ 10,531,351	$ 67,630	971,359	19,795
2016	48,210	4,134	3.4	9,375,633	60,964	1,006,304	20,873
2015	47,783	4,101	3.7	9,182,721	60,294	959,435	20,079
2014	46,623	4,022	4.3	8,795,194	58,603	942,421	20,214
2013	45,073	3,945	4.9	7,764,329	52,693	864,748	19,186
2012	44,471	3,914	5.9	7,493,869	51,255	819,390	18,425
2011	43,552	3,874	7.1	6,778,562	47,052	822,681	18,890
2010	40,745	3,915	6.9	6,463,200	45,282	814,017	19,978

* Information not available at this time.

Source:

(1) Weldon Cooper Center for Public Service, Demographics & Workforce Group
   http://www.coopercenter.org/demographics/virginia-population-estimates
(2) Fall Membership Charlottesville Public Schools
(3) Bureau of Labor Statistics Local Area Unemployment Statistics and represents unemployment
   for the calendar year
(4) Regional Economic Information System, Bureau of Economic Analysis, U.S. Department of Commerce:
   Albemarle County and City of Charlottesville
(5) Annual Report, Taxable Sales in Virginia Counties and Cities, Commonwealth of Virginia,
   Department of Taxation

PRINCIPAL EMPLOYERS CURRENT YEAR AND NINE YEARS AGO
JUNE 30, 2019

Employer	2019		2010	
	Rank	Number of Employee	Rank	Number of Employees
University of Virginia Medical Center	1	1000+	1	1000+
City of Charlottesville	2	1000+	3	1000+
UVA Health Services Foundation	3	1000+		
Charlottesville City School Board	4	500 to 999	4	500 to 999
Servicelink Management Com Inc.	5	500 to 999		
Aramark Campus LLC	6	500 to 999		
Lakeland Tours	7	500 to 999	5	500 to 999
Association for Investment Management	8	250 to 499		
Rmc Events	9	250 to 499		
Crutchfield Corporation	10	250 to 499		
Martha Jefferson Hospital			2	1000+
Region Ten Community Services			6	500 to 999
SNL Security LP			8	250 to 499
Pharmaceutical Research Association			9	250 to 499
United State Postal Service			7	250 to 499
Kroger			10	250 to 499

Source: Virginia Employment Commission 50 Largest Employers during 4th Quarter (October, November, December) 2017

Note: 2010 employer rank/number of employees received from 4th quarter 2009 Virginia Employment Commission
Labor Market Information

GOVERNMENT EMPLOYEES BY FUNCTION
LAST TEN FISCAL YEARS

Department		2019	2018	2017	2016	2015	2014	2013	2012	2011	2010
Management											
Council/Clerk of Council		4.00	1.00	1.00	1.00	1.00	1.00	1.00	1.00	1.00	1.00
City Manager's Office/Administration and Communications		12.00	11.00	11.00	9.00	9.00	9.00	8.00	8.00	8.00	8.00
Office of Economic Development		7.50	6.50	6.00	6.00	5.50	4.00	5.00	5.00	4.00	4.00
Office of the City Manager/Parking Entreprise Fund		1.00	1.00	1.00	-	-	-	-	-	-	-
City Attorney		7.00	6.00	6.00	6.00	6.00	6.00	6.00	6.00	6.00	6.00
Voting Registrar		3.00	3.00	3.00	3.00	3.00	3.00	3.00	3.00	2.50	2.50
	Total	34.50	28.50	28.00	25.00	24.50	23.00	23.00	23.00	21.50	21.50
Internal Services											
Finance Department: Purchasing/Risk Management/Warehouse		8.00	7.00	6.00	6.00	6.00	6.00	6.00	6.00	6.00	6.00
Information Technology		20.00	20.00	19.00	19.00	19.00	19.00	19.00	19.00	18.00	18.00
Human Resources		8.00	8.00	8.00	8.00	8.00	8.00	8.00	8.00	8.00	8.00
	Total	36.00	35.00	33.00	33.00	33.00	33.00	33.00	33.00	32.00	32.00
Financial Services											
Commissioner of Revenue		14.00	13.00	13.00	13.00	13.00	13.00	13.00	13.00	13.00	13.00
Finance Department: Management/Real Estate Assessment/Utility Billing Office		34.00	34.00	34.00	34.00	34.00	34.00	34.00	34.00	34.00	34.00
Treasurer		13.50	13.50	13.00	13.00	13.00	13.00	13.00	13.00	13.00	13.00
	Total	61.50	60.50	60.00	60.00	60.00	60.00	60.00	60.00	60.00	60.00
Healthy Families & Community											
Charlottesville/Albemarle Visitors Bureau [1]		10.00	10.00	10.00	10.00	10.00	10.00	10.00	10.00	10.00	10.00
Depart of Human Services		36.50	35.50	35.50	35.50	34.25	34.25	35.25	34.25	34.25	33.00
Children & Youth Commission/CCF		-	-	-	-	-	-	-	-	-	1.00
Department of Social Services		104.50	102.50	102.50	102.25	99.98	99.85	100.85	100.85	99.85	98.85
Neighborhood Development Services		39.00	39.00	37.50	37.50	36.00	33.00	32.00	32.00	32.00	32.00
Office of Human Rights/Human Rights Commission		2.00	1.50	1.50	2.00	2.00	2.00	-	-	-	-
Parks and Recreation/Parks Maintenance		40.00	40.00	39.00	39.00	37.00	37.00	37.00	37.00	37.00	38.00
Parks & Rec/Recreation and Programs		29.50	27.50	27.50	27.50	28.50	28.75	29.75	28.75	26.75	25.25
Parks & Rec/Golf Fund		4.00	4.00	4.00	4.00	4.00	4.75	7.00	7.00	8.00	8.00
CDBG/HOME Grant Coordinator (Grant Funded)		1.00	1.00	1.00	1.00	1.00	1.00	1.00	1.00	1.00	1.00
	Total	266.50	261.00	258.50	258.75	252.73	260.60	262.85	260.85	248.85	247.10
Infrastructure/Transportation											
Public Works: Administration, Facilities Development		26.86	21.86	21.86	21.86	16.73	15.73	15.73	15.69	16.00	16.25
Public Works: School Building Maintenance		19.28	19.28	19.28	19.28	18.28	18.28	18.28	18.28	16.00	16.00
Public Works: Fleet Management		11.00	11.00	11.00	11.00	11.00	11.00	12.00	12.00	12.00	12.00
Public Works: Public Service		49.00	51.00	51.00	51.00	51.00	51.00	51.00	51.00	51.00	51.00
Charlottesville Area Transit (CAT)		72.00	72.00	69.00	68.00	68.00	68.00	77.50	77.50	78.00	78.00
Public Works: Pupil Transportation		29.00	29.00	28.50	28.50	28.50	28.00	27.50	27.50	28.50	28.50
Public Utilities: Gas, Water, Wastewater		89.00	92.00	92.00	92.00	92.00	92.00	93.00	93.00	93.00	93.00
Public Utilities: Stormwater Utility		4.00	4.00	4.00	4.00	4.00	4.00	-	-	-	-
	Total	300.14	300.14	296.64	295.64	289.51	288.01	295.01	294.97	294.50	294.75
Public Safety & Justice											
City Sheriff		12.00	11.00	11.00	11.00	11.00	11.00	11.00	11.00	11.00	11.00
Commonwealth's Attorney		13.50	13.50	13.50	13.50	13.50	13.50	13.50	13.50	13.50	13.50
Courts and Other Support Service		11.00	11.00	11.00	11.00	11.00	11.00	11.00	11.00	11.00	11.00
Fire Department		95.00	91.00	91.00	91.00	91.00	89.00	89.00	89.00	89.00	89.00
Police Department		157.00	157.00	156.00	154.00	154.00	146.00	146.00	146.00	146.00	146.00
	Total	288.50	283.50	282.50	280.50	280.50	270.50	270.50	270.50	270.50	270.50
City-Wide Total		987.14	968.64	958.64	952.89	940.24	925.11	935.36	932.32	927.35	925.85

Source: Adopted Operating and Capital Improvement Budget

Note: FTE positions

[1] These positions are funded cooperatively with Albemarle County.

CITY OF CHARLOTTESVILLE, VIRGINIA

TABLE 18

OPERATING INDICATORS BY FUNCTION
LAST TEN FISCAL YEARS

General Government	2019	2018	2017	2016	2015	2014	2013	2012	2011	2010
Date of incorporation	1888	1888	1888	1888	1888	1888	1888	1888	1888	1888
Form of government	Council-Mgr	Council-Mgr	Council-Mgr	Council-Mgr	Council-Mgr	Council-Mgr	Council-Mgr	Council-Mgr	Council-Mgr	Council-Mgr
Area	10.4 sq miles	10.4 sq miles	10.4 sq miles	10.4 sq miles	10.4 sq miles	10.4 sq miles	10.4 sq miles	10.4 sq miles	10.4 sq miles	10.4 sq miles
Bond rating:										
Moody's Investor Services	Aaa	Aaa	Aaa	Aaa	Aaa	Aaa	Aaa	Aaa	Aaa	Aaa
Standard & Poor's Corporation	AAA	AAA	AAA	AAA	AAA	AAA	AAA	AAA	AAA	AAA
Number of employees:										
City (full-time)	967.1	958.6	958.6	952.9	940	925	935	932	927	925.9
School Board	840	635	767	797	772	767	765	753	754	795
Electors:										
Number of registered voters:										
Last general election - November, 2017	N/A	31,575	35,725	31,039	32,273	32,290	33,150	28,570	28,126	27,643
Last municipal election - November, 2017	N/A	31,575	31,039	31,039	32,291	32,290	28,570	28,570	N/A	23,506
Number of votes cast in:										
Last general election	N/A	18,067	22,692	6,077	10,816	12,494	21,797	7,522	13,852	20,122
Last municipal election	N/A	18,067	6,077	6,077	12,580	11,045	6,624	6,627	N/A	6,066
Percentage of registered voters voting in:										
Last general election	N/A	58.7%	63.4%	19.2%	33.5%	38.7%	65.8%	26.2%	49.3%	72.8%
Last municipal election	N/A	58.7%	19.6%	19.2%	38.9%	34.2%	23.1%	23.1%	N/A	25.9%
Public Safety										
Fire protection:										
Number of firefighters and officers (exclusive of volunteer firefighters)	90	90	88	88	88	88	86	86	86	86
Police protection:										
Number of police officers	125	127	129	127	127	119	119	117	117	117
Number of arrests	1,875	3,216	2,783	2,839	2,741	3,018	4,417	5,043	4,700	5,514
Traffic Citations issued	3,142	4,737	5,912	4,975	5,740	5,459	4,299	4,429	5,793	4,857
911 calls received	37,121	39,692	44,461	40,504	43,512	45,561	43,111	46,059	48,006	47,653
Cases Investigated	5,502	4,442	5,287	4,962	5,196	5,443	2,846	1,110	1,076	1,140
Parking Violations										
Violations written	17,141	17,853	16,637	16,734	17,847	12,633	15,813	20,657	21,696	15,501
Building permits issued	2,033	2,166	2,137	1,964	1,911	1,824	2,096	1,704	1,479	1,387
Education										
Schools:										
Number of teachers	478	456	440	429	421	415	424	434	423	429
Number of students	4,333	4,313	4,210	4,134	4,101	4,022	3,946	3,914	3,874	3,915
Pupil-teacher ratio	9.07:1	9.46:1	9.56:1	9.64:1	10.26:1	9.69:1	9.31:1	9.02:1	9.16:1	9.13:1
Public Utilities										
Municipal utilities:										
Gas:										
Number of customers	20,994	20,666	20,467	20,043	19,549	19,454	19,077	18,655	18,699	18,062
Average daily consumption	6,051 DTH	7,570 DTH	7,562 DTH	6,802 DTH	8,487 DTH	8,566 DTH	6,601 DTH	6,492 DTH	6,594 DTH	7,245 DTH
Water:										
Number of customers	14,661	14,639	14,756	14,692	14,652	14,554	14,446	14,377	14,396	13,814
Average daily consumption	561 MCF	569.4 MCF	579.2 MCF	569.4 MCF	569.3 MCF	569.1 MCF	577.8 MCF	587.9 MCF	604 MCF	601 MCF
Sewer:										
Number of customers	14,564	14,528	14,626	14,558	14,511	14,406	14,294	14,251	14,243	13,688
Average daily treatment	483 MCF	502.6 MCF	564.6 MCF	502.6 MCF	505.6 MCF	520.7 MCF	524.2 MCF	537.6 MCF	556 MCF	596 MCF
Public Works										
Refuse disposed at Zion's Transfer Station (City totals):										
Number of customers	13,200	13,200	13,200	13,200	13,200	13,200	13,200	13,200	13,200	13,200
Tons of domestic refuse	8,881	8,877	8,888	8,198	8,881	8,884	8,888	8,888	8,798	8,881
Tons of curbside recycling	4,429	3,866	3,866	3,647	3,557	3,254	3,342	2,471	3,331	3,330
Tons of stumps, demolition material & street sweeping [1]	1,300	866	1,150	2,117	1,048	2,063	1,664	1,532	1,505	1,423

Source: Departmental operational reports for the period ending June 30th.

[1] In FY2016, accounts for brush, street sweeping, and leaves In FY2017, the total accounts for street sweeping.

TABLE 20

CAPITAL ASSET STATISTICS BY FUNCTION
LAST TEN FISCAL YEARS

	2019	2018	2017	2016	2015	2014	2013	2012	2011	2010
General Government										
Miles of streets	159.91	158.76	158.45	158.1	157	156	156	156	156	156
Number of streetlights	6,070	6,070	6,070	6,040	6,025	6,016	6,016	6,010	5,985	5,960
Public Safety										
Fire protection:										
Number of stations	3	3	3	3	3	3	3	3	3	3
Police protection:										
Number of stations	7	10	8	4	4	4	5	6	6	6
Number of vehicular patrol units	58	50	64	68	67	63	55	64	64	64
Total vehicles	119	129	128	122	123	123	134	126	126	126
Motor Cycles	7	6	8	8	6	8	8	6	6	6
Unmarked cars	54	59	53	46	50	52	52	52	42	42
Bicycle patrol	14	14	14	24	17	17	18	15	15	15
Education										
Number of schools	9	9	9	9	9	9	9	9	9	9
Parks, Recreation, & Culture										
Number of parks [1]	36	36	36	36	31	31	30	31	26	26
Acres of park land [2]	904	900	900	902	872	822	785	1,979	987	987
Number of golf courses	1	1	1	1	1	2	2	2	2	2
Number of swimming pools	4	4	4	4	4	6	5	5	5	5
Number of recreation centers	5	5	5	5	5	5	5	5	6	6
Number of libraries	3	3	3	3	3	3	3	3	3	3
Public Utilities										
Gas:										
Miles of gas main lines	333	331	330	329	328	319	318	317	316	315
Miles of gas service lines	292	288	282	274	272	226	223	221	219	217
Water:										
Water treatment plant capacity (millions of gallons per day)	19	19	19	19	19	19	19	19	19	19
Miles of water lines	183	183	180	180	180.8	180	180	180.0	178.3	177.7
Number of fire hydrants	1088	1088	1,050	1,047	1,031	1,026	1,007	1,005	991	988
Sewer:										
Sewer treatment plant capacity (millions of gallons per day)	15	15	15	15	15	15	15	15	15	15
Miles of sanitary sewers	171	171	170	166	170	166	165	167	167	167

Source: Departmental operational reports for the period ending June 30th

Note:
(1) Includes 3 jointly funded parks with Albemarle County beginning fiscal year 2012.
(2) Includes City Parks and natural areas in FY2012

Appendix D

UNIVERSITY OF VIRGINIA — BASIC FINANCIAL STATEMENTS

UNIVERSITY OF VIRGINIA

STATEMENT OF NET POSITION *(in thousands)*

AS OF JUNE 30, 2019 (WITH COMPARATIVE INFORMATION AS OF JUNE 30, 2018)

	2019	2018
ASSETS		
Current assets		
Cash and cash equivalents (Note 2)	$ 148,191	$ 87,882
Short-term investments (Note 2)	235,288	84,831
Appropriations available	11,772	8,588
Accounts receivable, net (Note 3a)	384,774	387,387
Prepaid expenses	25,450	23,383
Inventories	33,654	31,336
Notes receivable, net (Note 3b)	6,045	6,113
Pledges receivable, net (Note 3c)	43,045	9,335
Total current assets	899,217	838,843
Noncurrent assets		
Cash and cash equivalents (Note 2)	12,654	22,880
Long-term investments (Note 2)	2,455,688	2,711,881
Endowment (Note 2)	5,088,081	4,838,142
Notes receivable, net (Note 3b)	29,189	33,118
Pledges and other receivables, net (Note 3c)	82,388	14,885
Capital assets - depreciable, net (Note 3d)	3,320,737	3,282,075
Capital assets - nondepreciable, net (Note 3d)	718,817	520,730
Derivative instrument asset (Note 6)	140	-
Investment in affiliated companies (Note 7)	87,510	85,442
OPEB asset (Note 12)	17,048	15,437
Other (Note 3e)	72,835	48,435
Total noncurrent assets	11,873,287	11,553,883
DEFERRED OUTFLOWS OF RESOURCES (Note 3f)	144,136	154,387
TOTAL ASSETS AND DEFERRED OUTFLOWS OF RESOURCES	$ 12,916,640	$ 12,345,113
LIABILITIES		
Current liabilities		
Accounts payable and accrued liabilities (Note 3g)	$ 472,830	$ 354,283
Unearned revenue (Note 3h)	80,038	74,080
Deposits held in custody for others	14,718	11,714
Commercial paper (Note 4)	243,800	121,845
Long-term debt - current portion (Note 5a)	10,186	8,581
Long-term liabilities - current portion (Note 5b)	101,469	81,946
Total current liabilities	923,139	663,449
Noncurrent liabilities		
Long-term debt (Note 5a)	1,980,382	1,895,829
Derivative instrument liability (Note 6)	35,068	27,880
Net pension liability (Note 11)	474,206	506,388
OPEB liability (Note 12)	255,875	283,545
Other noncurrent liabilities (Note 5b)	181,349	174,173
Total noncurrent liabilities	2,926,680	2,997,823
DEFERRED INFLOWS OF RESOURCES (Note 3i)	166,212	133,676
TOTAL LIABILITIES AND DEFERRED INFLOWS OF RESOURCES	$ 4,016,011	$ 3,794,948
NET POSITION		
Net investment in capital assets	$ 1,861,654	$ 1,881,811
Restricted:		
Nonexpendable	881,387	747,181
Expendable	3,238,088	3,081,428
Unrestricted	2,789,190	2,748,735
TOTAL NET POSITION	$ 8,900,829	$ 8,550,185
TOTAL LIABILITIES, DEFERRED INFLOWS OF RESOURCES, AND NET POSITION	$ 12,916,640	$ 12,345,113

Certain 2018 amounts have been restated to conform to 2019 classifications.

The accompanying Notes to Financial Statements are an integral part of this statement.

UNIVERSITY OF VIRGINIA

COMPONENT UNITS, COMBINED STATEMENT OF FINANCIAL POSITION *(in thousands)*

AS OF JUNE 30, 2019 (WITH COMPARATIVE INFORMATION AS OF JUNE 30, 2018)

	2019	2018
ASSETS		
Current assets		
Cash and cash equivalents	$ 110,415	$ 78,577
Receivables	180,038	148,352
Short-term investments	688,270	314,741
Other current assets	5,548	8,458
Total current assets	974,271	548,128
Noncurrent assets		
Pledges receivable, net	170,821	53,343
Long-term investments	9,532,821	9,625,569
Capital assets, net of depreciation	488,028	440,467
Other noncurrent assets	51,784	61,058
Total noncurrent assets	10,223,254	10,180,437
TOTAL ASSETS	$ 11,197,525	$ 10,728,565
LIABILITIES AND NET ASSETS		
Current liabilities		
Assets held in trust for others	$ 116,777	$ 115,456
Other liabilities	310,488	207,753
Total current liabilities	427,265	323,209
Noncurrent liabilities		
Long-term debt, net of debt issuance cost and current portion of $5,181 and $8,438	137,731	183,587
Other noncurrent liabilities	8,297,032	8,098,106
Total noncurrent liabilities	8,434,763	8,281,693
TOTAL LIABILITIES	$ 8,862,028	$ 8,584,902
NET ASSETS		
Unrestricted	$ 477,587	$ 485,187
Temporarily restricted	834,699	815,824
Permanently restricted	823,211	782,552
TOTAL NET ASSETS	$ 2,335,497	$ 2,143,663
TOTAL LIABILITIES AND NET ASSETS	$ 11,197,525	$ 10,728,565

Certain 2018 amounts have been restated to conform to 2019 classifications.
The accompanying Notes to Financial Statements are an integral part of this statement.

UNIVERSITY OF VIRGINIA
STATEMENT OF REVENUES, EXPENSES AND CHANGES IN NET POSITION (in thousands)

FOR THE YEAR ENDED JUNE 30, 2019 (WITH COMPARATIVE INFORMATION FOR THE YEAR ENDED JUNE 30, 2018)

	2019	2018
REVENUES		
Operating revenues		
Student tuition and fees, net of scholarship allowances of $143,810 and $128,228	$ 585,751	$ 585,081
Patient services, net of charity care and contractual adjustments of $4,252,871 and $3,889,038	1,718,128	1,842,115
Federal grants and contracts	304,008	284,183
State and local grants and contracts	6,845	8,882
Nongovernmental grants and contracts	66,082	70,208
Sales and services of educational departments	31,437	29,838
Auxiliary enterprises revenue, net of scholarship allowances of $22,088 and $18,851	140,787	140,484
Other operating revenues	50,988	47,280
TOTAL OPERATING REVENUES	2,915,028	2,788,829
EXPENSES		
Operating expenses (Note 9)		
Compensation and benefits	1,957,887	1,844,558
Supplies and other services	1,205,659	1,158,964
Student aid	104,793	100,373
Depreciation	243,820	232,478
Other	7,929	5,308
TOTAL OPERATING REVENUES	3,520,088	3,342,877
OPERATING LOSS	(605,062)	(553,848)
NONOPERATING REVENUES (EXPENSES)		
State appropriations (Note 10)	175,152	188,449
Gifts	187,181	170,454
Investment income	400,223	788,288
Pell grants	14,225	13,586
Interest on capital asset-related debt	(88,013)	(87,381)
Build America Bonds rebate	5,646	8,158
Loss on capital assets	(6,084)	(27,957)
Other net nonoperating expenses	(803)	(20,224)
NET NONOPERATING REVENUES	697,507	991,394
INCOME BEFORE OTHER REVENUES, EXPENSES, GAINS, OR LOSSES	92,445	437,548
Capital appropriations	48,379	15,148
Capital grants and gifts	129,788	38,200
Additions to permanent endowments	83,717	53,543
Special items	(4,875)	-
TOTAL OTHER REVENUES (EXPENSES)	258,019	106,889
INCREASE IN NET POSITION	350,464	544,435
NET POSITION		
Net position - beginning of year	8,550,185	8,205,417
Net effect of prior period adjustments (Note 1)	-	(199,687)
NET POSITION - BEGINNING OF YEAR AS RESTATED	8,550,185	8,005,730
NET POSITION - END OF YEAR	$ 8,900,829	$ 8,550,185

The accompanying Notes to Financial Statements are an integral part of this statement.

UNIVERSITY OF VIRGINIA
COMPONENT UNITS, COMBINED STATEMENT OF ACTIVITIES *(in thousands)*

FOR THE YEAR ENDED JUNE 30, 2019 (WITH COMPARATIVE INFORMATION FOR THE YEAR ENDED JUNE 30, 2018)

	2019	2018
UNRESTRICTED REVENUES AND SUPPORT		
Contributions	$ 28,718	$ 30,172
Fees for services, rentals and sales	441,239	483,105
Investment income	51,410	46,891
Net assets released from restriction	181,228	138,720
Other revenues	145,073	110,438
TOTAL UNRESTRICTED REVENUES AND SUPPORT	828,864	819,126
EXPENSES		
Program services, lectures and special events	548,863	535,348
Scholarships and financial aid	78,788	82,819
Management and general	38,400	42,848
Other expenses	148,588	108,217
TOTAL EXPENSES	818,417	770,128
EXCESS OF UNRESTRICTED REVENUES AND SUPPORT OVER EXPENSES	12,247	48,998
CHANGES IN TEMPORARILY RESTRICTED NET ASSETS		
Contributions	85,585	71,041
Investment and other income	81,307	155,218
Reclassification per donor stipulation	(2,435)	251
Net assets released from restriction	(151,811)	(138,882)
NET CHANGES IN TEMPORARILY RESTRICTED NET ASSETS	22,826	87,818
CHANGES IN PERMANENTLY RESTRICTED NET ASSETS		
Contributions	188,188	28,181
Investment and other (loss) income	(1,822)	531
Reclassification per donor stipulation	30	294
Net assets released from restriction	(8,815)	172
NET CHANGES IN PERMANENTLY RESTRICTED NET ASSETS	158,781	30,178
CHANGES IN NET ASSETS	191,834	186,792
Net assets - beginning of year	2,143,863	1,878,871
NET ASSETS - END OF YEAR	$ 2,335,497	$ 2,143,863

The accompanying Notes to Financial Statements are an integral part of this statement.

UNIVERSITY OF VIRGINIA
STATEMENT OF CASH FLOWS *(in thousands)*

FOR THE YEAR ENDED JUNE 30, 2019 (WITH COMPARATIVE INFORMATION FOR THE YEAR ENDED JUNE 30, 2018)

	2019	2018
CASH FLOWS FROM OPERATING ACTIVITIES		
Tuition and fees	$ 584,748	$ 572,877
Grants and contracts	385,487	355,889
Patient services	1,784,254	1,588,085
Sales and services of educational activities	36,724	18,724
Sales and services of auxiliary enterprises	133,847	145,241
Payments to employees and fringe benefits	(1,841,427)	(1,828,612)
Payments to vendors and suppliers	(1,202,231)	(1,184,703)
Payments for scholarships and fellowships	(104,783)	(100,373)
Perkins and other loans issued to students	(7,344)	(8,184)
Collection of Perkins and other loans to students	8,908	9,085
Other receipts	60,824	44,913
NET CASH USED BY OPERATING ACTIVITIES	(241,205)	(355,878)
CASH FLOWS FROM NONCAPITAL FINANCING ACTIVITIES		
State appropriations	188,878	188,332
Additions to permanent endowments	83,717	53,543
Federal Direct Loan Program receipts	133,178	181,881
Federal Direct Loan Program payments	(133,178)	(181,881)
Pell grants	14,225	13,588
Deposits held in custody for others	2,849	7,207
Noncapital gifts and grants and endowments received	181,350	147,889
Proceeds from noncapital debt	73,454	483,832
Repayments from noncapital debt	(137,745)	(175,000)
Other net nonperating expenses	(41,384)	(28,584)
NET CASH PROVIDED BY NONCAPITAL FINANCING ACTIVITIES	346,464	680,405
CASH FLOWS FROM CAPITAL AND RELATED FINANCING ACTIVITIES		
Capital appropriations	47,683	15,148
Capital gifts and grants received	43,778	37,088
Proceeds from capital debt	189,433	248,103
Proceeds from sale of capital assets	325	1,182
Acquisition and construction of capital assets	(488,684)	(485,947)
Principal paid on capital debt and leases	(10,802)	(32,432)
Interest paid on capital debt and leases	(83,127)	(87,718)
NET CASH USED BY CAPITAL AND RELATED FINANCING ACTIVITIES	(311,508)	(318,598)
CASH FLOWS FROM INVESTING ACTIVITIES		
Proceeds from sales and maturities of investments	1,051,806	544,805
Interest on investments	(15,898)	(4,808)
Purchase of investments and related fees	(776,358)	(544,504)
Other investment activities	(2,132)	(3,838)
NET CASH PROVIDED (USED) BY INVESTING ACTIVITIES	257,520	(8,145)
NET INCREASE (DECREASE) IN CASH AND CASH EQUIVALENTS	51,273	(216)
Cash and cash equivalents - beginning of year	110,772	110,988
CASH AND CASH EQUIVALENTS - END OF YEAR	$ 162,045	$ 110,772

Certain 2018 amounts have been restated to conform to 2019 classifications.

The accompanying Notes to Financial Statements are an integral part of this statement.

UNIVERSITY OF VIRGINIA
STATEMENT OF CASH FLOWS, CONTINUED *(in thousands)*

FOR THE YEAR ENDED JUNE 30, 2019 (WITH COMPARATIVE INFORMATION FOR THE YEAR ENDED JUNE 30, 2018)

	2019	2018
RECONCILIATION OF OPERATING LOSS TO NET CASH USED BY OPERATING ACTIVITIES		
Operating loss	$ (805,082)	$ (553,848)
Adjustments to reconcile operating loss to net cash used by operating activities:		
Depreciation expense	243,820	232,478
Changes in assets, liabilities, deferred outflows and deferred inflows:		
Receivables, net	14,838	25,020
Inventories	(2,318)	(3,082)
OPEB asset	(1,811)	(3,433)
Other assets	-	(2)
Prepaid expenses	(2,082)	5,324
Notes receivable, net	3,215	287
Capital assets, net	(5,142)	7,203
Deferred outflows of resources	732	18,214
Accounts payable and accrued liabilities	123,187	(85,573)
Unearned revenue	5,312	(11,482)
Long-term liabilities	21,030	(23,725)
Net pension liability	(32,180)	(45,400)
OPEB liability	(37,870)	43,734
Deferred inflows of resources	33,156	37,389
TOTAL ADJUSTMENTS	383,857	197,970
NET CASH USED BY OPERATING ACTIVITIES	$ (241,205)	$ (355,878)
NONCASH INVESTING, CAPITAL, AND FINANCING ACTIVITIES		
Assets acquired through assumption of a liability	$ 7,584	$ 42,738
Assets acquired through a gift	(12,755)	841
Change in fair value of investments	410,033	778,107
Increase in receivables related to nonoperating income	98,242	2,389
Gain on disposal of capital assets	(5,832)	22,044
(Loss) gain on investments in affiliated companies	(148)	(5,784)
Change in non-controlling interest in subsidiary	(558)	(74)
Amortization of bond premium and deferral	(121)	8,142
Trustee-held split interest agreements	-	3,838

Certain 2018 amounts have been restated to conform to 2019 classifications.
The accompanying Notes to Financial Statements are an integral part of this statement.

Exempt Organizations Glossary

Governmental terminology

accounting system. The methods and records established to identify, assemble, analyze, classify, record, and report a government's transactions and to maintain accountability for the related assets and liabilities.

accrual basis of accounting. The recording of financial effects on a government of transactions and other events and circumstances that have consequences for the government in the periods in which those transactions, events, and circumstances occur, rather than only in the periods in which cash is received or paid by the government.

ad valorem tax. A tax based on value (such as a property tax).

advance from other funds. An asset account used to record noncurrent portions of a long-term debt owed by one fund to another fund within the same reporting entity. (See **due to other funds** and **interfund receivable/payable**).

appropriation. A legal authorization granted by a legislative body to make expenditures and to incur obligations for specific purposes. An appropriation is usually limited in the amount and time it may be expended.

assigned fund balance. A portion of fund balance that includes amounts that are constrained by the government's intent to be used for specific purposes, but that are neither restricted nor committed.

basis of accounting. A term used to refer to *when* revenues, expenditures, expenses, and transfers, and related assets and liabilities are recognized in the accounts and reported in the financial statements. Specifically, it relates to the timing of the measurements made, regardless of the nature of the measurement. (See **accrual basis of accounting**, **cash basis of accounting**, and **modified accrual basis of accounting**).

bond. A written promise to pay a specified sum of money (the face value or principal amount) at a specified date or dates in the future (the maturity dates[s]), together with periodic interest at a specified rate. Sometimes, however, all or a substantial part of the interest is included in the face value of the security. The difference between a note and bond is that the latter is issued for a longer period and requires greater legal formality.

business type activities. Those activities of a government carried out primarily to provide specific services in exchange for a specific user charge.

capital grants. Grants restricted by the grantor for the acquisition or construction, or both, of capital assets.

capital projects fund. A fund used to account for and report financial resources that are restricted, committed, or assigned to expenditures for capital outlays, including the acquisition or construction of capital facilities and other capital assets. Capital project funds exclude those types of capital-related outflows financed by proprietary funds or for assets that will be held in trust for individuals, private organizations, or other governments.

cash basis of accounting. A basis of accounting that requires the recognition of transactions only when cash is received or disbursed.

committed fund balance. A portion of fund balance that includes amounts that can only be used for specific purposes pursuant to constraints imposed by formal action of the government's highest level of decision-making authority.

consumption method. The method of accounting that requires the recognition of an expenditure or expense as inventories are used.

contributed capital. Contributed capital is created when a general capital asset is transferred to a proprietary fund or when a grant is received that is externally restricted to capital acquisition or construction. Contributions restricted to capital acquisition and construction and capital assets received from developers are reported in the operating statement as a separate item after nonoperating revenues and expenses.

custodial fund. A fiduciary fund used to account for financial resources not administered through a trust or equivalent arrangement meeting specified criteria, and that are not required to be reported in a pension (and other employee benefit) trust fund, investment trust fund, or private-purpose trust fund.

debt service fund. A fund used to account for and report financial resources that are restricted, committed, or assigned to expenditure for principal and interest. Debt service funds should be used to report resources if legally mandated. Financial resources that are being accumulated for principal and interest maturing in future years should also be reported as debt service funds.

deferred inflow of resources. An acquisition of net assets by a government that is applicable to a future reporting period.

deferred outflow of resources. A consumption of net asset by a government that is applicable to a future reporting period.

deficit. (*a*) The excess of the liabilities of a fund over its assets. (*b*) The excess of expenditures over revenues during an accounting period or, in the case of proprietary funds, the excess of expenses over revenues during an accounting period.

disbursement. A payment made in cash or by check. Expenses are only recognized at the time physical cash is disbursed.

due from other funds. A current asset account used to indicate an account reflecting amounts owed to a particular fund by another fund for goods sold or services rendered. This account includes only short-term obligations on an open account, not interfund loans.

---

due to other funds. A current liability account reflecting amounts owed by a particular fund to another fund for goods sold or services rendered. This account includes only short-term obligations on an open account, not interfund loans.

enabling legislation. Legislation that authorizes a government to assess, levy, charge, or otherwise mandate payment of resources from external resource providers and includes a legally enforceable requirement that those resources be used for the specific purposes stipulated in the legislation.

encumbrances. Commitments related to unperformed (executory) contracts for goods or services. Used in budgeting, encumbrances are not generally accepted accounting principles (GAAP) expenditures or liabilities but represent the estimated amount of expenditures that will ultimately result if unperformed contracts in process are completed.

enterprise fund. A fund established to account for operations financed and operated in a manner similar to private business enterprises (such as gas, utilities, transit systems, and parking garages). Usually, the governing body intends that costs of providing goods or services to the general public be recovered primarily through user charges.

expenditures. Decreases in net financial resources. Expenditures include current operating expenses requiring the present or future use of net current assets, debt service and capital outlays, intergovernmental grants, entitlements, and shared revenues.

expenses. Outflows or other consumption of assets or incurrences of liabilities, or a combination of both, from delivering or producing goods, rendering services, or carrying out other activities that constitute the entity's ongoing major or central operations.

fiduciary fund. A fund that reports fiduciary activities meeting the criteria in paragraphs 6–11 of GASB Statement No. 84, *Fiduciary Activities*. Financial reporting is focused on reporting net position and changes in net position.

fund. A fiscal and accounting entity with a self-balancing set of accounts in which cash and other financial resources, all related liabilities and residual equities, or balances, and changes therein, are recorded and segregated to carry on specific activities or attain certain objectives in accordance with special regulations, restrictions, or limitations.

fund balance. The difference between fund assets and fund liabilities of the generic fund types within the governmental category of funds.

fund financial statements. Each fund has its own set of self-balancing accounts and fund financial statements that focus on information about the government's governmental, proprietary, and fiduciary fund types.

fund type. The 11 generic funds that all transactions of a government are recorded into. The 11 fund types are as follows: general, special revenue, debt service, capital projects, permanent, enterprise, internal service, private-purpose trust, pension (and other employee benefit) trust, investment trust, and custodial.

GASB. The Governmental Accounting Standards Board (GASB), organized in 1984 by the Financial Accounting Foundation (FAF) to establish standards of financial accounting and reporting for state and local governmental entities. Its standards guide the preparation of external financial reports of those entities.

general fund. The fund within the governmental category used to account for all financial resources, except those required to be accounted for in another governmental fund.

general-purpose governments. Governmental entities that provide a range of services, such as states, cities, counties, towns, and villages.

governmental funds. Funds used to account for the acquisition, use, and balances of spendable financial resources and the related current liabilities, except those accounted for in proprietary funds and fiduciary funds. Essentially, these funds are accounting segregations of financial resources. Spendable assets are assigned to a particular government fund type according to the purposes for which they may or must be used. Current liabilities are assigned to the fund type from which they are to be paid. The difference between the assets and liabilities of governmental fund types is referred to as *fund balance*. The measurement focus in these fund types is on the determination of financial position and changes in financial position (sources, uses, and balances of financial resources), rather than on net income determination.

government-wide financial statements. Highly aggregated financial statements that present financial information for all assets (including infrastructure capital assets), liabilities, and net assets of a primary government and its component units, except for fiduciary funds. The government-wide financial statements use the economic resources measurement focus and accrual basis of accounting.

infrastructure assets. Long-lived capital assets that normally are stationary in nature and can be preserved for a significantly greater number of years than most capital assets. Examples of infrastructure assets are roads, bridges, tunnels, drainage systems, water and sewer systems, dams, and lighting systems. Buildings, except those that are an ancillary part of a network of infrastructure assets, are not considered infrastructure assets.

Interfund receivable/payable. Activity between funds of a government reflecting amounts provided with a requirement for repayment, or sales and purchases of goods and services between funds approximating their external exchange value (also referred to as **interfund loans** or **interfund services provided and used**).

internal service fund. A generic fund type within the proprietary category used to account for the financing of goods or services provided by one department or agency to other departments or agencies of a government, or to other governments, on a cost-reimbursement basis.

investment trust fund. A generic fund type within the fiduciary category used by a government in a fiduciary capacity, such as to maintain its cash and investment pool for other governments.

major funds. A government's general fund (or its equivalent), other individual governmental type, and enterprise funds that meet specific quantitative criteria, and any other governmental or enterprise fund that a government's officials believe is particularly important to financial statement users.

management's discussion and analysis. Management's discussion and analysis, or MD&A, is required supplementary information that introduces the basic financial statements by presenting certain financial information as well as management's analytical insights on that information.

measurement focus. The accounting convention that determines (*a*) which assets and which liabilities are included on a government's balance sheet and where they are reported, and (*b*) whether an operating statement presents information on the flow of financial resources (revenues and expenditures) or information on the flow of economic resources (revenues and expenses).

modified accrual basis of accounting. The basis of accounting adapted to the governmental fund type measurement focus. Revenues and other financial resource increments are recognized when they become both *measurable* and *available to finance expenditures of the current period*. *Available* means collectible in the current period or soon enough thereafter to be used to pay liabilities of the current period. Expenditures are recognized when the fund liability is incurred and expected to be paid from current resources, except for (*a*) inventories of materials and supplies that may be considered expenditures either when purchased or when used, and (*b*) prepaid insurance and similar items that may be considered expenditures either when paid for or when consumed. All governmental funds are accounted for using the modified accrual basis of accounting in fund financial statements.

modified approach. Rules that allow infrastructure assets that are part of a network or subsystem of a network not to be depreciated as long as certain requirements are met.

net position. The residual of all other elements presented in a statement of financial position.

nonspendable fund balance. The portion of fund balance that includes amounts that cannot be spent because they are either (*a*) not in spendable form or (*b*) legally or contractually required to be maintained intact.

pension (and other employee benefit) trust fund. A trust fund used to account for a public employees retirement system, OPEB plan, or other employee benefits other than pensions that are administered through trusts that meet specified criteria. Pension (and other employee benefit) trust funds use the accrual basis of accounting and the flow of economic resources measurement focus.

permanent fund. A generic fund type under the governmental category used to report resources that are legally restricted to the extent that only earnings, and not principal, may be used for purposes that support the reporting government's programs and, therefore, are for the benefit of the government or its citizenry. (Permanent funds do not include private-purpose trust funds, which should be used when the government is required to use the principal or earnings for the benefit of individuals, private organizations, or other governments).

private purpose trust fund. A general fund type under the fiduciary category used to report resources held and administered by the reporting government acting in a fiduciary capacity for individuals, other governments, or private organizations.

proprietary funds. The government category used to account for a government's ongoing organizations and activities that are similar to those often found in the private sector (these are enterprise and internal service funds). All assets, liabilities, equities, revenues, expenses, and transfers relating to the government's business and quasi-business activities are accounted for through proprietary funds. Proprietary funds should apply all applicable GASB pronouncements and those GAAP applicable to similar businesses in the private sector, unless those conflict with GASB pronouncements. These funds use the accrual basis of accounting in conjunction with the flow of economic resources measurement focus.

purchases method. The method under which inventories are recorded as expenditures when acquired.

restricted fund balance. Portion of fund balance that reflects constraints placed on the use of resources (other than nonspendable items) that are either (*a*) externally imposed by a creditor, such as through debt covenants, grantors, contributors, or laws or regulations of other governments or (*b*) imposed by law through constitutional provisions or enabling legislation.

required supplementary information. GAAP specify that certain information be presented as required supplementary information, or RSI.

special-purpose governments. Legally separate entities that perform only one activity or a few activities, such as cemetery districts, school districts, colleges and universities, utilities, hospitals and other health care organizations, and public employee retirement systems.

special revenue fund. A fund that must have revenue or proceeds from specific revenue sources that are either restricted or committed for a specific purpose other than debt service or capital projects. This definition means that in order to be considered a special revenue fund, there must be one or more revenue sources upon which reporting the activity in a separate fund is predicated.

interfund transfers. All transfers, such as legally authorized transfers from a fund receiving revenue to a fund through which the resources are to be expended, where there is no intent to repay. Interfund transfers are recorded on the operating statement.

unassigned fund balance. Residual classification for the general fund. This classification represents fund balance that has not been assigned to other funds and has not been restricted, committed, or assigned to specific purposes within the general fund. The general fund should be the only fund that reports a positive unassigned fund balance amount. In other funds, if expenditures incurred for specific purposes exceeded the amounts restricted, committed, or assigned to those purposes, it may be necessary to report a negative unassigned fund balance.

unrestricted fund balance. The total of committed fund balance, assigned fund balance, and unassigned fund balance.

Not-for-profit terminology

board-designated endowment fund. An endowment fund created by a not-for-profit entity's governing board by designating a portion of its net assets without donor restrictions to be invested to provide income for a long, but not necessarily specified, period. In rare circumstances, a board-designated endowment fund also can include a portion of net assets with donor restrictions. For example, if a not-for-profit is unable to spend donor-restricted contributions in the near term, then the board sometimes considers the long-term investment of these funds.

board-designated net assets. Net assets without donor restrictions subject to self-imposed limits by action of the governing board. Board-designated net assets may be earmarked for future programs, investment, contingencies, purchase or construction of fixed assets, or other uses. Some governing boards may delegate designation decisions to internal management. Such designations are considered to be included in board-designated net assets.

charitable lead trust. A trust established in connection with a split-interest agreement in which the not-for-profit entity receives distributions during the agreement's term. Upon termination of the trust, the remainder of the trust assets are paid to the donor or to third-party beneficiaries designated by the donor.

charitable remainder trust. A trust established in connection with a split-interest agreement in which the donor or a third-party beneficiary receives specified distributions during the agreement's term. Upon termination of the trust, a not-for-profit entity receives the assets remaining in the trust.

collections. Works of art, historical treasures, or similar assets that are (*a*) held for public exhibition, education, or research in furtherance of public service, rather than financial gain; (*b*) protected, kept unencumbered, cared for, and preserved; and (*c*) subject to an organizational policy that requires the proceeds of items that are sold to be used to acquire other items for collections.

conditional promise to give. A promise to give that is subject to a donor-imposed condition.

contribution. An unconditional transfer of cash or other assets, as well as unconditional promises to give, to an entity or a reduction, settlement, or cancellation of its liabilities in a voluntary nonreciprocal transfer by another entity acting other than as an owner.

costs of joint activities. Costs incurred for a joint activity. Costs of joint activities may include joint costs and costs other than joint costs. *Costs other than joint costs* are costs that are identifiable with a particular function, such as program, fund-raising, management and general, and membership development costs.

donor-imposed restriction. A donor stipulation (*donors* include other types of contributors, including makers of certain grants) that specifies a use for the contributed asset that is more specific than broad limits resulting from the nature of the organization, the environment in which it operates, and the purposes specified in its articles of incorporation or bylaws, or comparable documents for an unincorporated association. A restriction on an organization's use of the asset contributed may be temporary in nature or perpetual in nature.

donor-restricted endowment fund. An endowment fund that is created by a donor stipulation (*donors* include other types of contributors, including makers of certain grants) that requires investment of the gift in perpetuity or for a specified term. Some donors or laws may require that a portion of income, gains, or both be added to the gift and invested subject to similar restrictions.

donor-restricted support. Donor-restricted revenues or gains from contributions that increase net assets with donor restrictions (*donors* include other types of contributions, including makers of certain grants).

economic interest. A not-for-profit entity's interest in another entity that exists if any of the following criteria are met: (*a*) The other entity holds or uses significant resources that must be used for the purposes of the not-for-profit entity, either directly or indirectly, by producing income or providing services, or (*b*) the not-for-profit entity is responsible for the liabilities of the other entity.

endowment fund. An established fund of cash, securities, or other assets that provides income for the maintenance of a not-for-profit entity. The use of the assets of the fund may be with or without donor-imposed restrictions. Endowment funds generally are established by donor-restricted gifts and bequests to provide a source of income.

functional expense classification. A method of grouping expenses according to the purpose for which the costs are incurred. The primary functional classifications of a not-for-profit entity are program services and supporting activities.

funds functioning as endowment. Net assets without donor restrictions (*donors* include other types of contributors, including makers of certain grants) designated by an entity's governing board to be invested to provide income for generally a long, but not necessarily specified, period.

joint activity. An activity that is part of the fund-raising function and has elements of one or more other functions, such as programs, management and general, membership development, or any other functional category used by the entity.

joint costs. The costs of conducting joint activities that are not identifiable with a particular component of the activity.

management and general activities. Supporting activities that are not directly identifiable with one or more programs, fund-raising activities, or membership development activities.

natural expense classification. A method of grouping expenses according to the kinds of economic benefits received in incurring those expenses. Examples of natural expense classifications include salaries and wages, employee benefits, professional services, supplies, interest expense, rent, utilities, and depreciation.

net assets. The excess or deficiency of assets over liabilities of a not-for-profit entity, which is divided into two mutually exclusive classes according to the existence or absence of donor-imposed restrictions.

net assets with donor restrictions. The part of net assets of a not-for-profit entity that is subject to donor-imposed restrictions (*donors* include other types of contributors, including makers of certain grants).

net assets without donor restrictions. The part of net assets of a not-for-profit entity that is not subject to donor-imposed restrictions (*donors* include other types of contributors, including makers of certain grants).

programmatic investing. The activity of making loans or other investments that are directed at carrying out a not-for-profit entity's purpose for existence, rather than investing in the general production of income or appreciation of an asset (for example, total return investing). An example of programmatic investing is a loan made to lower-income individuals to promote home ownership.

promise to give. A written or oral agreement to contribute cash or other assets to another entity. A promise to give may be either conditional or unconditional.

underwater endowment fund. A donor-restricted endowment fund for which the fair value of the fund at the reporting date is less than either the original gift amount or the amount required to be maintained by the donor or by law that extends donor restrictions.

Single audit and Yellow Book terminology

attestation engagements. Attestation engagements concern examining, reviewing, or performing agreed-upon procedures on a subject matter or an assertion about a subject matter and reporting on the results.

compliance supplement. A document issued annually in the spring by the OMB to provide guidance to auditors.

data collection form. A form submitted to the Federal Audit Clearinghouse that provides information about the auditor, the auditee and its federal programs, and the results of the audit.

federal financial assistance. Assistance that nonfederal entities receive or administer in the form of grants, loans, loan guarantees, property, cooperative agreements, interest subsidies, insurance, food commodities, direct appropriations, or other assistance, but does not include amounts received as reimbursement for services rendered to individuals in accordance with guidance issued by the director.

financial audits. Financial audits are primarily concerned with providing reasonable assurance about whether financial statements are presented fairly, in all material respects, in conformity with GAAP or with a comprehensive basis of accounting other than GAAP.

GAGAS. Generally accepted government auditing standards issued by the GAO. They are published as *Government Auditing Standards*, also commonly known as the Yellow Book.

GAO. The United States Government Accountability Office. Among its responsibilities is the issuance of GAGAS.

OMB. The Office of Management and Budget. The OMB assists the President in the development and implementation of budget, program, management, and regulatory policies.

pass-through entity. A nonfederal entity that provides federal awards to a subrecipient to carry out a federal program.

performance audits. Performance audits entail an objective and systematic examination of evidence to provide an independent assessment of the performance and management of a program against objective criteria as well as assessments that provide a prospective focus or that synthesize information on best practices or cross-cutting issues.

program-specific audit. A compliance audit of one federal program.

single audit. An audit of a nonfederal entity that includes the entity's financial statements and federal awards.

single audit guide. This AICPA Audit Guide, formally titled Government Auditing Standards *and Single Audits*, is the former Statement of Position (SOP) 98-3, *Audits of States, Local Governments, and Not-for-Profit Organizations Receiving Federal Awards*. The single audit guide provides guidance on the auditor's responsibilities when conducting a single audit or program-specific audit in accordance with the Single Audit Act, GAGAS, and the Uniform Guidance.

subrecipient. A nonfederal entity that receives federal awards through another nonfederal entity to carry out a federal program but does not include an individual who receives financial assistance through such awards.

Uniform Guidance. Formally known as Title 2 U.S. *Code of Federal Regulations* Part 200, *Uniform Administrative Requirements, Cost Principles, and Audit Requirements for Federal Awards*. The Uniform Guidance sets forth the requirements for the compliance audit portion of a single audit.

Index

FUNDAMENTALS OF GOVERNMENTAL ACCOUNTING AND REPORTING

BY BRUCE W. CHASE, PH.D., CPA

Solutions

The AICPA publishes *CPA Letter Daily*, a free e-newsletter published each weekday. The newsletter, which covers the 10-12 most important stories in business, finance, and accounting, as well as AICPA information, was created to deliver news to CPAs and others who work with the accounting profession. Besides summarizing media articles, commentaries, and research results, the e-newsletter links to television broadcasts and videos and features reader polls. *CPA Letter Daily*'s editors scan hundreds of publications and websites, selecting the most relevant and important news so you don't have to. The newsletter arrives in your inbox early in the morning. To sign up, visit smartbrief.com/CPA.

Do you need high-quality technical assistance? The AICPA Auditing and Accounting Technical Hotline provides non-authoritative guidance on accounting, auditing, attestation, and compilation and review standards. The hotline can be reached at 877.242.7212.

Solutions

Chapter 1

Practice question solutions

1. d.
2. b.
3. d.
4. d.
5. c.
6. b.

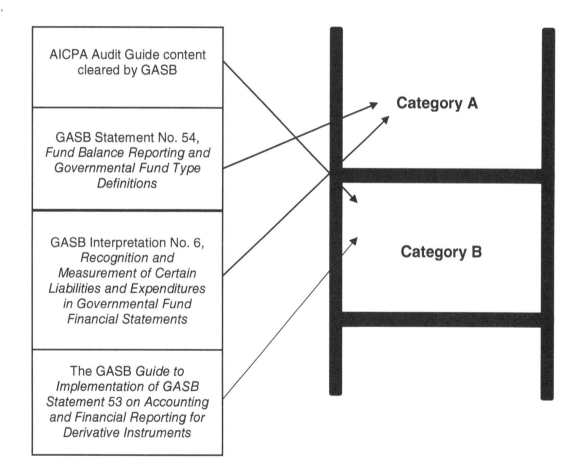

Knowledge check solutions

1.

    a. Correct. The state and local governmental environment is different in a number of ways from that of business; these differences influence financial reporting objectives.

    b. Incorrect. Many governments' resources come from taxes.

    c. Incorrect. The organizational purpose of a government is different than that of a business.

    d. Incorrect. Governments rarely go out of business because they have the ability to tax.

2.

    a. Incorrect. The primary source of revenue for a business is voluntary exchange transactions.

    b. Incorrect. A difference between government and business is how resources are provided.

    c. Correct. Governments are accountable to citizens and taxpayers and must provide them information on how financial resources are used.

    d. Incorrect. Governmental budget controls are achieved through budgets legally adopted by elected officials.

3.

    a. Correct. To meet one of the financial reporting objectives, governments must be able to compare actual financial results with the legally adopted budget.

    b. Incorrect. Budgets are often recorded in the accounting system.

    c. Incorrect. Budgets are often reviewed to compare actual financial results with the legally adopted budget.

    d. Incorrect. Budgets are legally binding on governments.

Chapter 2

Practice question solutions

1. d.
2. d.
3. c.
4. d.
5. c.
6. b.
7. c.
8. a.

---

9. General fund, a special revenue fund, or an enterprise fund would be the possible fund types for a new governmental park. The decision would be based on management's intentions for this activity. If management wants to report the full cost of this activity, an enterprise fund could be used. If management wants to demonstrate that the fees were used only for the park, a special revenue fund could be used. Otherwise, it would be appropriate to account for this activity in the general fund.

10. Enterprise fund – Water and sewer utility fund

    Permanent fund – Endowment fund for purchase of library books

    Capital project fund – City Hall construction fund

    Debt service fund – General long-term bond redemption fund

    Internal service fund – Central print shop fund

    Enterprise fund – Parking deck fund

    Special revenue fund – Federal grant fund

    Capital project fund – State grant for new bridge fund

    Private purpose trust fund – High school graduate scholarship fund.

    Internal service fund – Fleet center fund

    Pension (and other employee benefit) trust fund – Employee retirement fund

11. Coding for the following: governmental (G), proprietary (P), fiduciary (F).

    P Enterprise fund

    G Permanent fund

    G Debt service fund

    F Investment trust fund

    G General fund

    G Special revenue fund

    G Capital project fund

    F Private purpose trust fund

    P Internal service fund

    F Pension (and other employee benefit) trust fund

Knowledge check solutions

1.

    a. Correct. A grant or other restricted revenue source may require the use of a separate fund.

    b. Incorrect. A government may start a new activity that it wants to track separately.

    c. Incorrect. The governing board may create a new fund at any time during the year.

    d. Incorrect. A new fund can be established at any time.

2.

    a. Correct. Investment trust funds are used to account for the external portion of investment pools reported by sponsoring governments.

    b. Incorrect. Private-purpose trust funds are fiduciary funds.

    c. Incorrect. Custodial funds are used to account for resources held by the government in a purely custodial capacity.

    d. Incorrect. There are four fiduciary fund types.

3.

    a. Correct. There are separate fund financial statements for each fund category.

    b. Incorrect. Only proprietary funds report a statement of cash flows.

    c. Incorrect. All funds report fund financial statements.

    d. Incorrect. Fund financial statements use different MFBOAs.

Chapter 3

Practice question solutions

1. b.
2. b.
3. b.
4. a.
5. d.
6. c.
7. d.
8. d.
9. d.

10. Expenditures represent an actual outflow of current financial resources and result in a reduction in fund balance. An encumbrance represents only a commitment and not an outflow of current financial resources.

---

11. The budgetary comparison schedules are included as part of required supplementary information or may be included as part of the fund financial statements. If they are included as part of the fund financial statements, they are subject to the same audit requirements as other fund financial statements.

12. The amount of available appropriation is equal to the appropriation ($25,000) less expenditures ($5,800) less outstanding encumbrances ($2,500), which totals $16,700. Available appropriation represents the amount of the appropriation that still can be committed or spent.

Knowledge check solutions

1.
   a. Incorrect. Budgets consist of both estimated revenues and appropriations.
   b. Incorrect. The budget process typically involves several public hearings.
   c. Correct. Elected officials must balance the need for services against how much taxpayers are willing to provide.
   d. Incorrect. Once approved, budgets are legal contracts between the government and its citizens.

2.
   a. Incorrect. Budgets for proprietary funds are often not legally adopted.
   b. Incorrect. For business-type activities, there is a relationship between revenues and expenses.
   c. Correct. Proprietary fund budgets are usually flexible.
   d. Incorrect. Elected officials are usually more concerned with rates charged by business-type activities than with the amount of projected expenses.

3.
   a. Incorrect. Total appropriation represents the amount that can be spent for the year.
   b. Incorrect. It is not computed by subtracting actual expenditures from estimated revenue.
   c. Correct. It is computed by subtracting actual expenditures and outstanding commitments from the appropriated amount.
   d. Incorrect. It does not represent the amount spent.

Chapter 4

Practice question solutions

1. d.
2. c.
3. d.
4. b.
5. d.
6. a.
7. b.
8. d.
9. b.
10. d.

11. An expenditure is an outflow of current financial resources; an expense is a reduction of economic resources. Salaries, supplies, and utilities are examples of transactions that are both an expense and an expenditure. Purchases of fixed assets and payments of long-term debt are examples of an expenditure that would not be an expense.

12. Modified accrual accounting is used by governmental funds and requires that an item be both measurable and available to be recognized as revenue. Accrual accounting is used by proprietary funds and requires an item be measurable and earned to be recognized as revenue.

Knowledge check solutions

1.

a. Incorrect. Proprietary funds use a flow of economic resources measurement focus.

b. Incorrect. Proprietary funds would account for both current and noncurrent assets and liabilities.

c. Correct. The financial statements measure whether the economic resources have increased or decreased for the accounting period.

d. Incorrect. Proprietary funds report inflow of resources as revenue and gains.

2.

    a. Incorrect. Governmental funds recognize transactions using one basis of accounting; proprietary funds use another.

    b. Incorrect. The basis of accounting used by governments is linked directly with the measurement focus.

    c. Correct. The basis of accounting is concerned with when a transaction or event is recognized in the accounting system.

    d. Incorrect. The basis of accounting is concerned with when a transaction or event is recognized in the accounting system.

Chapter 5

Practice question solutions

1. a.
2. b.
3. d.
4. a.
5. c.
6. c.
7. d.
8. b.

9. The amount reported as property tax revenue would include amounts levied this year that were collected during the year or within 60 days after year-end. It would also include any amounts of prior-year taxes collected after the first 60 days of the current year.

10. This amount would include any interest or dividends earned and both realized and unrealized gains and losses. Governments are not permitted to report unrealized gains and losses separately from realized gains and losses.

11. The purchase method of accounting would report an expenditure when an item is purchased. The consumption method would report an expenditure when an item is consumed. Both methods can be used for inventories of material and supplies and for prepaid items. If the purchase method is used, significant amounts of inventory must be reported as an asset and nonspendable fund balance. This is not a requirement for significant amounts of prepaid items.

Knowledge check solutions

1.

    a. Correct. Governmental funds receive revenues from a variety of sources.

    b. Incorrect. Normally, two of the largest revenue sources for governmental funds are taxes and intergovernmental revenue.

    c. Incorrect. Governments report revenues by major source.

    d. Incorrect. The amount of revenue estimated to be uncollectible is recorded as a reduction in revenue.

2.

    a. Correct. GASB Statement No. 33 provides guidance on recognizing both receivables and revenues for nonexchange transactions.

    b. Incorrect. Sales taxes are a type of derived tax revenue.

    c. Incorrect. Nonexchange transactions are transactions that do not involve an exchange of value.

    d. Incorrect. Property taxes are a type of imposed nonexchange revenue.

3.

    a. Incorrect. The purchase of capital assets and payment of debt principal are recorded as expenditures.

    b. Correct. Expenditures are recognized in the period in which the fund liability is incurred.

    c. Incorrect. Governments should report expenditures by major function and major character.

    d. Incorrect. The consumption method or purchase method can be used for reporting the purchase of inventories.

Chapter 6

Practice question solutions

1. c.
2. a.
3. c.
4. a.
5. d.
6. d.
7. a.
8. b.

---

9. For an enterprise fund, the difference between the carrying value of the old debt and the cost to refund this debt is initially deferred. This amount is amortized over the shorter of the life of the old debt or the life of the new debt. Business organizations do not defer these amounts.

10. Proprietary funds report four types of cash flows: operating activities, noncapital financing activities, capital and related financing activities, and investing activities. Business organizations report three types of cash flows: operating activities, investing activities, and financing activities. In addition, interest income and interest expenses are not considered cash flow from operating activities for proprietary funds but they are considered such for business organizations. The statement of cash flows for proprietary funds must be done on the direct method. Business organizations may use either the direct method or the indirect method.

Knowledge check solutions

1.
   a. Correct. Either an enterprise or an internal service fund can be used any time there is a fee charged for goods and services.
   b. Incorrect. Internal service funds may be used to report any activity that provides goods or services to other funds, departments, or other agencies of the primary government and its component units, or to other governments, on a cost-reimbursement basis.
   c. Incorrect. Using a proprietary fund allows the government to measure the cost of providing such goods and services using a business model.
   d. Incorrect. There are three situations when the use of an enterprise fund is required.

2.
   a. Incorrect. Internal service funds generally operate on a cost-reimbursement basis.
   b. Incorrect. Internal service funds should be used only when the reporting government is the predominant participant in the activity.
   c. Correct. Governmental funds are used to account for the general operations of a government.
   d. Incorrect. Internal service funds usually provide services to internal customers.

3.
   a. Correct. Proprietary funds report change in net position as opposed to net income on a statement of revenues, expenses, and changes in net position.
   b. Incorrect. Proprietary funds report restricted net position on a balance sheet or statement of net position.
   c. Incorrect. Proprietary funds report net investment in capital assets on a balance sheet or statement of net position.
   d. Incorrect. Proprietary funds report unrestricted net position on a balance sheet or statement of net position.

Chapter 7

Practice question solutions

1. b.
2. c.
3. c.
4. b.
5. d.
6. d.
7. b.

8. Fiduciary trust funds report additions and deductions instead of revenues and expenses. These resources are held for others and do not represent resources of the government. The statement also reports net change and beginning and ending balance for fiduciary net position.

9. A government that holds a pension (and other employee benefit) trust fund reports a statement of fiduciary net position and a statement of changes in fiduciary net position. These statements report the amount of resources held in trust for others. In addition, actuarial information related to the funding status is also reported in schedules as part of required supplementary information. Footnote disclosures would also be needed.

Knowledge check solutions

1.

    a. Correct. There are four classifications of fiduciary funds: pension (and other employee benefit) trust funds, investment trust funds, private-purpose trust funds, and custodial funds.

    b. Incorrect. Governments are sometimes asked to act as fiscal custodian of resources for other organizations or individuals.

    c. Incorrect. There are fewer than five categories of fiduciary funds.

    d. Incorrect. Custodial funds usually operate under less formal agreements and resources are often held for only a short period of time.

2.
   a. Correct. Fiduciary funds report additions and deductions to net position.
   b. Incorrect. Fund financial statements are reported by fund type.
   c. Incorrect. Fiduciary funds report additions and deductions in the statement of changes in fiduciary net position.
   d. Incorrect. Fiduciary funds report amounts that belong to the fiduciary fund only.

Chapter 8

Practice question solutions
1. d.
2. b.
3. c.
4. a.
5. d.
6. d.
7. a.
8. d.
9. a.

10. The general fund is always reported in a separate column. In addition, any governmental or enterprise fund that meets the major-fund criteria must be reported in a separate column. Internal service funds and fiduciary funds are reported in columns by fund type. Also, a government may report in a separate column any governmental or enterprise fund it believes is important to financial statement users.

11. Governmental funds report a balance sheet and a statement of revenues, expenditures, and changes in fund balances. Proprietary funds report a statement of net assets (or balance sheet), a statement of revenues, expenses, and changes in net assets, and a statement of cash flows. Fiduciary funds report a statement of fiduciary net assets and a statement of changes in fiduciary net assets.

   Governments may elect to report budgetary comparison schedules for the general fund and major special revenue funds with legally adopted annual budgets as budgetary comparison statements included in the fund financial statements.

12. OA   Cash paid for supplies

    CA   Cash received from sale of equipment

    NC   Cash transferred from the general fund (noncapital)

    NC   Cash received from state grant (noncapital)

IA	Cash paid for investments
NC	Cash received from short-term borrowing
CA	Cash paid for interest on capital related debt
OA	Cash received from customers
IA	Cash received for interest from investment

Knowledge check solutions

1.

a. Correct. Generally, a government should have the minimum number of funds necessary for sound financial management and to meet legal and accounting requirements.

b. Incorrect. A government has three different types of funds: governmental, proprietary, and fiduciary.

c. Incorrect. The number of individual funds a government may have can vary from just a few to several dozen.

d. Incorrect. There are differences in how things are reported and measured in the financial statements of the different fund types.

2.

a. Correct. Reporting by major funds applies only to governmental funds and enterprise funds.

b. Incorrect. Major fund reporting does not apply to internal service funds.

c. Incorrect. The major fund approach allows the user to focus on the most important funds of a government.

d. Incorrect. Governments report information by major funds.

3.

a. Incorrect. There are separate sets of fund financial statements for each fund type: governmental, proprietary, and fiduciary.

b. Incorrect. The required financial statements for each fund type are different.

c. Correct. Financial statements for governments include both fund-based and government-wide statements.

d. Incorrect. Governmental funds do not report capital assets.

4.

    a. Incorrect. Governmental funds are used to report what financial resources were received during the year, how they were spent, and what amounts remain at year-end.

    b. Incorrect. Governmental funds are used to report what financial resources were received during the year, how they were spent, and what amounts remain at year-end.

    c. Incorrect. Governmental funds are used to report what financial resources were received during the year, how they were spent, and what amounts remain at year-end.

    d. Correct. Governmental funds are used to report what financial resources were received during the year, how they were spent, and what amounts remain at year-end.

Chapter 9

Practice question solutions

1. d.
2. c.
3. d.
4. d.
5. d.
6. d.
7. c.
8. c.

9. Blending combines the financial information of the component unit with the existing funds of the primary government in the financial statements. Therefore, financial information for blended component units is reported in both the fund financial statements as well as the government-wide statements. Discrete presentation reports the financial information of a component unit in a column separate from the primary government in the government-wide financial statements only.

10. Governments have three ways they can meet the requirement to present information about each major component unit. They can use separate columns for each major component unit in the government-wide statements, include a combining statement of major component units after the fund financial statements, or present condensed financial information about each major component unit in notes to the financial statements.

11. *A county transit authority. The authority is a separate legal entity; however, the governing board of the authority is made up of members of the county's board of supervisors. The authority receives no financial support from the county. The county does guarantee the debt of the authority.*

The transit authority is a component unit because the county appoints a majority of the board and there is a financial burden relationship. The authority should be blended because the two boards are substantially the same.

A tax-exempt foundation. A foundation that supports the county's public library raises funds for the purchase of books. The foundation receives requests for the director of the county's library systems and routinely funds those requests based on the amount of donations raised that year. The amount of resources raised and held each year is not significant to the overall county.

The foundation is not a component unit. It meets the first two tests for tax-exempt organizations but not the third. The resources of the foundation are not significant to the primary government.

Knowledge check solutions

1.

a. Correct. The primary government is at the core of the financial reporting entity.

b. Incorrect. The reporting entity for a government is defined as the primary government and its component units.

c. Incorrect. All state and general-purpose local governments meet the definition of a primary government.

d. Incorrect. A special-purpose government must meet all three criteria to be considered a primary government.

2.

a. Incorrect. There are two different methods: blending and discrete presentation.

b. Incorrect. Essentially, a blended component unit appears as just another fund in the financial statements of the primary government.

c. Correct. Once an entity has been determined to be a component unit of the primary government, the next decision is how it should be reported in the financial statements.

d. Incorrect. Some component units are blended with existing funds of the primary government.

Chapter 10

Practice question solutions

1. d.
2. b.
3. d.
4. b.
5. d.
6. c.
7. a.

8. Adjustments for an internal service fund's revenues and expenses must be done in such a way as to eliminate the double recording of expenses related to goods and services provided by internal service funds. The goal of this process is to have only the programs that consume the goods and services report the expenses.

   The statement of activities should be adjusted for the operating income or losses of the internal service fund by increasing or decreasing the expenses of the functions that purchase the goods or services. Most of the nonoperating items would be added to the statement of activities.

9. Program revenues reduce the expense of the different functions of government. They are generally generated from fees, fines and forfeitures, and charges for services from the different functions or come from parties outside the government's taxpayers or citizens (such as intergovernmental grants restricted to a particular function).

   They are reported in the statement of activities in three separate columns (charges for services, operating grants and contributions, capital grants and contributions) and are subtracted from expenses to show net (expense) revenues for the different functions of government.

10.

Reconciliation of the Statement of Revenues, Expenditures, and Changes in Fund Balance to the Statement of Activities

Net change in fund balances – total governmental funds		$300,000
Amounts reported for governmental activities in the Statement of Activities are different because		
Governmental funds report capital outlays as expenditures, whereas governmental activities report depreciation expense to allocate those expenditures over the life of the assets.		
Add capital acquisitions	1,500,000	
Subtract depreciation	(800,000)	700,000
Revenues in the Statement of Activities that do not provide current financial resources are not reported as revenues in the funds.		200,000

Reconciliation of the Statement of Revenues, Expenditures, and Changes in Fund Balance to the Statement of Activities (continued)

Bond proceeds provide current financial resources to governmental funds, but issuing debt increases long-term liabilities in the Statement of Net Position. Repayment of bond principal is an expenditure in the governmental funds, but the repayment reduces long-term liabilities in the Statement of Net Position.

Add debt principal repayment	2,000,000	
Subtract debt proceeds	(2,500,000)	(500,000)

Some expenses reported in the Statement of Activities do not require the use of current financial resources and therefore are not reported as expenditures in governmental funds (such as compensated absences). | | (50,000) |

Internal service funds are used by management to charge the costs of certain services to individual funds. The net revenue (expense) of the internal service funds is reported with governmental activities. | | 100,000 |

| Change in Net Position of Governmental Activities | | $750,000 |

Knowledge check solutions

1.

a. Incorrect. The government-wide financial statements are not used to address fiscal accountability.

b. Incorrect. Government-wide statements were created with the advent of GASB Statement No. 34

c. Correct. The purpose of the government-wide financial statements is to demonstrate operational accountability — to provide information on the results of operations and the financial condition of the overall government.

d. Incorrect. The fund financial statements are used to address fiscal accountability.

2.

    a. Correct. Fiduciary funds and fiduciary component units are excluded from the government-wide statements because these resources are not available to support the government's programs.

    b. Incorrect. The government-wide financial statements organize information by whether it relates to governmental activities or business-type activities (reported in proprietary funds).

    c. Incorrect. The government-wide financial statements organize information by whether it relates to governmental activities (reported in governmental funds) or business-type activities.

    d. Incorrect. The government-wide financial statements organize information by whether it relates to governmental activities (reported in capital project funds) or business-type activities.

3.

    a. Incorrect. The format of the statement of activities allows a government to report the net (expenses) revenues of the different functions of the government.

    b. Incorrect. The challenge in producing the government-wide statements is with converting governmental funds to governmental activities.

    c. Correct. The government-wide statements for governmental activities are generally produced each year using a worksheet approach.

    d. Incorrect. The government-wide statements for governmental activities report three separate columns of program revenue.

Chapter 11

Practice question solutions

1. c.
2. c.
3. b.
4. a.
5. d.

6. Governments are required to include management's discussion and analysis, basic financial statements, and required supplementary information in their general-purpose external financial reports to meet the minimum requirements for GAAP-based statements. However, governments are encouraged to go beyond the minimum requirements by preparing a comprehensive annual financial report (CAFR).

Governments can issue just the minimum requirements or a full CAFR (the minimum requirements are contained in the CAFR).

7. MD&A should focus on the activities of the primary government. The decision to include comments about a government's component units is a matter of professional judgment and should be based on the significance and relationship of the component unit with the primary governments.

    MD&A should discuss current-year results in comparison with the prior year. This is the only place in the general-purpose external financial report that governments are required to present comparative information.

8. In the basic financial statements, the fund financial statements would present separate information about major governmental funds, major enterprise funds, and major component units. The CAFR would report the nonmajor individual funds not separately reported in the fund financial statements as part of the combining statements. The combining statements would report nonmajor governmental funds, nonmajor enterprise funds, internal service funds, fiduciary funds, and nonmajor component units.

Knowledge check solutions

1.

   a. Correct. It is based on currently known facts, decisions, and conditions and must discuss both positive and negative aspects of current-year activity.
   b. Incorrect. Any information presented for a component unit should be clearly distinguished from that of the primary government.
   c. Incorrect. MD&A should be presented before the basic financial statements.
   d. Incorrect. Comparative financial information is reported in MD&A.

2.

   a. Incorrect. Government-wide financial statements are required to be included in a government's general-purpose external financial statements.
   b. Incorrect. Fund financial statements are required to be included in a government's general-purpose external financial statements.
   c. Correct. The Certificate of Achievement for Excellence in Financial Reporting is not required to be included in the general-purpose financial statements but would be included in the introductory section of the CAFR, if applicable.
   d. Incorrect. Notes to the financial statements are required to be included in a government's general-purpose external financial statements.

3.

  a. Correct. When a government uses the modified approach for certain networks or subsystems of infrastructure, certain information must be disclosed as part of RSI.

  b. Incorrect. RSI requirements exist related to pensions and OPEB.

  c. Incorrect. MD&A is presented before the basic financial statements. Other RSI is presented after the basic financial statements.

  d. Incorrect. Governments present budgetary comparison schedules only for the general fund and for each major special revenue fund with a legally adopted annual budget.

4.

  a. Incorrect. The Government Finance Officers Association (GFOA) provides guidance on what information should be included in the CAFR.

  b. Incorrect. The statistical section of the CAFR provides information that is useful in evaluating the economic condition of a government.

  c. Correct. The CAFR provides a variety of additional information outside the audited financial statements that is useful in assessing a government's performance and financial condition.

  d. Incorrect. GASB Statement No. 44 requires governments to report five categories of statistical information.

Chapter 12

Practice question solutions

1. d.
2. b.

3. Special-purpose governments engaged only in governmental activities that have more than one program are required to produce both fund financial statements and government-wide statements. However, if they have only one program, they may combine the fund financial statements and government-wide statements using a columnar format or they may present separate fund financial statements and government-wide statements. When they present separate statements, they may use a different format to report the statement of activities. Requirements would also include MD&A, notes, and RSI.

4. For a special-purpose government engaged only in business-type activities, the reporting requirements would include MD&A, the fund financial statements required for an enterprise fund, notes to the financial statements, and RSI, if applicable.

Knowledge check solutions

1.

    a. Correct. Special-purpose governments engaged in more than one program or that have both governmental and business-type activities should produce both fund financial statements and government-wide financial statements.

    b. Incorrect. Some special-purpose governments do not report government-wide statements.

    c. Incorrect. For special-purpose governments engaged only in a single program or only in a business-type or fiduciary activity, different financial statements are appropriate.

    d. Incorrect. Special-purpose governments are separate legal entities.

2.

    a. Incorrect. A cemetery district is an example of a special-purpose government engaged only in governmental activities.

    b. Incorrect. A levee district is an example of a special-purpose government engaged only in governmental activities.

    c. Correct. An electric authority is an example of a special-purpose government engaged only in business-type activities.

    d. Incorrect. A drainage district is an example of a special-purpose government engaged only in governmental activities.

The AICPA publishes *CPA Letter Daily*, a free e-newsletter published each weekday. The newsletter, which covers the 10-12 most important stories in business, finance, and accounting, as well as AICPA information, was created to deliver news to CPAs and others who work with the accounting profession. Besides summarizing media articles, commentaries, and research results, the e-newsletter links to television broadcasts and videos and features reader polls. *CPA Letter Daily*'s editors scan hundreds of publications and websites, selecting the most relevant and important news so you don't have to. The newsletter arrives in your inbox early in the morning. To sign up, visit smartbrief.com/CPA.

Do you need high-quality technical assistance? The AICPA Auditing and Accounting Technical Hotline provides non-authoritative guidance on accounting, auditing, attestation, and compilation and review standards. The hotline can be reached at 877.242.7212.

Continuing Professional Education

Thank you for selecting the American Institute of Certified Public Accountants as your continuing professional education provider. We have a diverse offering of CPE courses to help you expand your skillset and develop your competencies. Choose from hundreds of different titles spanning the major subject matter areas relevant to CPAs and CGMAs, including:

- Governmental and not-for-profit accounting, auditing, and updates
- Internal control and fraud
- Audits of employee benefit plans and 401(k) plans
- Individual and corporate tax updates
- A vast array of courses in other areas of accounting and auditing, controllership, management, consulting, taxation, and more!

Get your CPE when and where you want

- Self-study training options that includes on-demand, webcasts, and text formats with superior quality and a broad portfolio of topics, including bundled products like –
  - ➢ CPExpress® online learning for immediate access to hundreds of one- to four-credit hour online courses for just-in-time learning at a price that is right
  - ➢ Annual Webcast Pass offering live Q&A with experts and unlimited access to the scheduled lineup, all at an incredible discount.
- Staff training programs for audit, tax and preparation, compilation, and review
- Certificate programs offering comprehensive curriculums developed by practicing experts to build fundamental core competencies in specialized topics
- National conferences presented by recognized experts
- Affordable courses on-site at your organization – visit **aicpalearning.org/on-site** for more information.
- Seminars sponsored by your state society and led by top instructors. For a complete list, visit **aicpalearning.org/publicseminar**.

Take control of your career development

The AICPA's Competency and Learning website at **https://competency.aicpa.org** brings together a variety of learning resources and a self-assessment tool, enabling tracking and reporting of progress toward learning goals.

Visit **www.AICPAStore.com** to browse our CPE selections.

Your strategic learning partner

Let us help prepare your staff for the future.

What is your current approach to learning? One size does not fit all. Your organization is unique, and your approach to learning and competency should be, too. But where do you start? Choose a strategic partner to help you assess competencies and gaps, design a customized learning plan, and measure and maximize the ROI of your learning and development initiatives.

We offer a wide variety of learning programs for finance professionals at every stage of their career.

AICPA Learning resources can help you:
- Create a learning culture to attract and retain talent
- Enrich staff competency and stay current on changing regulations
- Sharpen your competitive edge
- Capitalize on emerging opportunities
- Meet your goals and positively impact your bottom line
- Address CPE/CPD compliance

Flexible learning options include:
- On-site training
- Conferences
- Webcasts
- Certificate programs
- Online self-study
- Publications

An investment in learning can directly impact your bottom line. Contact an AICPA learning consultant to begin your professional development planning.

Call: 800.634.6780, option 1
Email: AICPALearning@aicpa.org